Praise for *Murder in Matera*

"Filled with short, gritty sentences and portentous one-line paragraphs. . . . If the style [of *Murder in Matera*] is streetwise Hemingway, the theme is Faulkner in a nutshell: 'You could run, but the past would catch you soon enough and kick you in the ass when you weren't looking.' . . . [Stapinski] captures perfectly the 'simultaneous beauty and sadness' of Matera . . . its brutalizing poverty and superstition. . . . Food leads to family, family leads to motherhood. . . . In a virtuoso passage, she connects stolen pears to Genesis, Wallace Stevens, Homer, Lizzie Borden and the Harry & David catalog."   —*New York Times Book Review*

"Lively. . . . Engrossing. . . . In addition to solving the murder, Stapinski produces a vivid picture of the region's hardships, past and present."   —*The New Yorker*

"Tantalizing."   —NPR

"*Murder in Matera* is a remarkable family saga that captures the beauty and grit of Southern Italy. The powerful and complicated matriarch at the center of Stapinski's tale will stay with you long after you finish the book."   —Gay Talese, author of
Unto the Sons and *The Voyeur's Motel*

"This book is many things: a gripping murder story, an ancestral journey, a tender yet funny reflection on motherhood and love of country, family, and food. But mostly it's just a total page-turner. Helene Stapinski is incapable of delivering a dull moment. Bravissima to her and to this fine work!"
                                        —Meghan Daum, author of *The Unspeakable:
And Other Subjects of Discussion*

MURDER IN MATERA

ALSO BY HELENE STAPINSKI

Baby Plays Around:
A Love Affair, with Music

Five-Finger Discount:
A Crooked Family History

MURDER
IN MATERA

A True Story of Passion,
Family, and Forgiveness
in Southern Italy

HELENE STAPINSKI

DEY ST.
An Imprint of WILLIAM MORROW

HarperCollins books may be purchased for educational, business, or sales
promotional use. For information, please email the Special Markets Department
at SPsales@harpercollins.com.

A hardcover edition of this book was published in 2017 by Dey Street Books,
an imprint of William Morrow.

FIRST DEY STREET BOOKS PAPERBACK EDITION PUBLISHED 2018.

Designed by Suet Yee Chong

Library of Congress Cataloging-in-Publication Data has been applied for.

ISBN 978-0-06-243849-2

18 19 20 21 22 LSC 10 9 8 7 6 5 4 3 2 1

For Wendell, Dean, and Paulina

april 2 / 2018
second hand

And in that place of abundance
Believing he had been wronged . . .
He ate the fruit to his great regret, his eternal damnation.

—SERAFINO DELLA SALANDRA,
  ADAMO CADUTO (ADAM FELL), 1647

Contents

III

TRIAL

Cast of Characters

Now

HELENE

MA: Helene's elderly mother, the keeper of family legends, who travels with her to Bernalda, in the province of Matera.

DEAN: Helene's firstborn.

PAULINA: Helene's young daughter, also known as the Secret Weapon.

WENDELL: Helene's husband, whom she leaves behind in New York City.

BEANSIE VENA: Helene's career criminal grandfather, who tells the story of Vita to Ma.

ANGELO TATARANNO: Bernalda's town historian, who helps search for the murder.

ANTONIO SALFI: Bernalda's genealogist.

MARIA GALLITELLI: A neighbor and possible long-lost cousin.

MARIA NATALE: The kind downstairs neighbor, a widow who is best friends with Miserabila.

MISERABILA: The unhappy, unhelpful woman who lives around the corner.

LEONARDANTONIO GALLITELLI: Another possible relative and disgruntled neighbor.

CARLO LEVI: Physician and author of *Christ Stopped at Eboli,* Helene's bible and guide.

LEO: Beach bar owner and distant cousin.

FRANCESCO: Local lawyer whom Leo enlists to help find the murder.

IMMA: Young Bernaldan writer hired as a researcher.

GIUSEPPE: Farmer from Marconia also hired as a researcher.

MIMMO AND VIRGINIA: Imma's parents.

CARLA: Italian friend from Jersey City who introduces Helene to Giuseppe.

ANNA PARISI: Italian writer who knows the history of Bernalda.

EVARISTO: Policeman in Pisticci who helps with research.

THEN

VITA GALLITELLI: Helene's great-great-grandmother, alleged murderess from Bernalda.

FRANCESCO VENA: Helene's great-great-grandfather and alleged murderer.

TERESINA: Vita's mother, a weaver from Bernalda.

DOMENICO: Vita's father, a peasant farmer.

LEONARDO VENA: Helene's great-grandfather and Vita's son, who traveled to America with Vita as a boy.

VALENTE VENA: Leonardo's brother and Vita's eldest son, who also traveled to America.

LEONARDANTONIO GALLITELLI: Vita's brother and Francesco's friend.

CESARE LOMBROSO: Italian nineteenth-century doctor who studied physical traits of criminals.

GRIECO: The landowner.

FRANCESCO MIRALDI: Bricklayer and Francesco's friend.

ROCCO: Vita's firstborn son.

NUNZIA: Vita's daughter.

ANTONIO CAMARDO: The deceased.

I

PLEA

Chapter 1

ALL THE KNOTS COME
TO THE COMB

V ITA WAS A MURDERESS.

She took a life and ran.

Maybe she shot. Maybe she stabbed. No one was sure. But she took a life and ran.

She left her husband behind and crossed the Atlantic Ocean with her little boys, running from the crime. She made a home in the first place she found—an industrial city of train tracks and smokestacks and horse-drawn carriages with manure in the streets, where the bonfires burned as high as the rooftops on election night.

In the end she got hers. Boy, did she get hers. She paid the ultimate price.

Ma would tell me about Vita as we sat in our bright yellow kitchen in Jersey City, New Jersey, circa 1969. As she spoke she cooked sauce on the stove, slowly turning the red bubbling lava inside the pot with a big metal spoon, meatballs bobbing at the top. She'd dip some crusty Italian bread in the pot and give me a taste, the hot sauce burning and shredding the roof of my mouth because I was too impatient to let it cool off. Between bites, I listened, and nodded and colored in my coloring book.

It was before I had started school; those stories were my first lessons.

I saw Vita in my head: her wild eyes, her passion, long hair whipping in the wind off that ship on the blowing ocean as she held her boys tight.

Ma was a great storyteller—but nothing compared with her father, Grandpa Beansie.

He'd spent time in Trenton State, the Big House, and loved to tell us about prison life: guys who liked to crochet, guys who kept mice as pets on little leashes, men being carried off to the electric chair. His hands would shake and his knees would buckle and he would pretend to cry, as if making his way down the "last mile," the long corridor to the execution chamber. He was a real charmer, Grandpa.

But most of all, he loved to tell stories about Vita. And he told them to my mother.

Ma could have been a writer. She had studied journalism in high school, but never went on to college because she had to work to give her mother money and then decided she wanted a family of her own (a good, criminal-free family).

So Ma didn't tell her stories to a wide audience. She told them to anyone who would listen. And that anyone was me.

She told me everything she knew about Vita, and that was as much as anyone knew. Vita couldn't read or write. No letters or diary entries. I had never met anyone who couldn't read or write. Reading was important in our apartment and a great escape from the realities of Jersey City.

Grandpa's parents had passed the story of Vita down to him and he'd told my mother. Like a game of telephone, it was repeated from mouth to ear and mouth to ear, through the generations, changing, shifting, breathing—until it landed, finally, in my little ear. My orecchietta.

VITA GALLITELLI WAS MY GREAT-GREAT-GRANDMOTHER, THE FIRST on the Italian side to come over to America. She came in 1892 with her two teenage sons, Valente and Leonardo, my great-grandfather. Vita had had three boys, but Ma said the youngest was lost on the way over. Ma had no name, no proof. Only the story.

The myth, really.

They left for America because Vita and her husband, Francesco Vena, had murdered someone back in Matera, a province tucked away in the farthest reaches of Southern Italy. It was a place my mother and I knew nothing about, filled with such intense poverty that no one really liked to talk about it. The name Matera came from the Latin word for mother. It was the motherland, but no one in my family ever considered going back there. Tourists didn't visit, and even Italians from other parts of the country barely knew where it was on the map.

I looked in the atlas and found Matera at Italy's instep between Puglia and Calabria, in the region of Basilicata.

My mother told me the story of Vita over and over again. She would tell it to me when we went to visit my great-aunt Katie, who would fill in some blanks with her own details. She would tell it to me as we walked over to church for Mass, which we attended dutifully every Sunday at noon. She would tell it sometimes on weekday mornings before I went to school, dressed in my blue checkered uniform, while braiding my thick, dark hair.

I figured Ma told me the stories to kill time and to distract me while combing the knots out, to stop me from flinching and screaming to high heaven as she stood over me in the shag-carpeted living room. Don't cry, Ma would say. Vita had it so much worse. Poor Vita.

She told me that Vita's husband, Francesco, stayed behind in Southern Italy, though his last name, Vena, traveled with my family to America. In Italy, maybe because of all the red tape involved in changing their maiden names, women kept theirs. But the children took the husband's name. In our case, Vena.

One detail stuck in my head: my mother said the murder had happened over a card game.

It was unusual for a woman to travel to America without her husband or without him having gone to America first to scope things out. So just the fact that Vita went solo with the kids was a sign that something was a little crazy—*batz,* as Ma liked to say. Women were rarely in charge of their own destinies back then, or if they were, no one ever told stories about it.

In the movies of Martin Scorsese and Francis Ford Coppola, which my big brother loved, the Italian women were minor characters, usually in the kitchen cooking like my mother. While making chicken cacciatore, doing laundry, or combing their daughters' hair, maybe they were wishing they could tell the stories and make the decisions and have the adventures.

But Vita was different.

Vita had left. For better or worse, like many of our ancestors. I thought about her coming through New York Harbor, without her husband, seeing the Statue of Liberty for the first time, and wondering, Who the hell is that big lady?

When I looked at Liberty myself, from my neighborhood, I thought the same thing. Who the hell was she? I read somewhere once that Liberty was based on the sculptor's mother. What was she thinking, to make her brow furrow like that? And had she read that big tablet in her arms? A woman in mid-nineteenth-century Europe? Did she even know how to read? And did she have adventures? Had she brought her kids along, or had she left them behind for someone else to take care of, while she stood, so stoic and important, her feet firmly planted on that pedestal?

The same way I looked at that light green statue, I looked at Vita, with awe and a sense of mystery. Who the hell was she? This complete stranger whose genes I carried around with me every single day in my DNA. And why on earth had she killed someone? Maybe self-defense, to protect her children or her husband. Or was it out of hatred or revenge? My family had a very finely honed sense of vengeance and, if they didn't get even, they could hold a grudge for decades. Little did I know this trait—this never-forgetting, obsessive sense of revenge—was going to come in handy.

WHEN I WAS A TEENAGER MY MOTHER UPPED THE ANTE WITH A NEW chapter, a cautionary tale. I was old enough to get pregnant, so Ma told me that Vita had been a loose woman—or as Vita's own daughter-in-law, my great-grandmother, liked to call her, a *puttana*. (They didn't get along.) I imagined Vita on a busy street corner, giving passing men the eye.

Maybe this explained why my family was particularly good at making pasta puttanesca, which we called refrigerator pasta. We could whip up an amazing meal out of just a few random ingredients that were on hand—as the prostitutes once did for their hungry customers.

Ma said that Vita had sons by two different men. Someone named Grieco was involved. He was either a lawyer or a lover, and somehow helped Vita escape to America.

I took my first trip to Italy in college, studying at the University of Siena for a summer. I traveled no farther south than Rome, with no interest in finding my family's roots. I was trying to get as far away from them as possible, to untangle myself from the petty crooks and shysters who made up a good part of my family tree: the bookie uncle, the embezzling cousins, the mob consigliere, the political fixers, even a murderer or two.

After graduating, I landed a job as a police reporter at my

local newspaper, my family's crimes occasionally making their way across my desk. One day, on assignment, I walked across the construction bridge from Jersey City to the nearby, soon-to-be-opened Ellis Island museum. Out of curiosity, I checked the immigration records, but there was no trace of Vita, since she probably came under an assumed name. Maybe Grieco's name.

But I found Leonardo, thirteen, and Valente, fifteen, who arrived on separate ships in 1892—the year Ellis Island opened.

We had a couple of photos of Leonardo and Valente as adults in Jersey City, where they both lived and worked as barbers. Leonardo, my great-grandfather, looked a bit like Al Capone; he was a dapper guy with a round, pudgy face, a balding pate, full, shapely lips, and sad brown eyes. But he was much nicer than Capone. Leonardo's brother, Valente, had a longer face and a full head of hair, but those same full lips as his brother.

No photos survived of either Vita or her husband, Francesco. But everyone said Vita looked just like my great-aunt Mary, Beansie's older sister. She had a pretty face, but an underbite, thin lips, dark brown hair, and dark brown eyes, nearly black, like kalamata olives. So dark the light flashed off them like sparks. Like all the women on the Italian side of my family, she had soft, flawless skin. We laughed that this was due to all the pasta we cooked as mothers, the steam rising up out of the strainer and giving us facials.

Vita had the same crooked smile I had, and that many of the women in my family had, what we called our Mona Lisa smile, a hesitant smirk that didn't give much away. You didn't get the full-on smile until we knew you better, and then we would bend over backward for you, cook you elaborate meals, and do anything you asked. Well, almost anything.

Vita was short, not even five feet tall. We were all short. I was five feet and towered over some of my aunts. I would come to learn that this was due to centuries of poverty and no protein.

Like all the women in my family, Vita was tough but kind. We spoke, walked, and acted with purpose, usually while the men lollygagged along.

We took bullshit from no one. But we loved our men and our children and hugged them tight several times a day. We loved our sisters, but we could be catty sometimes and competitive, with a bit of a mean streak. But when it came down to it, we would do anything for them. Anything for our family, anyway. That's just the way it was.

I TOLD MY CHILDREN ABOUT VITA WHEN THEY WERE OLD ENOUGH to pay attention. And when my mother came to my house to visit, we told them together. Dean and Paulina had heard so many family stories by this point that another crime didn't really faze them.

I didn't tell the story on the way to visit Aunt Katie, since Aunt Katie was dead. And I didn't tell it on the way to church, since I didn't go to church anymore: I had a list of grievances with the Catholic hierarchy that was longer than the pope's robes.

I told the family stories while I cooked and the kids did their homework at the table in our own yellow kitchen. As I stirred a big pot of sauce, meatballs floating on top, my mother and I would tell them how Vita died at the age of sixty-four.

She was hit in the head with a sock full of rocks in Jersey City on Mischief Night, the night before Halloween when all hell broke loose and bonfires raged on its dirty streets. Had she not been smacked in the head, Vita probably would have lived longer. Due to genetics, and the Mediterranean diet, the women in my family lived long lives, well into their late eighties.

We all went to visit Vita's grave once, looking for the first clue to that family mystery. She was buried deep inside Holy Name Cemetery in Jersey City, Leonardo and a couple of grandchildren piled on top of her, her name not even written on the tombstone. Just VENA.

I realized, now that I had my own kids, that my mother told me the story of Vita and Francesco over and over not just to pass the time, or for pure entertainment value, but to teach me something. Vita and Francesco had been involved in a murder. She had been a puttana. And look how it all turned out. Hit in the head with a sock full of rocks on Mischief Night. Not even a name on your own gravestone. There was an Italian saying that went, "Tutti i nodi vengono al pettine," which meant "All the knots come to the comb." It was the Italian version of "what goes around comes around."

I searched for more clues about Vita and found her death certificate from 1915. It listed her birthday as August 22 and her mother as Teresina. Through a cousin, I also found the birth certificates of Vita's sons—Valente from 1877, born in the province of Matera, in the town of Bernalda "to Vita Gallitelli, wife of Francesco Vena," and Leonardo, from 1879, born in the neighboring town of Pisticci. The birth certificate said Vita had moved to Pisticci "for work reasons."

Valente's birth certificate said Vita was a weaver. And that Francesco was not present for Valente's birth. Or for Leonardo's birth two years later.

It was with these few meager clues—a few dates and street names—that I did something that surprised even me. I went to Basilicata with my mother and the kids on a long vacation to research that first family story. I left my husband behind, just like Vita had.

It would be fun, I told myself and my mother. We'll rent a house in the town of Bernalda. Spend some time on the beach in nearby Metaponto. Eat some gelato. We can poke around a little, and talk to the locals, do some archival research. My mother was seventy-three and had never been to Italy or anywhere, really, and had never tasted gelato. It was time she had an adventure.

We would be the first in four generations to visit the town of our ancestors, on the arch of Italy's boot. Vita had left and had never looked back. And neither had her children or grandchildren or even her great grandchildren.

I had no idea that I would cross the Atlantic again and again, that this trip was the beginning of an odyssey that would take me through ancient painted caves, over green volcanic mountains to dusty archives, to dead ends and the edges of cliffs, and to a valley of death where the drama all began.

I had no clue about the isolated world I was stepping into, or how long it would actually take to find Vita's true story, a story more tragic—and eventually more triumphant—than anything I could have imagined.

How could I have known there was something hidden at the end of my ten-year journey that would change my view of my children altogether, that would make me question my very own identity? That in the end, I would discover one shotgun blast and five dead bodies, most of them belonging to my family?

Chapter 2

DARK TO DARK

I WALKED OUT ONTO THE BALCONY TO CHECK THE HEAT BEFORE the kids were awake, the punishing sun barely making its way over the horizon. From my second-floor perch, with a hand on my hip, I surveyed the neighborhood, which was already stirring, unsmiling men and women quickly getting chores done before the inferno arrived. Women hung laundry and men swept the cobblestones, which were already immaculate.

Across the street from me, on her own balcony that first morning, was a long-lost cousin. Maria Gallitelli looked up from her humongous laundry pile, wiped her dark brow with the back of her thin, brown arm, noticed me, and waved.

"Buongiorno," she said, loudly, and smiled the exact same smile that my cousin Jill had back in New Jersey. Yeah, I thought. She's a cousin all right.

"Buongiorno," I said and smiled back. I told her I was visiting with my mother and two children and doing some family research. Young Maria Gallitelli had two sons and a husband, she said, gesturing inside with her head, so she was always hanging laundry, sentenced to a life of dirty undershirts and *mutande*—underwear—that would only get bigger and dirtier as her boys grew.

We chatted for a bit and finally I asked her, in my slow, stunted Italian, if she had ever heard the story of my great-great-grandmother Vita Gallitelli, who, with her husband, Francesco Vena, had been involved in a murder somewhere around here, somewhere in Matera province around the turn of the last century. They had killed someone, possibly in a card game? I raised my dark, bushy eyebrows, hoping she would nod and the details would come spilling out past her thin lips.

Maria Gallitelli scrunched her prominent Italian nose—a lot like my own prominent Italian nose—and thought for a second. She stuck out her bottom lip and shrugged. "No," she said, shaking her thick head of short black hair. "I don't know that story. I never heard it. But I will ask my family."

Maria owned a bomboniere shop on the corner, where, between loads of laundry, she sold expensive wedding gifts, the kind that the bride and groom give to their guests, crystal or silver trinkets that cost a small fortune. Her wooden sign, with a big *Gallitelli* calligraphied across it, hung over the corner and seemed to be a sign from God that I should live on this street, so I had rented this spacious, second-floor apartment in Bernalda, sealing the deal with the landlady with a shot of homemade limoncello.

Maria and the other locals pronounced the town name "Bare-NAL-da," with a little trill at the *r*. It was a perfect name for this bare-bones place still recovering from centuries of poverty and starvation, where life expectancy at the end of the nineteenth century had been thirty-nine years. My first day there I learned that the Basilicata region was also known as Lucania, its original Roman name. And residents were—and still are called—Lucani.

Bernalda sat on a small hill overlooking the fertile Basento

Valley. And now, in the summer of 2004, I'd arrived with my family. In theory it sounded fabulous: live in a small, sun-splashed Italian village with your kids and your mother for a month and research your family's roots.

But even on that first day, I noticed a darkness in Bernalda, as if a cloud were pressing down on its gray cobblestone streets and melancholy population. I wasn't sure if it was something I'd brought with me, like luggage, or if it was some vestige left from the malaria and *miseria* that had gripped its residents for centuries, a hangover that would take several more generations to shake.

Our apartment was on the same street where Vita had lived more than a hundred years before, Via Cavour. The name of the street had been on the birth certificate of her oldest son, Valente. It was in the Centro Storico, or historic district, the neighborhood on the edge of town.

I was thirty-nine (ready for the grave by nineteenth-century standards), around the same age Vita had immigrated to America with her two sons. But I was traveling in the opposite direction with my own two children, Paulina, who was one, and Dean, who was four. And Ma.

When I looked at my mother, it was like looking in a magic mirror that showed exactly what to expect in thirty years. Along with her work ethic, I shared my mother's temper, her impatience, her heartburn, her nice legs, thick middle, and face with its smooth, unwrinkled skin.

I had become who I had become because of her, not just through genetics, but because she took care of me every time I was sick and knew to call the doctor when I had pneumonia at age five. She took care of me when I wasn't sick, feeding me homemade chicken soup with pastina. She walked me to school every single day and brought me back again, until, at age fourteen, I begged her not to. And then she followed about a block behind me. She always listened to me and hugged me daily, but when I got snotty or did something bad, she yelled at me, in a very loud and scary voice. She found my stash of pot in my room as a teenager and let me know she had. I obeyed her not just because I was afraid of her wrath (which I was) but because she loved me so much, I couldn't bear to disappoint her. She had given me her best, and expected the best of me, so I gave it. People would say to my mother all the time, "You're so lucky. You have such great kids." And she would say, "Luck has nothing to do with it."

I tried to follow my mother's model of motherhood, and so far it seemed to be working. As far as I knew, my children had not inherited the criminal genes in my family and were not turning out to be sociopaths.

My husband, Wendell, had no criminals in his family. In fact, his great-grandfather had been a district attorney and his grandfather a judge. It was one of the many reasons I had married him, to help balance the larcenous side of my genetic code. Wendell was a newspaper editor, and that summer was helping to cover the Republican National Convention in New York. He would join us the last week of our monthlong trip to make sure we made it back to America and that I didn't decide to stay here.

He shouldn't have worried.

FROM THE TOWN'S CASTLE WALLS, YOU COULD SEE SILVER-TINGED olive trees and arthritic-looking vineyards and fig trees with those big leaves that Adam and Eve used as underwear. Light green and yellow rolling hills stretched into the distance, ending eight miles away in the flat plane of Metaponto and the Ionian Sea. On the outskirts of town, you could still make out some of the old narrow mule paths, called *mulattiere*, which the farmers once used to ride to work each day before the sun rose and then back home after it had set. (*Buia a buia* was the saying, dark to dark.)

I couldn't imagine why Vita would trade this country for a city as ugly and industrial as Jersey City. The landscape here was achingly beautiful, but uninhabited, and left you feeling forlorn and uplifted all at once, as if you'd just heard a favorite sad love song on the radio. This landscape made you want to sing sad love songs. Or maybe even write them.

When you approached Bernalda from the direction of the sea, from the south, as the pirates and invaders had long ago, the first things you noticed were the ginger-colored mother church, Chiesa Madre, which was now closed and under repair, the matching wall, and rounded medieval castle, which was no longer open to anyone.

These days, no one was out to conquer Bernalda. The few outsiders, like me, typically approached from the north, from either the city of Matera, the provincial capital, thirty-six miles inland, or from Bari, ninety minutes away on the Adriatic Coast, where you could rent a car.

On that route, you drove through desolate valleys and past badlands-like mountains called *calanchi*. The isolation and nothingness were interrupted by the occasional hill town hovering in the distance, and finally, by an immense white and red water tower, which looked like a giant poisonous mushroom. The tower was hideously ugly, an awful eyesore that ruined the natural beauty of the landscape but was a point of pride for the Bernaldans. It was their way of saying, "Hey! Look at us! We got water!" They were rightfully proud of their water tower, since running water had only arrived in most homes about fifty years earlier.

My balcony looked out over the historic district, a maze of cobblestone streets and tiny cavelike houses the color of old bones, some tumbling down. The houses were side by side, crowded together from the days when Saracen pirates and other invaders would launch sudden raids, forcing the frightened population to huddle together for safety. The region's history of constant attack helped explain the residents' mistrust of newcomers, including me.

Most of the twelve thousand people who lived in Bernalda were small and scrappy, like I was, with rough features and black hair and black eyes that darted about nervously and gave you the once-over the first time they spotted you. It was an animal-like quality that I recognized because I had seen it in myself, a searching, aggressive look that said, "I really don't trust you, so keep your distance. At least until I get to know you better."

Bernalda was still rough around the edges. People dumped their garbage over the wall of the city, a small band of local heroin addicts and dealers held court in the most secluded streets of the historic district, and a pack of stray dogs—sad and mangy—loitered not far from the main corso on Via Galileo Galilei.

Most houses in the district were the size of a walk-in closet, where people had lived in past centuries with their farm animals. When the beasts relieved themselves, a mix of straw and sand or soil was placed on top to absorb the stench. No real soap. No disinfectant. Disease had been rampant: cholera, tuberculosis, trachoma, smallpox. Hunger was a given, malnutrition common. Nearly half of the children born in the mid-1800s in Southern Italy died before the age of five.

It was the reason our family—and most Italian families—held huge bashes for the baby's first birthday. It was to celebrate that the baby—miraculously—had made it through the first year of life. In fact, we had had a big party for Paulina with the entire family and all our friends right before we left for Italy. I bought her first baby shoes in the city of Matera, and she took some of her first steps in them on these cobblestone streets.

Paulina was my secret weapon. She learned within the first few days in Bernalda how to wave the Italian way, palm facing in, scrunching her pudgy fingers up and down. People who would otherwise never talk to me smiled widely and started a conversation because I had Paulina with me. "Bella bambina!" is how they always started the exchange.

But most of the time, no one was out on the street to even start a conversation.

WALKING OUTSIDE MIDDAY WAS LIKE STEPPING INTO A PIZZA OVEN. It took approximately three minutes for laundry to dry when hung out on the line. Southern Italy was called the Mezzogiorno, aptly named for the time of day when the sun was highest in the sky. The fields were bleached yellow from a sun so strong it closed all the businesses from 1 to 7 P.M. The whole town retreated home for an epic lunch and nap.

This was a long siesta compared to the surrounding villages. Even Bernalda's toothless old women, the *anziane*, who especially loved Paulina and spent all their time outside on miniature wooden rush-bottomed chairs, pulled them inside their houses the entire afternoon. I soon learned that this siesta was not just in August, but every season in Bernalda, and helped contribute to the townspeople's reputation among the Lucani as being especially unmotivated.

Bernalda smelled of burning wheat stubble, as the farmers cleared their fields for the new crop. It was still an agricultural town, though many of the young men refused to work in those fields. Old women still put out woven baskets on straw chairs to sell produce from their latest harvest. That first week melons were in season, especially watermelon. The town was lousy with watermelon. We received three as housewarming presents from our kind, watermelon-plagued neighbors. Then came the figs. A tsunami of figs. Green figs, purple figs, yellow figs, and brown figs, which Paulina ate like candy.

But the produce chairs were becoming more and more scarce, especially outside this neighborhood. The chairs embarrassed the younger members of the farm families. Farming was beneath them, though unemployment was ridiculously high for the younger population—around 60 percent. Young men preferred to sit in cafés and bemoan the state of Italy's economy. I couldn't blame them. It was much cooler under the café umbrellas.

It was so hot on our first night in town that Dean, Paulina, and I fell asleep on the apartment floor, our faces pressed up against the cool marble tile. I woke up stiff after an hour and placed the kids in their respective playpen and bed, then stayed awake half the night wondering how I would survive this heat, but also how I would ever find Vita's story.

I had had visions of arriving and my long-lost relatives clamoring around me—perhaps with watermelons—to tell me their stories, which would jigsaw with what I already knew.

But it wasn't like that. Not even close.

YOUNG MARIA ASKED EVERYONE IN HER GALLITELLI FAMILY ABOUT the murder. She updated me one morning on the street, under the Gallitelli sign, as she was opening up her shop and I was heading out to the market to buy groceries for the day, the first of my many chores.

"I asked everyone," she said, shaking her head. "But no one has ever heard this story." I nodded and frowned. But Maria Gallitelli had a consolation prize for me. She told me to wait and quickly walked inside her apartment, which was next door to the shop. She emerged with the local phone book, a skinny volume she had pulled off a kitchen shelf and now handed to me.

"Take a look at the other Gallitellis listed here," she said, thumbing through to the G section. "And the Venas," she said, flipping to the back. "Maybe they know something."

Sixty-one Gallitellis were listed in the phone book. And in Pisticci, the neighboring hill town seven miles away, where my great-grandfather had been born, thirty-five Venas. They were the Smiths of their respective villages. I now knew that the Gallitelli sign hanging on this street was not a sign from God, not even a coincidence. So many Gallitellis lived here that it would have been unnatural not to see a Gallitelli sign somewhere in the neighborhood.

Over the next few weeks, I met many of those Gallitellis. To differentiate themselves from one another, each Gallitelli clan took on a nickname. A *soprannome*, they called it.

The Gallitelli man around the corner, the old guy they called Marinaro, had a seaman's history. God knows what happened to the family boat. But this guy had run aground ages ago. He owned a garage down the hill, his very own man cave, where he kept chickens and hung his homemade *soppressata*. You could see him hanging out in there amid the dried sausage, day after day. When we asked him if he knew about our Gallitelli/Vena murder, he shook his big round head no, pointed down the street, and said to try his cousin, the local butcher.

He was named Gallitelli as well and owned a shop called Paradiso. In Bernalda, the butcher shop was a kind of paradise. For centuries, these people had no meat to eat. Which helped explain why they barely broke the five-foot mark. Though the Paradiso butcher was very happy to talk, wiping his bloody hands on his white apron as he chatted, he smiled and said he knew nothing of my family murder. I took two pounds of veal cutlets and moved on.

Leonardantonio Gallitelli, who lived on our street, bumped into me one day and said he had heard I was asking a lot of questions. He said that his family nickname was Caschedette, which translates into casket, as in a funeral casket.

The name, Caschedette, refers to some long-forgotten Gallitelli who nearly died as a boy. His family had a casket made. But when he recovered, the casket was kept under his bed for the rest of his life, not as a reminder of his mortality, but for safekeeping, just in case he—or another relative—needed it. Nothing in Basilicata ever went to waste. Not the goat's head. Not the entrails. Not the ashes from the fire. And certainly not a perfectly made casket. Someone in the family—someone particularly short—was bound to die sooner or later.

Leonardantonio was friendly in a nosy, abrasive sort of way, with a comb-over and a long, horsey face. We chatted one night over a drink in one of the local cafés, though Leonardantonio said he had never heard of a Vena-Gallitelli murder.

The pretty young painter, Luciana Gallitelli, who had a show in a gallery nearby, had never heard the story either. The old Gallitelli woman who lived around the corner barely answered me when I asked her about the murder, turning away with a grunt and a frown. I didn't know her *soprannome,* but I gave her one myself: Miserabila.

Nearly bald, with the face of a bulldog, Miserabila usually sat with my downstairs neighbor, Maria Natale (Mary Christmas), who saw everything that went on. Maria Natale perched outside on her small wooden chair and sewed each morning and night, looking up from her stitch to watch, like women here had done for centuries.

Maria Natale was a widow, but her husband had died so long ago in a crop-dusting accident that she was no longer *in lutto* (dressed in widow black). She wore bright colors and was happy-go-lucky, though she did wear a picture of her husband in a gold locket around her neck, just like the other widows in the neighborhood. Her hair was the color of ginger, the same shade of the nearby church tower.

Over the four weeks we lived on Via Cavour, Maria Natale made us stewed snails, tomato bruschetta, and Italian profiteroles and introduced us to her family members, who visited regularly. Though not as regularly as Miserabila, her best friend.

Miserabila gave me and my mother the hairy eyeball the very first day we moved in. And every day after that. Sometimes more than once a day. The *malocchio,* my mother called it. The evil eye. I wasn't usually superstitious, but if anybody had the *malocchio,* it was this woman.

"I don't trust that one," my mother said to me in English. I smiled and nodded and pretended she'd said something else, something nice. And hoped Miserabila was not a long-lost cousin.

Chapter 3

PUBLIC MOCKERY

WE HIT THE CEMETERY FOR CLUES.

I knew Vita was buried back in Jersey City, but the bones of Francesco were somewhere around here. If we could find his grave, we could find out the year he died, which might give us a lead on the murder. We drove to the outskirts of town for a family outing to the high iron gates of Bernalda's *cimitero*.

Its tall white, immaculate tombs were called loculi. The dead were stacked six high, in long drawers, the fronts of which were dutifully decorated with fake flowers and framed photos of the deceased—like a yearbook photo, smiling out at you from Beyond the Beyond High School. We walked up and down the endless rows looking for Francesco Vena, passing old women on their knees scrubbing their family graves.

The cemetery caretaker told us that if the tombs weren't maintained and visited regularly, cemetery officials would exhume the bones and replace them with a newly deceased person. Space was at a premium. Harsh, I thought to myself.

With Vita gone to America, I imagined Francesco's grave was never kept up. God knew where his bones were scattered now.

After several hours of searching through the loculi and then the cemetery records with the caretaker, we found no photo or trace of Francesco. I would have settled for seeing Francesco's ghost.

We headed over to Bernalda's comune, or city hall, near the center of town to search for records there. Birth records, marriage records, death records. I would have been happy to find an old dog license.

The Comune was a yellow building with a clock tower that lit up, but blinked on and off because of faulty wiring. A plaque on the building read CITTA DI BERNALDA 1497, the year the city was founded. Three flags hung outside: the Italian green, white, and red; the blue European Union flag with a circle of yellow stars; and the blue Bernalda flag, which had a cow on it. I hadn't seen a single cow on my trip here. Eaten long ago, I figured. Beef was hard to come by in town. There was plenty of horsemeat, though I was on a strict no-horsemeat diet.

Swordlike agave and some bushes sat in a sad clump outside the Comune. Squat palm trees—which looked like giant pineapples—ran down the middle of the Corso. The outdoor courtyard, which took up the center of the Comune, had long porticoes on either side, where the paint was chipped and the walls were worn and dirty. The place had a run-down bandito beauty to it, like something you'd see in Mexico, inspired by the Spanish invaders who passed through here centuries ago.

While the kids played on the brown patches of grass out front with Ma, I went inside to talk to the clerk. She looked incredibly tired and unhappy, though you could see past the scowl and the bags under her eyes that she had once been very pretty.

When I asked to see the book for the year of Vita's birth, the clerk frowned and shook her head.

"What?" I asked.

"It's unavailable," she said.

"Why?" I asked.

She just shrugged.

I took a deep breath and began again. I asked for the span of years around the time Vita and Francesco would have been married—the late 1860s, probably—but the frowny clerk shook her head again.

"Come back in three weeks," she said and began to walk away from me.

"But I'll be gone in three weeks!" I shouted after her. "Wait." But she just kept on walking.

We traveled to Pisticci, where Leonardo was born, to try our luck there. The locals pronounced it "Pis-TEECH." And though the Comune and the staff there were in much better shape, all we could find was Leonardo's birth certificate, which I already had. We found no traces of a marriage between Francesco and Vita.

Then suddenly our research was cut short. Over and out. Arrivederci, amore.

We were swallowed whole by the annual feast of San Bernardino, Bernalda's patron saint, who had saved the town from famine and plague in the 1600s. When we had made plans to come here, I thought it would be fun for everyone: marching bands and costumed townspeople in medieval garb and parading farm animals and long skewers of mystery meat and strings and strings of colorful lights. But of course, it meant the city offices were closed for an entire week.

Bernalda's festivities grew and grew, until they exploded, finally, in a fireworks competition on the last night, rockets flying right above our bedroom, so close and so loud it felt like we were being shelled. They went on and on for hours, as each team tried to blast the hell out of the other. Paulina, who could sleep through anything, snored away to the racket. But Dean was having a hard time.

I lay in bed with him and stroked his big head of dark, thick hair to try to comfort him. Dean had the same sad eyes that seemed to look back at you everywhere you turned in Southern Italy. (We called them Dondi eyes in my family, after the comic strip character, an Italian war orphan.) His Dondi eyes were more downturned than usual, tired and especially sad. A sadness so deep, several generations of American prosperity hadn't erased it. When he turned a certain way, Dean looked an awful lot like Grandpa Beansie. I wondered how old Beansie had been when he'd turned to a life of crime. Certainly not four. I pushed the thought from my mind.

Dean asked me when the fireworks would stop and why, why it was even happening to begin with. I told him the people of Bernalda were celebrating his arrival. That they were just so happy to see him.

"Really?" he asked, suspicious, just like his mother.

"Really," I lied, stroking his head. He smiled and promptly passed out, bombs and all.

I HAD THOUGHT THAT THE FEAST WAS THE REASON BERNALDA'S streets were so crowded at night. But long after the feast ended, its streets grew crowded each and every night with the *passeggiata*, as old people, teenagers, children, and their parents made their way down the Corso, exchanging hellos, gossip, and small talk. Cafés were packed until midnight, giving the town a lively vibe that it lacked during the oppressive afternoons.

Despite the late *passeggiata*, the Bernaldans were up very early due to their long midday nap, sweeping the streets and shopping at the local food vans. The fish man or the meat and cheese man arrived on alternate mornings, announcing their arrival through a bullhorn at 7 A.M. That was my alarm clock.

I did my shopping, fed the kids, and then went out to do some research, interviewing the locals or digging through church records here and in Pisticci. Then, most afternoons, while the rest of the town was inside sleeping, I took my family to Metaponto to a place called Spiaggetta, which means Little Beach. I needed a nap myself, but felt guilty for having the kids and my mom cooped up in the hot apartment all morning, Dean playing with his toy plastic soldiers and Power Rangers we'd brought along, Paulina listening to Ma's songs and stories, the first of several hundred rounds to come in her lifetime.

The salt air usually revived me once I got near Metaponto. We could smell and taste the sea before we could see it, the saltiness of the Ionian coast filling our rental car. Leading down to the beach was a long line of tall trees, a forest that replaced the marshes Mussolini had drained back in the 1930s to combat malaria.

The sea was turquoise blue and bathtub-warm, the cloudless sky a deep azure, the sand clean and fine like the talcum I put on Paulina's bottom, and the beach empty except for the occasional Speedo-clad German tourist.

I chased the children into the mild surf and bought everyone gelato at the empty wooden lido café, which also rented out beach chairs. The locals hardly ever went to the beach. Centuries of malaria and pirate invasions had left them landlubbers.

Spartacus had once rested on the sandy beaches of Metapontum with his troops between battles with the Romans in the first century BC. I told stories of Spartacus to Dean, who loved battles and military history. I shared the little I knew from the Kubrick film I had seen years ago, and we imagined him here, looking an awful lot like Kirk Douglas, chin dimple and all, lounging on the beach next to us with his slave army.

It seemed everyone had passed through because of the topography of the Ionian coast—a wide-open mouth, unintentionally welcoming ship after ship of invaders.

The philosopher and mathematician Pythagoras had settled here; Hannibal made his way through, but retreated when his brother's head was delivered to him. They were followed by the Lombards, the Normans, the Aragonese, the pirates.

The locals joked that they talked with their hands for good reason, after centuries of trying to communicate with strangers. Now I was one of those strangers.

BACK ON VIA CAVOUR, I WASHED THE KIDS IN A BIG PLASTIC BASIN, scrubbing the sand from their hair. I made sure to remove all traces of gelato from their faces, or else the flies—which flew freely into our apartment, since there were big windows with no screens—would feast on their cheeks.

I cooked dinner or got the children dressed for eating out, then headed back for another round of research, making my way from house to house, like a detective searching for a suspect. If I took Paulina and Dean with me, people opened up easier, but it was harder to follow the conversation when I had to constantly keep an eye on them.

I grew exhausted from being a single parent in a strange and foreign land. Everything was a struggle, from changing diapers and figuring out what the right size was to buy, to food shopping, haggling with the fish man, cooking the fish, translating baby food labels (prosciutto and cheese flavored!), doing laundry, hanging it out to dry, driving a stick shift on roads I didn't know, and reading signs I didn't understand. My brain hurt from constantly translating. At night in bed, I read to Dean, then lay awake until the early morning hours, staring at the ceiling, praying to the saints that the next day I would find some tiny morsel of information about Vita. I wasn't normally a religious person. Angry, estranged Catholic was the box I checked. But in Bernalda, you couldn't avoid religion. And I needed every bit of help I could get.

Stations of the Cross, each carved with a Roman numeral, and a picture of Jesus making his way to his fate, step by painful step, were posted on the corners of the historic district, as were murals and dioramas dedicated to the Blessed Mother and the saints: Santa Lucia with her gouged out eyes on a dinner plate. St. Rocco with his pet dog, who liked to lick the plague sores on his master's leg. And a doctored photo of Padre Pio, with blood dripping not just from his hands, but from his eyes. They were a gruesome bunch, those saints.

When someone was sick, you went to church—either the Chiesa Madre over near the castle or to Mount Carmel, a smaller, seventeenth-century church in the historic district—and lit a votive candle to pray to your patron saint for help.

One night, Dean had a high fever. I ran to the local pharmacy to buy the Italian version of Tylenol and waited impatiently on line at the counter. But when my turn came, the pharmacist said I needed a doctor's prescription. "But I'm not from here," I explained, using my hands for emphasis. "I have no local doctor. Please, help me. My son is very sick."

The pharmacist shrugged and moved on to the next customer. I wanted to put him in a headlock and insist he give me some medicine. But I figured it would only land me in the town jail. Instead I stormed out, stomped all the way home, put a cold rag on Dean's head, and resorted to prayer.

All night I lay awake, checking his forehead and saying the Rosary. What if it was something serious? What if he'd been bitten by a bad mosquito and had malaria? What kind of mother was I, dragging him and his baby sister here on some cockamamie genealogy field trip? What was I even thinking?

After hours of mom guilt and worry, after several hundred

rounds of the Hail Mary, I finally fell asleep, Dean's small, hot body tucked into mine. Whatever he had, I was bound to catch it. If he had something bad, I wanted it, too.

Of course, when we woke up in the morning, the fever was gone.

SOME DAYS I PRAYED TO ST. LEONARDO, THE PATRON SAINT OF PRIS- oners, to help protect us and to help me find my family murder. Thousands of children in Bernalda had been named after Leon- ardo, including my great-grandfather. St. Leonardo protected the site of the old town jail, which was marked by a giant clock with Roman numerals and a brick tower with two small bells. It was where I'm sure my relatives passed many a day, behind bars. Now it was a garage for motorbikes and bicycles, its vaulted ceiling painted in orange and purple graffiti by Bernalda's disaf- fected youth.

Three hundred years ago, at the sound of its small bells, pris- oners were paraded out to the barred window of the jail up on the third floor, subject to public humiliation. It was the perp walk of its day, before people had the six o'clock news, and was called *pubblico ludibrio,* public mockery. Their hands were tied, honey was spread on their bare torsos, and they were forced to stand in the window as bees and flies and other insects attacked them. The townspeo- ple watched and pointed and laughed. It seemed insanely brutal. But daily life in Basilicata—pronounced Boz-ee-lee-GOD—was so brutal, I figured lawmakers had to go to extremes to make the prisoners suffer a bit. Life in a quiet, dry jail cell, with a meal of bread and water, was a step way above normal life in town. As I gazed up at that jail window, I wondered if the honey torture had happened to anyone in my family.

But no one would tell me about my family's crimes. Those with stories to tell told tales that had happened too late, long after Vita had left for America.

I heard the story about the Fascists chasing a Gallitelli man into his home, finding him under his bed and dragging him out by the heels and beating him and then shooting him in the head. Not our story.

I met a mechanic by the name of Beano Vena (Beansie Vena; Beano Vena; maybe he was related!), who told me the story of the great-grandfather who was woken at night by a knock at the door. When Vena went to see who it was, the visitor refused to answer and he became frightened. Vena fired one shot through the closed door and killed the visitor instantly, who, it turned out, was a deaf mute peddling olives. But the story had happened after the turn of the century.

An eye doctor named Vena from Pisticci told me about the Vena murder that happened out in the countryside, a lover's triangle that ended in the husband being slaughtered with a scythe by his wife and her lover. But there was no Vita or Francesco involved.

We found, in three weeks, nothing that had to do with our Gallitelli or Vena. Maybe it was my fault, I thought, as I lay awake sweating night after night. Maybe I was too forward, too demanding and brusque. Women didn't usually ask the questions around here. Or maybe I wasn't bold enough. Maybe I should offer bribes.

The less I found, the more fixated I became on finding something, anything, about Vita.

I ventured farther afield, scouring the dusty records in the archives of Matera, where I flipped through every criminal case file from the end of the 1800s. I turned up many of the crimes the locals had told me about.

But not mine.

Then, just when I began to worry that Vita had never even lived here, I discovered one scrap of evidence, a simple piece of paper, sewn inside an old leather-bound book. I found it with the help of the town historian, right around the time of Vita's birthday in late August, in a small annex to city hall. Proof of a newborn baby girl buried deep in the dusty files of antiquity.

Vita's birth certificate.

Chapter 4

IN THE NAME OF THE FATHER, SON, AND HOLY SPIRIT

T ERESINA STIGLIANO WAS UP EARLY AS USUAL THAT FRIDAY, August 22, 1851, earlier than anyone else in the house. The day was guaranteed to be a scorcher, even at 6 A.M. She lay on the elevated, lumpy, straw-filled mattress in the only bed in the back part of their one-room hovel. Besides the bed, and maybe a bench or a wooden chest, there wasn't much furniture. A small straw and wood chair was kept out on the street to make room for the eight to ten people who slept inside—and to have a good seat to the drama that unfolded now and then in the *rione,* or neighborhood.

The couple's farm tools, a mattock and hoe—called a *zapp*— their cheese forms, baskets, and pots hung from rusty metal hooks all around Teresina on the cracked, darkened walls, made black by the smoke from the small hearth, where they cooked their meals.

But that day there would be no cooking. Just pain. And a knotted cloth shoved into Teresina's mouth by the midwife, so that she wouldn't scream out loud. Thirty-three-year-old Teresina knew it was a dishonor to scream out in pain during childbirth. But the farm animals, the ones who lived under the high bed, sensed her pain—the skinny, dying chicken, which they kept for her occasional egg, which was usually sold or given to a sick child, and the half-starved goat, used now and then for a squirt of milk, though hardly ever enough for cheese. The goat hunkered down, its head on its hooves, with worry. The chicken clucked more than usual, in a nervous panic, emerging from beneath the bed and making anxious circles around the room.

Like a Nativity scene, the animals were there for the birth of this little baby. Except there was no smiling baby Jesus, no figures frozen in pastoral poses, and no happy mother dressed in blue with outstretched arms.

This was the real deal. Madonna and child, as it had transpired for millennia and no doubt would for centuries to come. Forever and ever, amen.

All that pushing and all that pain. So much so that the animals finally left their cover under the bed and escaped out front, away from the thrashing and silent tears, the torn bedclothes and bloody rags. Teresina's other children would clear out but would stay close to the house just in case their mother needed them or was near death and wanted to say a last goodbye, give them a final hug.

The men—Teresina's thirty-six-year-old husband, Domenico Gallitelli, his brothers, Grandpa Donato, and whoever else was alive at the time—sat out front and smoked and drank homemade wine and waited for that little girl to come out into the world, her wet, slippery head finally sliding out into the warm August air.

Teresina, already crying from the pain, now shed happy tears at the sight of her. She marveled at the tiny head, with a thick shock of black hair, and a grimace that opened up into an operatic solo. Still dizzy from the pain, aching from past childbirths, the memory of some babies placed dead in her arms, or soon to die,

Teresina smiled down at her newborn daughter. This one came out yelling. Fighting. Fists tight and as small as walnuts.

A little girl so full of life that they called her just that: Vita.

Vita!

Her mother struggled up in bed and laughed at the sight of her, as the midwife wiped the baby clean. Teresina then took Vita in her unsteady arms and offered a weak smile to the local priest, who was called right away for the baptism, combined with last rites, since the rate of infant mortality was so high. This one won't need last rites, her mother thought to herself. Not this one.

Vita was a pure baby, but like all of us, was born with original sin, and so the priest placed some blessed oil on her red forehead and mumbled a few words in Latin—"In nomine Patris et Filii et Spiritus Sancti"—and suddenly her soul was wiped clean like a blackboard and she was welcomed into the dirty old world. After a few more mumbles, and some more oil, she was protected from going to limbo in case she died anytime soon. Just like that, saved with a few simple words and a shiny smudge.

You couldn't take any chances. To make sure that no special curses were placed on her baby or on her mother's milk, Teresina that week would put a talisman inside the baby's crib—a cross, made of straw, blessed by that same priest before he left the house. There were just too many dangers out there and too many ways to die.

You had to be strong just to survive the birth and the first few months of life in Bernalda. Because Bernalda was a terrible place to be born in 1851. Mothers sometimes smothered their infants to spare them the awful life that lay ahead: the constant hunger and malaria, the searing summer heat and the *pebrina* silkworm disease and the earthquakes. In fact, a big earthquake had destroyed the Basilicatan hill town of Melfi just a week before, killing a thousand people. Teresina no doubt had felt the tremors and thought her labor had come early.

Most towns, like Melfi, were set up on tall hilltops to guard from pirates and malaria. But not Bernalda. People in Bernalda were called "green faces" because of their malarial symptoms, their monstrous pallor. In Teresina's day, two million Italians were sickened by malaria each year, a good number of them from low-lying Bernalda. Those who survived were left blind, deformed, infertile, never really whole again.

Vita was born in the last, dying days of the Kingdom of the Two Sicilies, a decade before Italy's unification. There was no Italy as we know it, but a complicated collection of independent kingdoms and duchies and states.

Into this kingdom, this disenchanted hell of a kingdom, Vita Gallitelli would—like my own daughter—take her first baby steps.

Chapter 5

YOU HAVE THE FACE
OF THE GALLITELLIS

PROFESSOR ANGELO TATARANNO CUT WHAT THE ITALIANS called *una bella figura*. The first night we met he was dressed in linen slacks, a collarless button-down shirt, and very stylish bowling shoe–type sneakers. He was in his fifties and had hair the color of pepper, with some grains of salt tossed in near the temples, a long face, and a big forehead, with wavy lines across it like a thick strip of bacon, lines that betrayed years of concentration and study. His lips were pursed, as if he were thinking, and his narrow eyes, which always looked like he was focusing on a problem, were covered in rectangular, rimless glasses.

I met Professor Tataranno the last week in August at Pitagorici, a restaurant named for the Greek philosopher Pythagoras. It had an outdoor café and two stucco-walled rooms, separated by an arched doorway, with a glowing, brick pizza oven at the back. It was one of dozens of restaurants and cafés to choose from in Bernalda. But it had the best pizza and was close to our apartment, so the family and I ate there most nights when I was too tired to cook.

Pythagoras ($a^2 + b^2 = c^2$) had lived in nearby Metapontum—not far from our favorite beach—and eventually died there around 500 BC. Every Italian schoolchild was reminded of him every time the multiplication table—*tavola pitagorica*—was mentioned. But around here, streets and restaurants were named after Pythagoras and his philosophy was held in high esteem. He was a Christ-like figure, five centuries before Christ, and a cult leader, back in the days when religious cults were a new sensation. He believed in reincarnation, vegetarianism (except for beans, which, for some strange reason, he hated and forbade his followers to eat), the therapeutic use of music, and in long communal dinners, where women were invited to the table.

Professor Tataranno, much like Pythagoras, had been a philosophy student when he was young and was now a revered teacher. A professor of literature at the local high school for many years, he was everyone's favorite teacher in Bernalda—and everyone's favorite storyteller.

By the time we connected, he knew that I was the American in town searching for her nineteenth-century roots. My family and I were the only Americans, in fact. I should have gone looking for Professor Tataranno the first day I got there. But Tataranno came looking for me my last week there and found me over a plate of lightly fried calamari.

He introduced himself when he approached my family's table. By then I knew his reputation around town. He had written several history books on the region and was the premier expert on Bernalda. I was thrilled to meet him.

"Piacere," I said.

"Hai la faccia di Gallitelli," he said.

You have the face of the Gallitellis.

"Really?" I asked.

"It's true," he said. "You look just like the niece of a famous Gallitelli who was killed."

"A murder?"

"Yes," Professor Tataranno said, shaking his head. "But it's not your story. This is from 1923." I could feel my Gallitelli face fall.

"This man was killed for political reasons," said the professor, taking a drag from his cigarette. "It was a day of terrible bloodshed. Three people were killed that same day, all by the Fascists. When you are done with your dinner, let's take a walk. There's a plaque dedicated to those murdered." Professor Tataranno wasted no time. He was my kind of man.

I paid the bill and gathered the family together for our evening *passeggiata*. I strapped Paulina into her stroller and my mother grabbed Dean's hand. Tataranno, a chain smoker, lit another Benson & Hedges from the one burning down in his fingers.

He puffed and talked, and talked and puffed, and I nodded and listened to his every word, breathing in his offhand history lessons as if they were secondhand smoke. A few blocks away, near the Paradiso butcher shop, was a beautiful old building, big and white, four stories high, which was tall for Bernalda. It had flowerpots outside and large green shutters, and on it a brass plaque, which I hadn't noticed before. ECCIDIO FASCISTA, it said. Fascist slaughter. JANUARY 31, 1923. And the names of those slaughtered:

Maria Distasi
Pasquale Gallitelli
Giuseppe Viggiano

The first, Maria Distasi, had been inside nursing her baby that day when the Fascists began shooting in the street. A stray bullet entered her one-room house and killed her, baby still at her breast, Professor Tataranno colorfully recounted. The last victim, Giuseppe Viggiano, was the father of the mayor of Bernalda. "When he looked outside on his balcony, the Fascists just shot him," Tataranno said. "For no good reason." He turned his palms up, cigarette still in hand, and shrugged.

Pasquale Gallitelli had been killed that day as well. His story was the worst of the three, really. "He was killed in an atrocious way," Tataranno explained. He shook his head, and for a moment I thought maybe it was too atrocious to tell. But after another cigarette drag, he spilled it.

Pasquale was chased down the street by the Fascists, then ran into a house to escape. He hid under the bed, but the Fascists found him and pulled him out. They beat him to death and then, just to be sure, shot him in the head. I had heard this story before. But Professor Tataranno knew the gruesome details.

"What did he do to deserve that?" I asked.

"The strange thing was that he wasn't really a political guy," he said. "Some say that maybe it was a private situation, a lover's quarrel. That someone already had it in for him. And that the Fascists simply used political motives to kill him." He shrugged again. "I haven't really researched that one completely yet. But you do look like the man's niece. You look exactly like her, in fact. I once saw a photo of her."

"I would love to see that photo," I said.

"Maybe," Professor Tataranno began. "We—" He was suddenly cut off by Paulina, who let out a bloodcurdling screech from the stroller. Dean moaned, as if sympathizing with her.

"My feet hurt," complained Dean, a staunch opponent of the evening *passeggiata*. I stuck a pacifier into Paulina's mouth.

"I'm sorry, honey," I said, patting Dean's big head. "We'll go home soon. Just a little while longer."

Paulina spat the pacifier into her tiny lap in protest and let out another screech as if to say, "You're full of it, Mommy. Quit dragging us around." Paulina was an even-keeled kid but could have a mean temper when she wanted. She looked a lot like my aunt Victoria, one of the big troublemakers in our family. Aunt

Victoria was beautiful but bad. She liked to "stir the pot," as my mother would say. I jiggled the stroller to keep Paulina quiet and kept walking.

WE HEADED BACK TO THE CENTER OF TOWN AND TOWARD THE CO-mune. Professor Tataranno took out his flip phone and dialed a number. And within minutes Professor Antonio Salfi was standing outside the Comune. Salfi was a thin old man with white stubble and a receding tangle of white hair on a small round head. He had dark bushy eyebrows, the thick glasses of those who do too much close reading, and a light in his eyes from the knowledge that those books had imparted. His pants were too long and sagged at his leather shoes and he wore a standard white button-down dress shirt, the left breast pocket filled with pens for easy access. Professor Salfi wasn't quite as stylish as Professor Tataranno but was his comrade and fellow scholar. He was the local genealogist. I would come to think of him as the grandfather I wished I'd had, since mine had spent most of his time in prison.

"Meet Professor Antonio Salfi," Professor Tataranno said, proudly.

"Piacere," I said, extending my hand.

"Piacere," he said, smiling a pained smile and putting his hand out. He was so old, it probably even hurt to shake hands.

Tataranno brought Salfi up to date, in proper Italian, which I understood, then asked him whether he thought I had the *faccia di Gallitelli*. Salfi looked straight at me for a moment, then turned back to Tataranno and said I looked just like the photo of Pasquale Gallitelli's niece.

Professor Tataranno looked at me and raised his dark eyebrows, as if to say, "See? Didn't I tell you?" By now Paulina had fallen asleep in the carriage and Dean was practically sleepwalking, so my mother went back to the apartment with them while I went to an outdoor café with my two new best friends.

Professor Salfi ordered us a round of *cedrata*, a yellow-green fluorescent drink that looked a lot like antifreeze. Though it was past 10 P.M., the streets were still packed with families and small energetic children, the air warm and humid. The *cedrata*, Salfi insisted, would help me to cool down. Though I was skeptical, I took a sip. It was syrupy and sweet, with a strong citrus flavor that was cool and bracing.

Between sips, I told them all I knew about Vita, that she had been a weaver. Professor Tataranno explained that most women in town were weavers and made their own clothes.

I told them that her husband, Francesco, was not present for the boys' births. That the birth certificates said he was "far from the town" at the time. But Professor Salfi said that was not so strange and that he was probably busy working on the farm, where men often stayed for weeks at a stretch.

I said Vita had come to America with her two sons without Francesco. It was strange, they said, for a woman to travel alone. "Maybe Francesco stayed behind and took the blame for the murder," suggested Tataranno.

I repeated the family rumor that the murder had occurred during a card game. They raised their eyebrows simultaneously and blurted, "Passatella!"

It was a very popular card game that was played in the 1800s, and as far back as Roman times really. Salfi was convinced that if the family crime happened over a card game, then this was the one.

Passatella often ended in violence. Sometimes murder.

"But it would be very unusual for a woman to be playing passatella, or any card game," Tataranno said, taking a sip of his *cedrata*.

I looked around at the other tables and noticed, not for the first time in Southern Italy, that I was the only woman among dozens of men at the bar.

"I know," I said, nodding. "You have a good point." I waved my arm. "But you'll notice I'm the only woman here now." Tataranno and Salfi laughed, bowing their heads, embarrassed. "Maybe Vita worked in the tavern. . . ." I added.

"Maybe," said Professor Tataranno, his head still bowed. "But it is very unlikely. Here today, and even America years ago, they are both much different than Bernalda at the turn of the century." Here the working men would gather at night at places called *osterie* (taverns) while the women were at home with the children. "The men would play cards by lamplight, and drink."

"And drink and drink," Salfi said, draining the last of his cedrata.

"Maybe Francesco had been playing and was insulted," I theorized, "and Vita took revenge later. Or maybe a fight broke out that night and the women ran to stop their husbands from killing each other, and one thing led to another. . . ."

They collectively stuck out their bottom lips and gave it some thought. It was not a crazy theory, really.

"Maybe that's what happened," Salfi said with a shrug. "Who can say?"

Passatella was sometimes called Padrone e Sotto and was based on the tortured relationship between the landowners—the *padroni*—and the worker—*sotto,* or underling. The relationship was basically a slave-landowner relationship, fraught with tension.

Passatella was a little drama played out every night to help the *braccianti*—the day laborers—get out their frustrations with the class system without actually confronting the boss and hitting him in the head with a hoe. Rather than fight with the actual padroni, they fought with one another over a friendly—and sometimes not-so-friendly—game of cards.

The game required more than four players and was incredibly complicated. The man with the most points is called the padrone. A person who wins again and again is called *furbo*—which means cunning. (*Furbo* meant so much more than that, though. It meant you were like a fox, able to get over on the person sitting next to you, not just in the card game, but in life. It meant making the best of a bad situation and turning things around to your advantage.)

The top two padroni of the evening are given control of the wine at the table, at which point the cards are cleared away and glasses are placed on the table, always a smaller number of glasses than there are players. The padrone drinks first and then decides who else may drink and in what order. This continues until the bottle is empty, at which point the cards are brought out again and another round is played, repeating the cycle until most people are plastered. Those who are not allowed to drink are called *ulmo*—foolish.

The padrone explains why the drink is being withheld, insulting the *ulmo* with jokes and personal cracks that often hit too close to home: you're too stupid to drink, or too crafty, too young, or too old, too hairy, or too bald, your teeth are too crooked or your head is too lumpy, your nose is too big, or your nose is too small, you're too clumsy or too proper, too macho, or a cuckold.

At any point, the game can end in a fight or a full-blown riot. And because of this, it was actually illegal to play passatella in Italy for many years.

As Professors Tataranno and Salfi described the game, I just listened and nodded. They talked about the landowners in the region and their poor relationship with the workers. "Many of the properties in this area," said Tataranno, "were owned by the Grieco family."

"Grieco?" I asked.

They nodded.

"My family always said there was a Grieco involved in our story," I said. "Either the lawyer who helped Vita escape or maybe a lover."

"What do you mean a lover?" asked Tataranno.

I looked around to see if anyone else was listening and lowered my voice. "My family always said Vita was a *puttana*," I whispered, "and that there were two different fathers for her sons."

Tataranno and Salfi were silent for a moment and looked at one another. I wondered if they were judging me and my promiscuous ancestor. But after a few more beats, Salfi finally said, "It's very likely that Vita had an affair with the local landowner."

Tataranno jumped in. "It was not uncommon for the landowner to sleep with the wives of the farmers. In fact, it was normal. Concubines were typical in this region."

He and Salfi told me about *prima notte*—or first night—a tradition that allowed the landowner to sleep with the virgin wife of his worker on the couple's wedding night. A special dish called the Lamb of the Husband, Agnello del Marito, was typically served to distract and satisfy the farmer while the landowner ravaged his young, innocent bride. In a place where you ate meat only twice a year—on Christmas and Easter—maybe it was considered a good deal. After all, the landowner was going to sleep with your wife whether you liked it or not. It was a sacrifice that was expected of most farmers, and their wives. I figured the lamb, that universal symbol of innocence and sacrifice, was no coincidence, but the padroni's cruel inside joke.

At the start of the twentieth century, when guns were easier to come by, *prima notte* began to fade. But in small, poor towns, this way of living—this feudalism—continued right into the 1950s, Tataranno said.

They theorized that Valente was the son of Grieco, since he was firstborn. But we had no way of really knowing. "Such things," said Salfi, shaking his head, "are not recorded on birth certificates."

Chapter 6

GO BACK TO AMERICA AND
LEAVE THE DEAD IN PEACE

I STARED INTO THE BATHROOM MIRROR AT NIGHT. MY DARK,
normally curly hair was even curlier because of the humidity. My face looked more worn out than usual, with circles
beneath my eyes, my skin an even darker shade because of the
Basilicatan sun, the whites around my black eyes bloodshot from
reading through so many files. I wished I could peel away the layers, the generations of skin and bone, to get at the hidden facts
deep within my genetic code, there, no doubt staring right at me
from my *faccia di Gallitelli*.

A mystery was hidden here, in me and in Matera, a truth buried so deep that I couldn't find it. All of us, I thought, are made
up not only of what we know, but of all that we don't know as well.
Generations of unknowing. Centuries and millennia of secrets
hidden just below the surface.

The answer to my questions was there, right there, staring
back at me in the mirror. It was the story that might help explain away the generations of vice and violence that had settled

in the roots of my family tree. But I couldn't seem to dig down far enough, or find anyone who knew this story.

What started out as a fun family trip and genealogy project had morphed into something else, something I had never really experienced. My morbid curiosity about Vita had slowly become an obsession, with each passing, unproductive day.

I felt, looking into that mirror, as if there was some dark stain on my soul and on the souls of my children, and instead of walking away from it and ignoring it, I wanted to stare deep into the abyss. And the more time I spent here, the more determined I became.

Maybe coming here had been a mistake. It was like Bernalda and Vita had taken possession of me.

I was convinced someone here knew Vita's story but was refusing to tell me. What were they hiding? And who were they not to give me the information I needed about my family? This was my family. Not just theirs.

I wanted to know the horror, so I could accept it or somehow make it right. Not just for myself but for my kids. What if the resemblance to my bad relatives wasn't only skin deep when it came to them? I worried I had passed on some dirty, fatal flaw, and I wanted them to be prepared to deal with it if it ever came to the surface. Crime and tragedy had swirled around my family for generations, but it had never pierced the core of our immediate family. It had come close.

I wanted to keep it away from me and mine. Not with talismans and magic spells. And not by moving away from it, but by getting as close to it as possible, hunting it down and inhabiting it. I wanted to find it and crush it, turn it inside out and on its head.

I wanted to mourn it. Right it. Forget it. Go into therapy about it. But without the goods, there was no doing that. I had to know what I was dealing with in order to deal with it. You didn't get rid of cancer by pretending it wasn't there. You had to find it and cut it out. Or zap it until it was gone.

I had met Professors Tataranno and Salfi too late. I felt I was only getting started with my research when it was time to leave. They told me everything they knew about life in Bernalda in the nineteenth century, but I hadn't found the murder. Maybe it didn't even exist and I would just search forever for something that wasn't there. It's not like there was a card in the archives that said, "Stop looking. There is no Vena-Gallitelli murder." When would I know to stop searching?

Part of me wanted desperately to stay and finish what I had started. But another part—the more logical maternal part of me—simply wanted to go home and retreat, just like Hannibal had centuries ago, his brother's head in his ancient luggage.

Dean was starting kindergarten in a few days in Brooklyn. We had to go back. Establishing a normal, respectable life had been a real accomplishment for my mother, my siblings, and me.

Ma would go back to her day job at the Hudson County Prosecutor's Office, where she helped record pleas in court and pulled files for lawyers during the discovery phase of criminal cases. She loved to regale Dean with tales of murders from work.

I would go back to my regular routine and resume my freelance career writing for newspapers and magazines. I would teach college classes in creative writing and take care of my kids and make meatballs and clean the house and make the beds.

But the mystery of Vita—the core to the identity of my family, the criminal core—would go unsolved. I had to take care of my own family before solving that mystery. I had to choose between my past and my kids.

And so, naturally, I chose my kids. I would leave Bernalda with my two children, just like Vita had over a century ago.

I HAD ONE FINAL TASK BEFORE I LEFT: SALFI AND TATARANNO IN-
sisted I see the photograph of the Gallitelli woman whose face
was identical to mine. They were both busy on our last night in
Bernalda, but told me what door to knock on in our neighborhood, that I should ask the woman there to show me the photo. It
wasn't until after I knocked that I learned the door belonged to
the family of Miserabila, the lady with the bulldog face and the
hairy eyeball.

Miserabila appeared, her grimace firmly in place.

Oh no, I thought. She *is* a relative. Had she seen my face that
first day and known immediately we were related?

I explained, politely, why I was there, laughing nervously
about what Professor Tataranno called my *faccia di Gallitelli*. But
before I could finish, Miserabila exploded in a stream of shouts.
Between her strong dialect and rapid-fire delivery, I couldn't understand what she was saying. But I knew she was not inviting me
in for some homemade biscotti. She stepped into the lamplight
and I thought for a minute she might try to wrestle me onto the
cobblestones. Suddenly Leonardantonio Gallitelli, the guy with
the horse face, appeared and joined in the shouting. I hadn't even
known they were related.

"Gallitelli has nothing to do with your story!" he shouted,
waving me off with his hand. "The murder is a Vena story. Not a
Gallitelli story. Gallitelli has nothing to do with it." He had said
he knew nothing about the murder. So what was he even talking
about? It didn't seem the right time to ask. I was afraid he might
haul off and sock me.

"Tornar America e lasciar in pace i mord!" Miserabila
screamed at me in dialect. It was the only sentence of hers I could
understand. It was the only one I needed to hear. In meant, "Go
back to America and leave the dead in peace!"

The words echoed off the clean, gray cobblestones and tiny

eighteenth-century houses, and eventually in the recesses of my brain for years to come.

I WENT BACK HOME TO NEW YORK, NOT EMPTY-HANDED, BUT WITH fists tightly clenched. I knew that one day, when my kids were old enough to leave behind, I'd come back to Bernalda. It was too hard to bring the kids and take care of them, plus do all the research I needed to do. I couldn't change diapers and flip through files simultaneously. I needed a wife, goddamnit, someone to take care of me while I took care of business. But I was the wife.

And mother.

So I went back home and learned patience. I waited year after year, as my children grew inch by inch, and as I worried that every fib they told and every tantrum they threw was the potential beginning of their life of crime. I wouldn't stop worrying until I was able to solve the mystery of Vita and deal fully with the past.

So I read all about Basilicata, the history, the daily struggles of the Lucani. When I finally did return, I would be ready, like a ninja, primed for battle.

I read a biography of Pythagoras and anthropological studies of the region, hoping I might stumble upon a clue to my own story. I read a stack of books about the economic struggles of the Mezzogiorno—what was called the Southern Question. So much had been written on the topic, but an answer still hadn't been found.

I read everything about Basilicata that I could get my hands on, including Carlo Levi's *Christ Stopped at Eboli*, about the time the author had spent in the province of Matera, in the tiny villages near Bernalda.

The Fascists had exiled Levi to the towns of Grassano and Aliano, where he worked as a doctor for ten months, traveling from village to village, tending to the sick and dying. Life there had been grim, but he had a maid, a woman who took care of him and cooked for him and even bathed him. Lucky bastard. There were times when I wanted to throw his book across the room, I was so jealous of his freedom. What was a political prisoner compared with being a full-time mother?

But I soaked in every poetic word that Levi wrote and then re-read the book a second time, underlining passages as if it were my Bible. Passages about passatella, illegitimate children, evil spells, and the poor, melancholy people who inhabited this no-man's-land. My ancestors.

The book's title referred to a town farther north, Eboli, where Levi claimed civilization had stopped, leaving the peasants in Basilicata abandoned and without hope.

"But to this shadowy land," he wrote, "that knows neither sin nor redemption from sin, where evil is not moral but is only the path residing forever in earthly things, Christ did not come. Christ stopped at Eboli."

I read the books of Ann Cornelisen, who had spent two decades in Italy in the 1950s and '60s working with its poverty-stricken women. I watched and rewatched all of the Godfather movies, because, I had discovered, Francis Ford Coppola's ancestors were also originally from Bernalda. Maybe we were related. I studied the neo-Realists, and any other movies that were filmed in or about Italy.

For my birthday one year, Wendell gave me an old Baedeker's travel volume about Southern Italy from 1887, right before Vita left. There was not much about Basilicata, since hardly anyone ever went there:

> The fields once extolled by Sophocles for their richness
> and fertility are now sought for in vain, and the malaria
> exercises its dismal sway throughout the whole of this

neglected district. The soil belongs to the nobility, who let it to a miserably poor and ignorant class of farmers. The custom of carrying weapons is universally prevalent here and brigandage was carried on until the year 1870. The villagers are generally wretched and filthy beyond description. No one should therefore attempt to explore the remoter parts of this country unless provided with letters of introduction to some of the principal inhabitants.

I read an anthropological study of magic in Southern Italy, about the curses and spells people put on each other. I learned about *monacelli* and *succobi*, the mischievous dwarfs who would sometimes appear at night and sit on the chest of a sleeping person, pressing on their solar plexus and paralyzing them. The *monacello* was believed to be the spirit of a baby who died before being baptized.

I reread Greek history, about Magna Graecia, the Greek settlement in Basilicata centuries ago, and reread the mythology that had always fascinated me as a kid. I'd adored Edith Hamilton's *Mythology*, whose stories of all those related Greek gods and goddesses and heroes—which I traced in the family tree she provided—were a match for my own family's crazy stories. I got lost in the tales of Zeus and Hera and Hercules and Pandora and read them to Dean aloud for the first time.

Eventually, I moved on to the Greek philosophers: Socrates, Plato, and Pythagoras. As a student at New York University, I had discovered Plato's Allegory of the Cave, in which he says that most humans are like prisoners chained inside a cave facing a wall. Shadows are projected onto the wall. The prisoners think the shadows are reality and don't even know there's another world outside the cave, filled with truth and beauty and light. I considered myself one of the lucky kids from Jersey City who had escaped into the light of the outside, educated world.

To make money, I wrote stories for newspapers and magazines and essay collections, stories about jazz musicians and ballerinas and spaghetti tacos and dinosaurs and robots and lots of things I stumbled upon because I was a mother, when all the while I wanted to research Vita and her murder.

I plotted and planned, making long-distance connections over social media, using it to line up my "letters of introduction." My family thought I was crazy. And maybe I was. Batz. But I had my reasons. I was stubborn, of course. But it was more than that.

I would tell the story to my son and daughter, use the story of the first family sin to immunize them, so they would never commit sins so mortal.

Of course, when I was being honest, I knew there was another reason: I wanted revenge against the two long-lost relatives who had screamed at me that night on the street in Bernalda. I wanted to find the story, walk up to Miserabila and Leonardantonio, and stick it right in their miserable faces and say, "Here. Here it is. I found it without your help. Thanks for nothing. Here is the family story. *My* family story." Then I would give them the finger and yell, "Vaffanculo!"

Chapter 7

A TURNED-UP NOSE
IS WORSE THAN HAIL

A S MANY AS NINE MILLION SOUTHERNERS FLED ITALY BE-
tween 1871 and 1951. Nine million. A crowd bigger than
the population of New York City.

Most of them were dirt poor.

And some of them were criminals.

A congressional study started in 1907 drew a link between the
high crime rates in Southern Italy and immigration numbers.
The authors of the study claimed that as the emigrants left the
South, the crime rates in those parts of Italy dropped substan-
tially. "Certain kinds of criminality are inherent in the Italian
race," the report concluded in 1911. "In the popular mind, crimes
of personal violence, robbery, blackmail, and extortion are pecu-
liar to the people of Italy."

Was Vita one of those criminals? Was Matera happy to see
her go?

Vita's sons, Valente and Leonardo, would become upstanding citizens in Jersey City. Had the criminal gene skipped a generation?

Grandpa Beansie, Leonardo's son, was by far the biggest and baddest character in the Rogues' Gallery that was my family album. As a kid, he stole a crate of beans off the back of a truck—hence the nickname. But that was just his first crime. He was a career criminal who stole, beat people up, and even murdered a guy once during a fight. Ma said Grandpa did it with his bare hands, that he beat the guy so badly that he eventually died.

There were tales about Beansie's siblings, particularly his sister, Aunt Katie. She worked for the corrupt administration of Jersey City mayor Frank Hague, "getting the vote out," which usually involved either bribes or beatings. But there were so many stories about Katie, I couldn't even keep track of them all.

My favorite was the one about her rigging the St. Mary's parish bingo game with the help of her son, my cousin Mike, who was blessed with a photographic memory. He would memorize the bingo boards of the women who paid Katie a kickback before the game started. He would whisper the "winning numbers" to his mother. Katie would then call out the fake winning numbers to reward the women who had paid their tribute. She made a killing every week.

Cousin Mike later went to Harvard Law School, where he studied beside Antonin Scalia. Instead of a chief justice, Mike became a mob consigliere.

His brother, my cousin Chubby, had the dubious distinction of being Jersey City's first heroin addict. He stole to support his habit. One time he knocked on our apartment door and tried to sell my mother a pot roast from Aunt Katie's freezer.

I had witnessed firsthand the petty crimes that my Polish father committed each day. He stole frozen food—sometimes lobsters and steaks—from the warehouse where he worked near the mouth of the Holland Tunnel in order to feed us at home.

Burglars and bookies, killers and con men filled the Polish, Italian, and Russian sides of my family. But sad to say, most of the criminals came from the Vena side, the Italian side. I hated to admit it, but it was true. Overwhelmingly so.

The name Vena can be translated a number of ways. It can mean mood, either good or bad. Or it can mean streak, as in having a lucky streak or a wild streak. *Vena poetica* means having a turn for poetry. But Vena's main meaning is vein, as in a vein that runs through a family, a trait passed down from one generation to the next. In our case, a penchant for crime.

CESARE LOMBROSO'S THEORIES WERE RACIST, REPUGNANT, AND crazy. He claimed, for instance, that the reason Southern Italians were more likely to be murderers than their brethren in the north was the heavy concentration of African and Asian blood in their veins. But I couldn't help reading every word he wrote, since those words were written around the same time Vita and Francesco were committing their own crime.

I stumbled upon the work of Lombroso, a nineteenth-century Italian doctor, while doing research at the New York Public Library. He had studied seven thousand different cases, many of them Southern Italian criminals and brigands, and developed a detailed theory on what a typical criminal looked like. According to him, criminals were throwbacks to more primitive savages and apes. And he believed that criminal behavior was inherited.

Lombroso forged his theory while working as a doctor at an asylum in northern Italy. As he was performing an autopsy on a criminal named Vilella, Italy's version of Jack the Ripper, Lombroso came across a small hollow at the base of his skull, which was not found in normal specimens, and an enlarged spinal cord near the same spot, which was typical in lower primates. He claimed to find it in other criminals as well and so began his life's work.

Lombroso's research, though embraced in the United States, was eventually debunked in most of Europe. His work gave me insight into the incredible ignorance and mind-set of that time and place. But mostly, I thought one of my relatives might pop up in one of his illustrated studies.

Since I didn't know what Francesco looked like, and had very little to go on with Vita, I substituted their physical characteristics with Lombroso's descriptions of the natural-born criminal, using his books as if they were a family album.

Typical criminals were short in stature and usually skinny, with several of these traits:

* an asymmetrical face
* a large, jutting jaw with strong canine teeth
* high cheekbones
* deep, arched eye orbits with drooping eyelids
* handle-shaped ears that stuck out (like a chimp's)
* apelike long arms
* an elongated big toe
* a hairy body but a lack of much facial hair (except in female criminals, who tended to have mustaches and beards)
* either an extremely large head or an unusually small head, with a lined forehead and lots of wrinkles
* dark hair (rarely bald or with gray hair)
* bushy eyebrows
* thin lips
* missing or extra ribs
* extra nipples in men, and flabby breasts in women

The nose varied depending on the crime. Murderers tended to have flat noses, whereas thieves had birdlike noses that often pointed up. Turned-up noses were so typical of criminals in Italy that there was a saying that went: "Naso che guarda in testa è peggior che la tempesta," which translated as "A turned-up nose is worse than hail." Hail being the archenemy of farm owners.

Criminals were also more likely than the general population to be left-handed.

My family had a large contingent of southpaws, including Grandpa Beansie, who was forced by his teacher to write with his right hand as a child. They would scold and beat him if he tried to write with his left hand. (The Italians called the left *sinistra*, a Latin word that by the Middle Ages had come to mean evil or sinister.)

Forcing a little kid to write with his right hand when he was really left-handed could lead to learning disabilities and, of course, terrible frustration. It seemed cruel and could likely drive a normally precocious kid over the edge. Beansie was held back in school several times and finally dropped out at thirteen.

He also suffered a head injury as a child when he was hit by one of the only cars in Jersey City. My relatives were convinced the accident left him bipolar, which might explain his violent outbursts. Ma had tons of excuses for why her father turned out the way he did. But my favorite excuse was the one about him being a twin, conceived separately, and his mother giving birth to a dead baby a month before Beansie was born. When Beansie finally was born, his mother was so depressed about losing that other baby that she was unable to breastfeed him. So Beansie was suckled by his Zia Maria, Valente's wife, a kind woman to whom he stayed attached for years.

Ma claimed that all that formative psycho baby trauma had caused Beansie to become the criminal and murderer that he would become. Separation anxiety from his twin and separation anxiety from his cold, depressed mother had both taken their toll and made him no good. I worried he was simply born that way, the murderous gene passed down from our ancestors.

LOMBROSO MEASURED HEAD SIZE AND ARM LENGTH AND TOOK DE-tailed notes on other physical attributes to prove that criminal character was indeed inherited. He found criminals had worse hearing, sense of smell, and taste. Their eyesight was more acute than the average Joe, though they tended to be color-blind and their field of vision more limited.

Criminals were incredibly lazy, Lombroso said, and would rather starve than put in a good day's work. They were reckless and often sloppy in their handiwork, leaving bloody weapons lying around, or in some extreme cases, even tattooing their criminal exploits on their bodies.

They loved tattoos and were much more likely to be tattooed than the normal person. They also were big drinkers and were often violent when drunk.

Lombroso also found that natural-born criminals had the uncanny ability to heal their wounds more quickly than the average person. One case involved a man who ripped out his mustache, including a big chunk of skin, only to have it heal a few days later. Lombroso thought that maybe this was some throwback in evolution. Criminals were like salamanders and lizards who were able to regrow tails and other body parts.

When I read that, I cringed. Doctors in Jersey City had marveled at the speed with which my Italian relatives healed. Beansie, for instance, would be beaten by the cops on a regular basis, but within a day or two his bruises and cuts would miraculously disappear. His sisters were known to heal extremely quickly as well. And my mob consigliere cousin Mike—he of the bingo game fix—recuperated so fast from open heart surgery that his doctors were astounded. He hardly even had a trace of the incision on his chest.

The ability to heal his wounds quickly was only one of many Lombrosian criminal traits Grandpa Beansie possessed. The laziness and refusal to work, the perfect eyesight, the tattoos and violent alcoholism described Beansie to a tee. He also had thin lips and very little facial hair, and was pretty short.

In Lombroso's books were photos of his various patients, whose faces I scanned for any family resemblance whatsoever. I knew Vita was supposed to have had an underbite, so the enlarged-jaw theory worried me right off the bat. Lombroso claimed that nearly half the criminals he studied had a jaw that jutted out beyond the forehead.

Women, when they turned to murder, could be much more vicious than men, Lombroso claimed. The female brigand, Ciclope, chastised her partner for murdering his victims too quickly. And a subject by the name of Rulfi killed her niece by stabbing her with long pins.

But women rarely became criminals, Lombroso said. He believed the equivalent to criminal behavior in women was prostitution.

The most common form of murder for women was infanticide, rampant in Southern Italy. Women with no means of feeding another child, and without access to abortion, sometimes smothered a newborn rather than watch it die a slow, painful death from hunger and disease.

I hoped the family murder in Italy didn't involve Vita killing one of her children. Killing someone in a card game was one thing; killing your own kid was another.

Lombroso wasn't a big believer in environment, though he did admit that growing up in a poor place, surrounded by other criminals, didn't help your chances. But he didn't cut the poor much slack. "If thieves are generally penniless, it is because of their extreme idleness and astonishing extravagance, which makes them run through huge sums with the greatest ease, not because poverty has driven them to theft," he said.

It seemed obvious to me that people with misshapen heads, giant jaws, and such were more likely to be shunned by society, which would lead, inevitably, to them participating in antisocial behavior. And that because they were antisocial, chances were their kids would be, too. But Lombroso didn't see it that way. They weren't criminals because they looked this way and were mocked. They looked this way *because* they were naturally born criminals. Criminal behavior wasn't learned and passed down, but was in the blood.

Climate, he thought, played a bigger role. Murder was more frequent in warmer climates, while theft was more prevalent in the north, where food was harder to come by.

Hunger, I knew, was a prime criminal motive. My father stole all that food from work every day to feed us. Beansie's first foray into the criminal underworld was stealing that crate of beans. All you needed was to think back on the story of Adam and Eve and their stolen fruit.

Most of the world disregarded Lombroso's theories, but Germany and America accepted them. The Germans used them in the study of eugenics and the Americans in drafting strict immigration laws. By the turn of the century, crime in America was on the rise and the immigrants—particularly Southern Italian immigrants—were taking the fall.

Thanks in good part to that 1911 congressional report and to Lombroso, the United States passed the Immigration Act of 1924, more or less ending immigration for Southern Italians and Eastern European Jews. After the turn of the century, around two hundred thousand Italian immigrants were pouring into the country every year. After 1924, only four thousand were allowed in each year.

A drop of over 90 percent.

By this time, the Italian government was happy to stanch the flow. Emigration had devastated the small landowners, who were unable to find young men to work the land—since most of them had left for the Americas.

Wages doubled in Southern Italy for farmers, who also demanded better food. Because of the exodus, many of the small landowners either had to work the land themselves or abandon it, since they were making hardly enough to pay the land tax.

The situation led one politician from Reggio in Calabria to tell the U.S. congressional commission that emigration from Italy had gotten out of control. He regretted, he said, that Columbus had ever discovered America.

Chapter 8

YOU'LL NEVER BE SATED WITH BREAD AND OLIVES

L ITTLE VITA WAS ALWAYS HUNGRY.

Each morning Teresina would feed her and the whole family a thin minestra soup made with tomato and oil. Then Vita's father, Domenico, trudged into the piazza, with his hat pulled tight over his head, where he would get in line for the shape-up with the rest of the town's *braccianti*, waiting to be called as a day laborer by one of the village agents. The only thing worse than working the *latifondi* (estates) was not being called to work the *latifondi*. This was the 1850s, before the sea of workers began flooding into America.

The luckiest had a mule, who slept at the back of the house. He would trudge along with his master to the farm each morning, both man and beast practically sleepwalking.

But Domenico was too poor to own a mule. Maybe a chicken or a goat.

Because they lived and slept so close to their animals, the *braccianti* smelled like them and were considered barely human by the landowners—the padroni. In the summer, the animals stayed inside, while the family slept out on the cool cobblestones on the street, sometimes on a bed of straw, to avoid the stench and the body heat of the animals.

If he found work for the day, Domenico would walk alone the two or three miles to the farm. Sometimes farther. If it was raining when they got there, the *braccianti* were sent back home without pay. If the weather was good, they worked all day—even on Sunday—and then were fed a lunch of cornmeal polenta.

When work was more than ten miles away, Domenico would spend half the month in a tiny country hovel provided by the padrone. And when they were desperate, Teresina would go, too. Sometimes the workers would all live together in a larger house, a *masseria*, locked in at night, sleeping on the floor like animals, with a piece of canvas to cover them all, a tarp separating the men from the women.

In the cold months, from November through March, they would eat bread soup cooked by the women. In the hottest months, they ate bread with a crushed-up tomato or pepper, some olives. Maybe a little cheese.

Domenico worked like a mule all day in that punishing sun, beside a real mule that didn't even belong to him, but who recognized him, who saw in him the same weary look. The two of them worked the fields together, with a small wooden plow that barely scratched the surface, and depending on the season, sowed wheat or harvested it, or sowed tomatoes or harvested them, the mule stopping every few minutes in his stubbornness and Domenico waiting, always waiting, never hitting him or yelling at him. With the patience of his patron saint, San Domenico, the Italian monk and healer of snake bites. This mule was his partner, his friend, and Domenico even had a name for him. Though that name has been lost to the ages.

Just because you worked like a beast didn't mean you thought like one. Domenico—whose nickname was likely Mimmo—had hopes for his children. He worried about them and prayed Vita's life would be better than his had been. It had to be. It couldn't get much worse. Or so he thought.

Like most of the farmers, Domenico was kind and gentle, his face creased and tanned, a tan so dark and deep that it reached down to future generations, guaranteeing they would never burn.

Vegetables, fruit, and citrus were grown on what was called the corona, a small area surrounding the *latifondi,* and were harvested in winter for the padrone's personal use. Winter was also hog-slaughtering time. Domenico killed the pigs, even though the pork wasn't his to keep.

On the larger parcels of land, Domenico planted tobacco, dried it on huge wooden frames, then threaded the leaves for hours, until his fingers bled and his eyesight started to go. In fall he harvested the grapes in tight bunches and turned them into wine with the other men on his crew. They sang songs while they worked, about sneaking to a lover's window in the night, or about meeting a pretty girl in the fields, or about being in love with three sisters, each one prettier than the last. Anything to take their mind off their grueling job.

Then came olive season. Domenico built a *lunetta*—a half-moon wall of stones—around every single silver-leafed olive tree to protect it from erosion. He placed a blanket under each when harvest time came, and shook the olives from the branches. You never picked the olives off the ground that were there before the shaking of the tree, because that meant they were old and dead. That is, you never picked them for the padroni. You picked them for yourself and your family. The freshest olives made the best and longest-lasting oil, since they were ripe with natural preservatives. The older the olives, the lower the quality of the oil. Your oil.

Domenico pressed them with the other farmers, using a mule

or cow to turn the huge stone wheel that squeezed out the precious golden liquid. When there was no cow or mule, the men used their own strength to push it, singing a rhythmic call and response to help them move in unison, grunting after every erotic line to push harder.

Come on
Another press
Come oooooon
See how it comes out
Press gently, like a kiss
Give another press
So that the young girl can marry

DOMENICO AND HIS FELLOW *BRACCIANTI* WERE PAID IN WHEAT, olive oil, or wine, sometimes a little salt, rarely actual money. And on feast days and holidays, Domenico had to bring an offering to his padrone, hat in hand, to thank him for the work he had given him throughout the year. It was usually some produce or cheese. Some even gave sausage, those lucky enough to live with a pig or two in their own house. It was outrageous, really, having to give gifts to the rich padroni. But you had to show the proper respect. Those who didn't could be beaten or whipped. Or worse, not chosen to work the *latifondi*, their families left to starve.

If a husband had any money at all, his wife and daughters didn't work the land, but rather stayed behind in town, since women could get into all kinds of trouble on the farm. But Vita's family had no money. Teresina often worked in the country and would sometimes bring Vita along, especially during the wheat harvest, when everyone worked—men, women, children, animals.

Domenico and Teresina couldn't read the newspapers from Naples, so they usually had no idea what was really happening on the rest of the peninsula that would soon become Italy. But they heard the gossip. Beyond the farms where they worked, they knew that changes were coming that might one day affect little Vita's life.

By the 1860s, a bearded man named Giuseppe Garibaldi was leading something called the Risorgimento—or resurgence—out of Sicily, employing a mighty army of volunteers known as "the redshirts," who fought their way to Naples and beyond. They were victorious in their battles, uniting the north of the peninsula with the south and creating one nation, called the Kingdom of Italy.

They were promising a better life for the peasants, fewer taxes, land for everyone. Maybe soon, Vita's life wouldn't be so hard.

WHEN VITA WENT TO THE COUNTRY TO HELP HER MOTHER WORK, she wore long skirts and woolen stockings, even though the heat was so hot and the sun so strong that it felt like it might crack your skull open. If your legs were bare, the wheat sliced them like a razor, like the one the local barber used to shave the *galantuomini*— the gentlemen in town.

Vita helped her mother bundle the wheat, using a long piece to wrap around and tie each bunch. The wheat was tricky because if you didn't harvest it fast enough, it would overripen and burn. Her mother never planted, since it was thought to be unlucky for a woman to sow. But she would harvest. Everyone harvested, from the end of May sometimes until the end of July.

The wheat was cut by many hands, then taken to the *aia*, the square on the farm bordered by bricks, where it was beaten with sticks to separate the chaff. The straw was thrown to one side and the grain to the other. Then it was placed in the *granaio*, the open-windowed building used to keep the air flowing onto it and keep it dry.

Teresina made flour at the communal gristmill using the

small bits of grain Domenico was paid, and then baked the family's homemade bread—*pane casareccio*—in the communal stone oven in town once or twice a week, gossiping with the other women as she waited for the loaves to be done. Then she carried them home on her head on a big wooden board. The dough was stretched to feed the whole family with anything she found that week—some corn, chestnuts. The most desperate even used sawdust. Salt was used sparingly because it was highly taxed. The children were given bread according to how big they were, another inch for every inch they grew. Tiny Vita prayed to the saints that she would grow faster.

If there was enough work and pay, a good night's dinner consisted of a round loaf of bread, cut usually by Vita's father, placed up against his chest, the knife making its way toward him, but stopping just short of a nipple-ectomy. The bread—never enough to go round—was rubbed with a found pepper or maybe some garlic and a quick brush of olive oil. And if they were really lucky that day, a bit of crushed tomato or a few olives.

It was placed on one big plate in the middle of the small wooden table. There were many mouths to feed. Vita's siblings, her grandmother and grandfather. Domenico, if he was not off on the masseria. You shared your space, everyone sleeping and eating in that one room. If you weren't fast, you didn't get any food. But Vita was smart and quick. She got some. Though never enough to satisfy her. There was an Italian saying that went, "You'll never be sated with bread and olives." And it was true. It was never enough for Vita.

Until she was four years old, Vita slept in a small hammock above her parents' bed, where her mother could easily reach up and rock her daughter when she cried out in hunger, that black hole in her belly growing deeper and wider with each passing hour. Sometimes she cried out in thirst for water that wasn't there. Teresina soaked a sponge in wine to quench her thirst, like the Romans had done to Jesus on the cross. But that's if there was any wine.

Usually, Teresina just sang her daughter a lullaby, because lullabies were free. The town favorite was "Ninna Nanna," which never failed to get Vita to sleep, her thirst fading only when she faded.

> Do the ninna, do the nanna
> Your real mother is the Virgin
> Do the ninna, do the nanna
> The wolf ate the little sheep
> Oh, my little sheep
> What did you do
> When you saw yourself in the mouth of the wolf,
> Who ate the skin and who ate the wool?
> Poor little sheep how it screamed.
> Sleep, my sweet friend
> sleep for a long time
> and don't make me suffer.

II

DISCOVERY

Chapter 9

THE TRUTH ALWAYS RISES
TO THE TOP

T HE PALM TREES ON THE CORSO WERE TALLER, STRETCHING into the powder blue sky. They had grown over the past ten years, just like my children had back in Brooklyn. I couldn't believe a decade had passed, but here I was, back in Bernalda. It was the fall of 2014. I was here on a solo vacation, a mommy break, I told people. Though it was really a reconnaissance mission: to poke around for a week and see if it was finally time to take another stab at finding the family murder.

Bicycles had taken over. In many of the other hill towns, like Pisticci, you couldn't ride a bicycle because of the steep hills. But Bernalda was flat and perfect for biking. In typical Bernaldan boldness, the cyclists rode without helmets in the center of the mile-long Corso, defying the gods and the drivers at every turn. It was a miracle more people weren't lying dead in the middle of the street.

Gaggles of local boys, in jeans and gaudy T-shirts with gold swirly American slogans that they didn't understand, roamed the main drag. Girls pushed baby carriages or moved in giggling groups, trying to get a look at the groups of boys. Old café owners in white aprons swept the still-spotless pavement outside.

A few more tourists had arrived in Bernalda, since Francis Ford Coppola had opened a luxury hotel, Palazzo Margherita, on the main Corso. Coppola's family had grown up just a few blocks from Via Cavour, on Via Eraclea.

The new hotel was an old palace built the very same year Vita had left for America, 1892. It had nine rooms, a private courtyard, a Baroque fountain, and a fragrant garden filled with jasmine, lilac, and rosemary. Its outdoor bar was the new hotspot in town.

Coppola's hotel rates were too expensive, especially for a peasant town. At five hundred euros a night, it was more than my immigrant ancestors had made their entire lives. I decided to stay on a farm outside of Pisticci, in an old masseria called San Teodoro Nuovo, on the Metapontan plain. I hadn't spent much time in the Materan countryside last time around—had only glimpsed it from hilltops and through car windows—and thought it might be a good idea to see what it was like up close, since my ancestors had spent so much time on the farm.

I chose San Teodoro because it looked like the Garden of Eden on its website, and in real life it looked even more so. I arrived between olive and grape harvesting time, driving past pomegranate trees, stretches of kiwi and strawberries, cornfields, red prickly pears, and row after row of twisted grapevines and mournful olive trees. I kept all the windows to my rental car wide open and let the fragrant air wash over me.

The farm was incredibly lush, with palm trees and flowering cactus and tall pine and olives and figs, the air sweet from its lemon and orange groves. I had forgotten how beautiful it was down here; when you first arrived, how striking it could be. I had known, through memory, but seeing the landscape again was like being Judy Garland in *The Wizard of Oz,* stepping out of the black and white of reminiscence and into the colorful reality that was Basilicata.

It was October and I was the only guest at the farm/bed and breakfast. The days were warm and gentle, what the Italians called Ottobrate—their version of Indian summer.

A tight-knit group of farmers helped till the red soil of San Teodoro, which still produced fruit, vegetables, olive oil, grapes, wheat, jam, and honey—much of which was served in the dining room on the premises, in the old stable, across from my room.

The soil here was called *precoce* and was rich in iron, which helped crops grow at twice the rate as on other farms in the area. Pisticci's soil was more clay based and its fields broken up by the *calanchi,* which quickly eroded in the rain. Bernalda's land was better and flatter and more fertile than Pisticci's, though not as good as Metaponto's.

In the eighth century BC, just after Homer's *Odyssey* was written, the Greeks began arriving and colonized the area in what became known as Magna Graecia. They came because the land was so fertile.

The Roman poet Horace, who had been born in Basilicata in the first century BC, wrote of "the rich wealth of the countryside's beauties," of long, sloping valleys, safe woodland groves, golden fields, green sprays of vine, dark figs, and flowing honey.

Some believed the founder of Metapontum was Epeius, the soldier who built the Trojan horse. So entrenched was the Greek culture here that one of the most popular surnames was Grieco. And still, millennia later, many of the Griecos were well-off and owned much of the land.

Being in the middle of the countryside here for the first time gave me a new perspective. It was so gorgeous and lush that it occurred to me that maybe Vita loved it amid the citrus and pines, the grapes and olives. Life in the country seemed so much better than life in Bernalda.

Of course, I wasn't harvesting crops, slaughtering animals, and pressing olives beneath a giant stone wheel.

A RUSTED CHAIN STRETCHED ACROSS THE ENTRYWAY. NO GUARDS. No visitors. Just a few small lizards darting back and forth. I hopped the chain and made my way down the path past the fluffy white and pink oleander bushes, which were planted everywhere in the area because they were so easy to maintain. They didn't need a lot of water or love, but they looked bright and cheerful and smelled like giant bouquets of bubble gum. But the oleander was deadly poisonous. Local legend was that when foreign troops invaded, they sometimes used the oleander branches to cook their meat over the fire—accidentally poisoning themselves.

Even the plants were lethal weapons here.

Ten years ago, I had become so obsessed with finding Vita's story that I hadn't been able to enjoy the beauty of Basilicata. This time, instead of going to the archives and the cemetery, I visited all the tourist spots, and even stopped to smell the deadly flowers.

Past the oleander, at the end of the path, I found what I was looking for: the pillars. The area's most famous ruins were the fifteen Doric columns in Metaponto, left over from a grand temple to Hera, Zeus's wife. It was known as Tavole Palatine, and had been built in the sixth century BC. Some locals believed it had been built on the site of Pythagoras's home, to pay tribute to him after his death. Though no one was paying tribute these days.

For people who live in Basilicata, visiting the Greek ruins is like a New Yorker visiting the Statue of Liberty. It just wasn't done. She was there, all the time, staring at you from the harbor, but you just appreciated her from afar.

Over at the deserted archeological park in Metaponto was a temple to Athena, a sanctuary dedicated to Apollo and a rounded amphitheater. In Metaponto and nearby Marina di Pisticci—and even in Bernalda—streets were named after the Greek and Roman gods and goddesses: Via Atena, and Hera, Neptune, and Hercules. And one named Ulisses, the Roman name for Odysseus, who had traveled in nearby waters in *The Odyssey*.

With Odysseus in mind, I headed over to the beach. It hadn't changed much since my last visit, and probably not a hell of a whole lot since Spartacus's time here, either. The sea was tranquil and turquoise, the sand powdery and soft. Again, there were no tourists. Which was fine with me. I had the whole stretch of beach and Ionian Sea to myself.

I ate a solitary picnic of soppressata, mortadella, runny burrata cheese, triangles of tangy provolone, and some local peasant bread, all wrapped in a dish towel, the waves quietly lapping against the shore—the only sound for miles.

I looked out into the Ionian Sea and thought of Odysseus, sailing from spot to spot over ten years during his odyssey. Ten years. How could ten years have passed since I had been here last? It seemed only months ago I had been chasing the kids on this same stretch of sand. They were eleven and fifteen now, in middle and high school. My job raising them was nearly done. Most of the time, they didn't want me around so much, which made me waver between deep despair and incredible relief. It was like I had finally been reissued the driver's license to my life, but I wasn't sure what direction to drive.

Though my children didn't seem to be exhibiting any antisocial traits, I was still slightly nervous that they might take a wrong turn. It was every mother's nightmare that you'd wind up with a bad egg, no matter how much you loved or cared for them. And with my family's track record, it wasn't such a crazy nightmare to have.

But I would be gone only a week. They wouldn't turn to a life of crime in such a short period of time. I would just enjoy myself and learn what it was like to be me again—without them by my side.

In the distance I saw a small wooden building amid some palm trees, like an oasis. Maybe it was a new restaurant. I pulled my shorts over my bathing suit, covered my picnic and left it on the sand, then headed toward the bent palms.

As I got closer, I saw a young guy and an older man sitting at a table next to the rounded lido building, which had a thatched roof and porthole windows. "Ciao!" I yelled, waving. I walked up and introduced myself and said I was from New York doing research on my family. We shook hands.

"My name is Leonardo," the young man said. "Leo to my friends." He had dark curly hair and was dressed in a blue linen oxford and ripped faded jeans. His eyes were sad and his smile was guarded and more of a smirk, like the one we had in my family. "This is my place," he said, waving his arm, "Riva dei Ginepri." Thatched roof umbrellas hovered over small square restaurant tables, two white-cushioned wicker couches, and a few brown beanbag chairs, all part of a Hamptons-like lido with a bar, restaurant, and rented beach chairs. The place was empty, the season just ended.

Leo explained that *ginepri* meant juniper and showed me that the area behind the beach was filled with juniper trees studded with tiny berries—which were typically used to make gin. Legend was that centuries ago, right on this spot, Saracen pirates had invaded, but were conquered by the wily locals who had hidden behind the juniper trees and then launched a surprise attack. These days, it was a trendy summer spot for the few tourists who wandered past, the place where Sofia Coppola had had her pre-wedding cocktail party.

I told Leo my own story, about Vita Gallitelli and Francesco Vena killing someone and about the name Grieco. He opened his eyes wide and exclaimed, with a full-on bright smile this time, "My family is Grieco! That is *my* family story!"

I had been waiting to hear this sentence for a decade. And I actually took a step back in the soft sand. I looked at him through narrowed eyes and laughed. "Really?" I didn't believe him. Though I wanted to. Was this guy for real?

"My grandmother on the Grieco side used to tell us a story about a family murder involving a Gallitelli woman and a Vena man," he said, excitedly, talking with his hands. "I don't know any of the details. It's been years since I heard it. But I will ask my mother," he promised.

"Maybe we're related," I said, laughing and shrugging.

"You look very Greek," he said to me. "Grieco. Even the design on your bathing suit is Greek." I looked down at the turquoise blue wave motif cresting across my chest.

"Oh yeah, I guess I never noticed that before," I said, smiling, my hand across my breasts.

"We are probably cousins," he said, spreading his arms out. I thought for a minute he might hug me, but we had just met, and I was wearing a bathing suit after all. So I didn't lean in. I didn't want to give Leo the wrong impression, that I was a *puttana* like Vita.

But I took his number and his email address and told him that we would meet again before I left for America. "It's just a matter of time before you find your story," he said. "In Basilicata, there's a saying that goes, 'La verità viene sempre a galla.' The truth always rises to the top."

Chapter 10

TAKE A COFFEE

NIGHT FELL AND BERNALDA CAME ALIVE. IT WAS AS IF THE town were full of vampires, who only came out after dark. Mopeds, bicycles, and Vespas sped past, young women and men laughed and moved in unison like schools of fish down the street. The cafés were packed. *Passeggiata* was in full swing.

In the chic outdoor bar in front of Coppola's hotel, handsome white-jacketed waiters took my order while I waited for Leo. The tall palm trees, nearly as high as the streetlights, cast shadows onto the Corso and the thick crowds promenading past. Leo was late.

I ordered a glass of the local Aglianico del Vulture, the rich red wine from grapes grown in the volcanic soil near Mount Vulture to the north. I took a sip and tried to look as laid-back as everyone else in town. But until Leo showed up, I couldn't really relax.

Finally, more than a half hour late, he appeared with a friend beside him. I wanted to skip the formalities, forget the drinks, and just find out what Leo had learned from his mother. I had hoped he would bring her along with him tonight.

Instead he brought this tall, skinny, birdlike man around my age with thick glasses and a baseball cap covering a receding hairline. "This is Francesco," said Leo. We shook hands and I smiled. But Francesco looked pained and uncomfortable. I abruptly turned to Leo and asked if he had spoken to his mother.

"Yes," he said, sighing. "But my mother does not remember any of the details of the murder story." I groaned but I wasn't surprised. Just another dead end. I hadn't really expected much. I decided then that if I did return to do more research, I would have no expectations, that I would try to be much more Zen than I had been last time around. I needed to try to calm down and not force the facts, but let them come to me—if they existed. Try to enjoy the scenery, the food, the wine, the company. I needed to be more patient. More Italian.

"I think my friend Francesco can help you," Leo said. "He is a local lawyer and is doing his own family research right now." Francesco smiled his difficult smile and looked embarrassed, or maybe angry, I couldn't tell. Either way, he looked like he really didn't want to be here. Leo explained that Francesco knew the workings of the local legal system and was a history buff. He didn't know my story, but he might be able to help me find it.

Francesco didn't speak any English but was married to a Croatian woman named Natasa, who spoke perfect English. After we finished our drinks, we walked over to their home, the big palazzo at the end of the Corso near the town's St. Rocco statue, the one with the dog licking his master's plague sores. The palazzo reminded me of that Sicilian mansion from *The Godfather Part II,* where Don Ciccio is gutted like a fish.

Past the mansion's own grove of seven palm trees, Francesco shyly invited me and Leo inside to see the antique murals, ceiling frescoes, and wrought-iron balconies. I had passed this place dozens of times ten years ago and had often wondered who lived in it. That mystery was solved. Francesco and Natasa also owned a small hotel on the other side of town, named Giardino Giamperduto, a former cheese-making factory—a *caseificio*—which Francesco's family had owned for decades.

After the house tour they took me on a tour of the hotel. The cheese factory was now a garden oasis inside a scrappy neighborhood, with 11 rooms, a swimming pool, a café, a giant chessboard, and a view of the Basento Valley farms, from which you could see olive groves and the old mule paths.

Francesco, who seemed to be warming up, explained to me himself that he was doing his own research into the Fascist history of his family. He suggested, in proper Italian, that I visit Potenza, the capital of the region, on my next trip. If there had been a murder trial, it probably would have taken place in Potenza, he explained. "In fact," he said, "I will be in Potenza in a few weeks doing my own research. I would be happy to look for your murder when I am there."

"That's too much to ask," I said. "I'm sure I'll be back soon to do my own research and you can point me in the right direction."

"It's no trouble at all," he said, bending his head and staring down at his running shoes.

I reached into my brown leather backpack, which I used as a purse, and took out my new beige leather wallet, which I had just bought during a shopping spree for family souvenirs. I thumbed around until I found my business card and handed it over to Francesco. "Well, here's my email, just in case you do find anything," I said. "Anything at all."

I HEADED AROUND THE CORNER AND STOPPED IN AT THE OLD HOUSE on Via Cavour where I had lived years before, to say hello to Maria Natale and Maria Gallitelli, my old neighbors. Gallitelli was away for the weekend, but Maria Natale was home—as always—and greeted me warmly, as if I'd seen her just last week. She had a friend inside with her and insisted I come in and sit with them and "prendi un caffè."

I went down the steps into her parlor, which was cluttered with knickknacks and old furniture. The place hadn't changed and neither had Maria Natale. Her hair was still the color of ginger, though it no longer matched the mother church, which had undergone a cleaning and was now the color of sand. Maria was as lively and as talkative as always, the locket with her husband's photo still pressed to her tanned chest.

When I turned to greet her friend, I realized with a start that it was Miserabila, the one who had screamed at me in the street. I took a breath and held it as if diving underwater, preparing myself for her attack. But Miserabila didn't recognize me. I breathed out and tried to relax. Had I changed all that much in ten years? A little chubbier maybe, but I still had that same round *faccia di Gallitelli*. Maybe she was senile.

Miserabila looked the same, though, same nasty bulldog face, same balding head, same miserable frown.

Maria and I chatted, about my mother, about New York, about the kids, whose photos I showed her on my iPhone, Paulina with braces on her teeth but still a "bella bambina."

"She's a ballet dancer," I told Maria, using my arms and doing a little step to make sure she understood me. "And an A student, just like her brother." I showed her a picture of Dean, tall and lanky, under a thick head of dark hair and a pair of black-rimmed hipster glasses. Dondi all grown up.

"He plays bass guitar and is in a band, but he also loves history," I said. Dean's love of battles had evolved into an appreciation of world history.

I looked closely at his face and felt a stab of homesickness. "I wish I could have brought them with me," I said, half-meaning it.

"I don't think they remember Bernalda. They were too little when we came last time."

Maria shook her head and said, "I can't believe how big they've gotten." Some days, neither could I.

We talked about Maria Gallitelli across the way, who had given birth to a third son (poor Maria with all that laundry to hang), and about my possible return to do more research.

All the while, Miserabila looked on and tried to follow along with my broken Italian, and slowly, slowly, it began to dawn on her just who I was. With a sideways glance, I saw the gradual recognition and then outright disgust fill her face. I could hear the words echoing in her head, not just mine: "Go back to America and leave the dead in peace." But she said nothing. She finally stood up and told Maria Natale she had to go.

Maria seemed puzzled, perhaps having forgotten the screaming rant on the street. Or maybe she was just being polite. But she said goodbye to Miserabila and ushered her outside. When Miserabila was halfway down the cobblestone street, I turned to Maria Natale, shook my head, and said, "I don't think she likes me."

Chapter 11

THE CRYPT OF THE ORIGINAL SIN

A NTONIO TURNED ON SOME SPOTLIGHTS AND THE CAVE lit up like the inside of a jack-o'-lantern. A chill ran through me.

A skinny man in his thirties, with downturned eyes and short dark hair, Antonio was my guide for the day. He had been part of the team that had restored this painted cave ten years earlier.

We had driven together that morning to the edge of a cliff near the cave city of Matera, the last stop on my reconnaissance trip, just to see this place—this Crypt of the Original Sin. Since I was searching for my own family's original sin, it seemed a poetic and fitting final destination.

Matera was home to more than 150 painted caves, whose frescoes were created between the eighth and thirteenth centuries AD. But this one—this Crypt of the Original Sin—was supposed to be the most intact and beautiful, known as the Sistine Chapel of cave paintings.

From the highway, Matera resembled a collection of skulls, all looking out into the distance. The rounded doors and windows to many of its hushed caves were black, and against the chalky, treeless landscape resembled eye and nose holes.

Once you got up close, you could see that the caves—called *sassi*—were carved from tufa rock inside two giant sunken pits, one house haphazardly built atop another like in an Escher drawing. You climbed long, worn stone staircases to get from top to bottom.

Though the caves were created in Paleolithic times, some were painted with religious murals in the Middle Ages by troglodytic monks hiding from persecution. In the seventeenth century, Matera was named the regional capital of Basilicata. But in 1806, Napoleon's brother, Joseph, declared Potenza the capital. Materans were still angry about it.

Less than a century ago, some of the poorest people in the region lived in the *sassi* with their farm animals, but they were evacuated in the 1950s because of Carlo Levi's book.

He had written about Matera and the poverty and disease there, the children's eyes closed shut with trachoma, the flies crawling all over them, the levels of the *sassi* like Dante's rings of hell. Because of his depiction, its residents were moved to more healthy living quarters. The *sassi* were called "vergogna nazionale." A national shame.

But in the 1980s, local politicians and citizens started a movement to renovate the *sassi* and have families move back in. The caves were now filled with spas and hotels, luxury apartments and pizzerias, but were quiet as a graveyard.

These days, Matera was the capital of Basilicata's movie industry. Its rocky exterior was hauntingly beautiful and was often used as a stand-in for Jerusalem and Rome in biblical films. If you saw a movie with ancient Israel as the backdrop, there was a good chance it was actually its stunt double, Matera. The walls of many restaurants were covered in autographed photos of Hollywood stars, the latest invaders to pass through the city's eroded, shiny stone streets.

The upper reaches of Matera, above the *sassi*, were more typical of a modern Italian city, bustling and very sophisticated, with upscale wine shops, expensive specialty grocers, and luxury shoe stores. In those upper reaches were the archives, kept in a modern building with a red gate on a quiet side street where I had searched years ago for the murder.

But I had been looking in the wrong place.

ANTONIO'S SPOTLIGHT ILLUMINATED A SMALL CROWD OF FACES ON the amber, glowing cave walls. They greeted me as if I had arrived at some unexpected bizarre family reunion. The faces looked like mine. My *faccia di Gallitelli*.

The hermit monks who had painted these people in the ninth century likely modeled them on the shepherds and shepherdesses they had encountered on their less hermity days. The monks' models were my ancestors.

I recognized the portraits of the archangels as if they were my uncles, with their wings spread mightily, and a haloed St. Peter and St. John the Baptist, whose images were slightly chipped, done in bright gold, poppy red, and vibrant blue. Staring back at me was a painting of the Blessed Mother with her baby on her lap, looking sad, as usual, maybe knowing that her son would one day die in front of her. She had high cheekbones and a long nose, like mine. Her portrait was completely intact and looked like it had been painted last week.

"You'll see that connecting one scene to the next," said Antonio, pointing at the wall, "are strings of blue and orange flowers that the monks painted in ochre and lapis lazuli, a motif repeated on the edges of all the stories."

On the right side of the rocky cave mural was the main

attraction—Adam and Eve, the most distressed of all the characters, with large swaths missing from their limestone faces and bodies. But you could tell they were naked, covering themselves with big blue bunches of leaves with one hand, and exchanging the forbidden fruit with the other.

A Basilicatan monk had published a dramatic poem about the fall of Adam back in the seventeenth century and I wondered if he had come here to see this cave, if its beautifully simple, elemental version of good and evil had inspired him. His name was Serafino della Salandra and somewhere along the line, the English poet John Milton either met him or stumbled upon his work while visiting Southern Italy. Milton borrowed heavily (some would say stole) from Salandra's opus—*Adamo Caduto*—for his own *Paradise Lost,* published twenty years later.

Here in this cave paradise, Adam and Eve were very relaxed and natural looking, Eve's breasts full and sagging, Adam's head tilted up at the tree of knowledge, the serpent in blue and red tightly slithering up the trunk. Eve offers the stolen fig to Adam, not an apple, naturally, since this was Southern Italy—land of a billion figs.

Beneath them was the line of ochre and lapis flowers. "A symbol," Antonio said, "of the rebirth, regeneration, and forgiveness that comes after mankind's fall. The crypt, with its frescoes, speaks of original sin that man has committed, but it also speaks of rebirth and regeneration that follows the awareness of being wrong."

It was as if Antonio knew all about me and my sinful family. "Thanks to error, man has the ability to grow and mature," he explained. Without the sin, he said, there is no knowledge, no growth. No learning curve. No making things better. No forgiveness. "And that's the intimate message that the monks were trying to send us, and have sent us, these twelve centuries later. With their flowers."

We're all connected, they say. One story leads to the next. One generation to the next. But we learn from our stories and our past. We learn from our sins. And we grow. Hence the tree of knowledge. We were put here on earth to have our eyes opened.

And though I could see the images, I couldn't see that right before me was the actual key to my own family story. It was hanging right in front of my eyes, a piece of ripe fruit just waiting to be picked. It was as if Antonio, along with God and Salandra and Milton and all the angels and saints, was yelling in my ear, "Here it is. It's the clue you've been looking for, right up there on the wall. Can't you see?"

But I couldn't see it. Not just yet.

Chapter 12

THERE'S NO TWO
WITHOUT THREE

T WO GENES LINKED WITH VIOLENT CRIME, THE HEADLINE
read.

It was a small story, which most people probably missed,
and it broke the week after I got back from Italy. I read it once and
then read it twice, thoughts of Cesare Lombroso spinning in my
head.

> A genetic analysis of almost 900 offenders in Finland
> has revealed two genes associated with violent crime.
>
> Those with the genes were 13 times more likely to have
> a history of repeated violent behaviour. The authors of
> the study, published in the journal *Molecular Psychiatry*,
> said at least 5–10% of all violent crime in Finland could
> be attributed to individuals with these genotypes.
>
> The study, which involved analysis of almost 900 crim-
> inals, is the first to have looked at the genetic make-up of
> so many violent criminals in this way.

This group had committed a total of 1,154 murders, manslaughters, attempted homicides or batteries. A replication group of 114 criminals had all committed at least one murder.

These all carried a low-activity version of the MAOA gene, which previous research has dubbed the "warrior gene" because of its link to aggressive behavior.

The warrior gene. Is that what it was called? And did we have it in my family? Dean had always been especially obsessed with military history. Was this why?

I DIDN'T MENTION THE STORY TO ANYONE BUT MY HUSBAND. I DIDN'T want the kids to know that Mommy's crazy rantings about her criminal family genes might actually have some basis in reality.

But the story pushed me over the edge in some strange, emotional way. I decided right then and there that no halfway measures were going to get me what I wanted. No more reading books from 4,500 miles away. Or searching for cryptic clues in prehistoric caves.

Lying in bed at night, my body still tanned from the beach, I decided to dive back in, headfirst, to find my family murder. I couldn't wait for another ten years to pass. I was going to find Vita's story, to solve the question once and for all of whether my family was genetically flawed. It seemed counterintuitive, but I had to leave my family to make sure they were safe.

I needed a month—at least. Maybe two. Maybe even six. I announced my plans to my stunned family and booked my return flight to Rome. I bought my train tickets to and from Metaponto and arranged to have Leo, my long-lost cousin and beach bar owner, pick me up at the station.

As if getting ready to give birth, for the next eight months

I prepped and researched and hunkered down for the blessed event. I contacted everyone I knew there and planned my strategy. The owner of the San Teodoro farm knew a woman who rented an apartment in Pisticci for fifteen dollars a day. I took it. I contacted a professor in Potenza—a friend of a friend of a friend—who could help me search the archives there.

I emailed Professors Tataranno and Salfi and everyone else I had ever met in Basilicata and asked for recommendations on hiring a researcher/translator. I made list upon list, with names and numbers and email addresses, then interviewed a dozen candidates over Skype.

I found two—one from each of the towns my family lived in a century ago. I hired Imma, a twenty-eight-year-old writer from Bernalda, and Giuseppe, a farmer whose family were landowners from Pisticci, who would help me between his apricot and wheat harvests.

We strategized over Skype and they got started immediately, searching town records and quizzing the locals. Meanwhile, I downloaded translating apps, texting apps, and used the Internet to brush up on my Italian and connected with countless Bernaldans and Pisticcesi over Facebook. I went to Chinatown and bought a duffel bag full of baseball hats and T-shirts with New York emblazoned on them to hand out as gifts to anyone who might help once I got off the train in Metaponto.

I packed and repacked, including my favorite books on Basilicata, then checked and double-checked my itinerary, my flights and train rides, the places I would stay, and the contacts for the people who, I hoped and prayed, would help me find my family murder.

When I told my mother I was going back to Italy for a month alone, I could hear the disapproval and worry in her voice. What kind of Italian mother left her kids behind for a month? Now I was slightly sickened by the thought. I didn't eat on the day of my departure, though the refrigerator and freezer were crammed with food. I left frozen dinners I had prepared in the weeks before, meatballs, beef stew, sausage and peppers, pasta fagiole. It was a greatest-hits medley of my Italian family classics, for fear my family wouldn't survive without me. In keeping with my family credo, passed down from the prosperous days following centuries of poverty and hunger, it was always better to make too much than not enough. Basta!

Being without my children on that last weeklong trip had been incredibly freeing, but unnerving the whole time, as if I were missing a limb or had forgotten my purse somewhere. But I knew I shouldn't worry so much. My kids were good kids and they were in safe hands with my husband. Maybe the criminal gene had luckily skipped over them, like it had over me and my siblings and Leonardo, my great-grandfather, or maybe it was because I had been there to yell at them when they did something wrong and hug them the rest of the time. Nature versus nurture. We would never know.

But maybe, just maybe, that warrior gene was buried deep inside them, or one of them, slowly ticking, ticking, until finally it exploded in some tragedy or drama that I couldn't foresee or control. Maybe it would happen while I was gone.

SO I LEFT AMERICA IN SLOW MOTION.

First I was stopped at airport security because they inexplicably found explosive traces on my hands. After an "over the clothes" body search and some tough questions in a private room, I was allowed to proceed to the gate, only to have my flight delayed, and finally, because of a raging thunderstorm, canceled. I rescheduled my flight and texted Leo, Imma, and Giuseppe that I'd be a day late.

Though a part of me—mostly my stomach—didn't want to go at all.

What if my plane crashed? What if someone else, someone they *should* be inspecting for explosive traces, had a bomb? Would my children ever recover if I never returned home? Would Wendell remarry?

He would have to remarry. He could never raise them alone. Maybe my mother would move in. I imagined that scenario and thought it would make a good premise for a TV pilot. What happens when a mother dies on her way to Italy and her eighty-three-year-old mom moves in to raise the kids? Hilarity ensues. Tuesday nights at eight on Lifetime.

Maybe I should just stay home, I thought that night as I pulled up to our house in Brooklyn, back from my unsuccessful visit to Newark International Airport. Forget Italy. Forget the crime. Maybe this was a sign I should forget the search for Vita. First the explosive traces and now the canceled flight. Leave the dead in peace, like Miserabila had said.

And then it hit me: maybe she had understood what I was saying to Maria Natale back in October in my broken Italian, knew I was returning, and had put a curse on my plane.

I laughed at the thought of it, trying to shake the idea from my head.

That evening, with Paulina sleeping next to me, curled inside me like a shrimp, I couldn't help but think of all those curses I had come across in the book I'd read on magic in the South. The evil eye. The potions. The spells. The horrible little people who tried to suffocate you.

I pressed Paulina closer to me.

I fell asleep and dreamed strange dreams. I most vividly remember one in which I rent a mule instead of a car when I get to Italy. The mule moves so slowly that I decide to simply walk everywhere I go, from town to town, much like my ancestors.

Buia a buia. Dark to dark.

Chapter 13

WILD THINGS

VITA LOVED TO HEAR ABOUT THE KILLERS.
With her front teeth missing and her messy hair in dark knots, Vita loved a good story as much as she loved the country. And usually the two went *mano nella mano*. While they worked in the fields, her mother would tell her incredible legends.

Tales of magic and wolf men and witches, of love and betrayal and the local criminals, the brigands—the folk heroes of Southern Italy. On the best days, Teresina would sing the stories to her daughter, her voice high and nasal and oscillating, rising up like a Middle Eastern call to prayer.

She recited legends of *monacelli, succobi,* and the local witches—or *streghe*. Every town had a witch, a woman or a man who could cast spells and remove them, who could cure your headache with a few words and cause your breast milk to flow freely after it had been cursed and stopped up by a jealous neighbor or mischievous dwarf. Vita heard stories of the werewolves who howled from mountaintops every time the moon was full but spent most days walking among the *cristiani*—civilized people—in town, disguised as regular, respectable men. Though slightly more hairy.

Teresina told Vita about the dragon whose bones were kept in an old church farther north and whose magnificent cave was said to be near Maratea. Vita had never seen it, but she knew all about it because of her mother's stories. The dragons must have been frightening, Vita thought, but no more awful than everyday life.

The best stories were the ones about the killers, whom she had seen with her own eyes. They were the best stories because she knew they were true.

TERESINA SPENT MOST DAYS AS A GATHERER, GLEANING IN THE fields—picking off the ground the bits and pieces of what was leftover after a harvest, or teaching Vita what wild plants and herbs were safe to eat. This was the thing that Vita loved most, wandering the fields with her mother in search of wild things, the smells of what they found clinging to her hands and fingertips. When she got back to dirty old Bernalda, Vita would hold her tiny fingers up to her nose to remember the smells of the country.

Selvatico, or wild things, included dandelions, sorrel, mint, prickly pears, wild asparagus, forest fennel, rosemary, arugula, nettles, chicory, thistle, radicchio, and *lampascion,* soft little onions that Teresina would pickle. And mushrooms, though you had to be careful to pick the right ones. The brighter, more colorful designs were practically yelling at you, "Leave me alone! I'm poisonous!"

Teresina also taught her daughter what herbs and roots to pick when she or anyone in the family was sick. When someone was in pain, you picked the red poppies from the side of the road. Sometimes a sick baby died, not from illness, but from an overdose of those poppies. There were no doctors and no pediatricians. Only the richest traveled the 150 miles to the hospital in Naples. The local witch said incantations over deadly insect bites, and laid on hands for almost anything, even snakebites. Some even worked at bloodletting. But you were better off simply praying to one of the dozens of saints and martyrs, whose suffering the Bernaldans identified with and understood. You had to choose the right saint, depending on what ailed you: St. Rocco for plague and pestilence, Santa Lucia for eye and vision problems, San Biagio (St. Blaise) for the throat.

Along with the herbs and mushrooms and found treasures, Vita carried firewood home each day in a giant, four-foot-high bundle atop her tiny head. It was much lighter than the water her mother carried most days in a tall, earthenware jug upon her own head. And much easier to find.

Bernalda had no running water or public fountains. You had to be careful, since water was sometimes muddy and contaminated, and was one of the reasons children died so often.

Men with mules fetched water from the two distant wells and fountains, Fontana Nuova and Pozzo di Torrone, more than a mile away. They traveled back and forth for the townspeople, trading their services for food. But when you had so little food to go around, you searched for your water yourself. Bernalda wouldn't get its own fountain for another thirty years.

Wine—*vino casereccio*—was homemade and easier to come by, which was why the children in Italy drank it. There was more of it and it was less likely to be contaminated because the alcohol killed many of the germs. Wine gave the children good color in their faces and made Teresina think Vita and her siblings were healthier than they actually were.

But water was ever sought after, for cleaning and cooking, not just drinking. It was so much better than cleaning with sand mixed with ashes from the fire. The sea was nearby, though its water was off-limits. Because the government taxed the salt, it guarded the coastline and forbid people from taking salt water. Only those with a doctor's note, signed by the mayor, could retrieve seawater for medical reasons. (Never mind that most towns didn't have a doctor.)

The sea, rich with fish and shellfish, was so close, but yet so far for the natives of Bernalda. It wasn't worth getting hassled by the police, captured by pirates, or bit by a malarial mosquito.

In Basilicata, mothers told their daughters stories to teach them morality lessons, just like mine had. Being promiscuous would always end in disaster. There were plenty of local stories about that, about the teen who was loose and had a baby with two hearts, or the girl who had slept with so many men she was now the town whore.

Aside from breastfeeding, birth control didn't exist. Sex was one of the only pleasures you could wring out of a life of *miseria.* Though no one talked about this, of course. Sex was forbidden until marriage and even then, you weren't supposed to enjoy it much.

Younger kids heard stories of marawall, the monster who came and got you if you were bad or if you stayed out too long on the streets during "the hot hour"—around three thirty—and didn't listen to your mama to come inside already.

But Vita's favorite stories were the ones about the brigands, the outlaws and killers who roamed the countryside. Sometimes, on their most exciting days gleaning, Vita and Teresina would see a brigand, high on his horse, with a pointed hat. They trotted by sometimes on the road where she and her mother stopped to pick up snails after it rained, to make the dish *o vavalic' po pulej*—snails with mint. The brigands were fierce and launched attacks on the landowners with their weapon of choice—socks filled with rocks, which they twirled above their heads as they galloped on their horses onto an estate. The guns came out later, when the padroni resisted and refused to turn over their money and crops.

But the brigands were always polite and bowed deeply from

atop their horses when they encountered a peasant family, sometimes even removing their hats. Vita couldn't understand why the military police killed the brigands and impaled their heads on sticks, which she glimpsed now and again in the countryside. Teresina usually shielded Vita's eyes, though sometimes she was too late.

It was done to scare them, the poor country folk, the *cafoni,* so that they wouldn't give shelter to the brigands—the Robin Hoods of Southern Italy, who stole from the rich but didn't really give much back to the poor, except a hope that they, too, could triumph over the padroni.

Brigands kidnapped only rich people, the *pezzi grossi* (or big shots), never the poor ones, since they could never provide a ransom. But somedays Vita wished they would kidnap her. And keep her. She would miss her parents, it was true, but it would be worth it. The romance. The intrigue. She would brandish the knife. If only she could grow a little taller.

BY THE TIME VITA WAS FULL GROWN, OLD ENOUGH TO START WORKing the masseria, old enough to pull weeds and help clean for the padrone's wife, Garibaldi's Risorgimento and his redshirts were proving to be a disappointment. The north of Italy was building railroads and funneling money into work projects and the military, but the South hardly ever saw tracks laid or any improvements. In fact, day-to-day life was even harder. A new grist tax was put in place, forcing the peasants to pay for simply grinding their own wheat at the local mill.

The communal lands, given over to the poor, sat fallow because the peasants didn't have the money to properly farm them. They had to buy their own fertilizer, seeds, and other equipment. And land was often broken into too small a parcel—handkerchiefs, they were called—to even support the family.

The sharecropping families, those who paid the padroni to work their own soil, had it just as bad. The padroni were usually so wealthy they didn't care if the land was profitable to those working it, and when the farm failed, sometimes after a single bad harvest, a new poor family just came along and took the old family's place.

Much of the land became infertile and depleted, without proper irrigation and crop rotation. So even those who were given land wound up selling it back to the large landowners for a small profit.

With the communal lands gone, gleaning scraps of food and collecting firewood became nearly impossible.

There seemed to be no hope, not from Garibaldi, not even from the brigands. By 1870 most of them were dead, the rest in prison or in exile, headed to America. Some said their treasures were buried deep in the Montepiano and Gallipoli woods. But no one ever found any of that treasure. All that was left of the brigands, really, were their stories.

It seemed that all Vita ever had were the stories.

Chapter 14

IN THE MOUTH OF THE WOLF

ROME LOOKED LIKE IT HAD BEEN SEIZED BY A MILITARY junta. Most streets were eerily calm but others were crowded with officers dressed in their finest regalia, with tall caps, and gold braids, pins, and medals on neatly pressed uniforms. Large groups of very stern-looking men in camouflage and black berets marched in formation. Huge Italian flags waved atop buildings. Jets soared overhead, spewing green, white, and red exhaust. I half-expected to see Benito Mussolini pouting, with his arms crossed, on one of the government balconies.

"What's going on?" I asked my cabdriver, a woman named Katia, one of the few female cabbies in the city.

"It's a holiday!" she said, twisting her bleached-blond head around. "The celebration of the republic."

"Ahhhh," I said. Italy's version of Fourth of July.

I checked my bags at the train station, bought my new ticket south at a vending machine, and went off into the deserted streets to meet a new friend for lunch. Her name was Rosa Parisi, an anthropologist who had written a study of Bernalda years ago. I had read her book and emailed her this past spring.

Over spaghetti and baby clams, we discussed my destination. I hoped Rosa could shed some light on my quest. I didn't want this visit to be a string of dead ends and blind alleys. With some guidance from people like Rosa, maybe I could find what I was searching for.

She had written a book about Bernalda's class system when working in the Mezzogiorno and knew the town's entire history and its inner workings. She had worked closely with Professor Tataranno and knew where many of the ghosts of the past resided.

The original inhabitants of the area, she explained, were part of the Oenotri tribe, which had settled before the ancient Greeks, during the Iron Age as early as the eleventh century BC. The name Oenotri meant "the people from the land of vines." Lovers and growers of wine.

The original town where Bernalda now stands was named Camarda. In the beginning, it was just a series of village groupings made up of the Oenotri and other native peoples who banded together against the Greeks, who were the annoying newcomers, the yuppies of their day. In the third century BC, the Romans invaded the area and continued to invade, often pushing the Greeks and natives into the nearby hill towns. Camarda was always on the side of the Romans.

The Barbarians invaded after the Romans left, until Frederick II took charge of the South in the thirteenth century. He was its first modern ruler, a man of reason and reform, lover of both science and literature, tolerant of Jews and Muslims. But after Frederick's death, civil war followed and eventually Charles of Anjou, from France, took over. The Florentine banks backed Charles and so he repaid them using the area's resources, and gave them power to tax the peasants heavily.

Charles's reign caused the Southerners to grow a deep hatred of all public institutions—a hatred that was still ingrained now after all those years, Rosa said. No one in the South trusted the government and it seemed they never would. Especially after the Spanish invaded.

The Aragonese proved to be the worst, levying even higher taxes because of their rich tastes. King Alfonso II, the oldest son of Ferdinand and Isabella, decided to give a gift to his secretary of state, Bernardino de Bernaudo. Looted gold or jewels weren't enough. So Alfonso gave him Camarda—which Bernaudo renamed Bernalda, after himself.

Bernaudo built the ginger-colored castle and Chiesa Madre on the edge of town. Sucking up to their new feudal lord, the townspeople moved everything closer to the new church and changed their patron saint from St. Donato to San Bernardino. The statue of San Bernardino of Siena, a new, trendy saint at the time, was placed inside the mother church, the church of St. Donato. It was all for show, that name change, to garner favor with the aristocracy in the hopes of making life a little better, a little worth living.

The saint switch was probably one of the reasons for Bernalda's town nickname. Each town had one. And the Bernaldans had no shortage of nicknames. People in the neighboring towns called them *pagliacciunn*. Fakers. Superficial. Two-faced posers.

Rosa said the Bernaldans didn't mind their nickname and were actually proud of it. They believed their town to be prettier and their countryside more fertile than any of their neighbors'.

The Bernaldans also believed they were all equal, that there were no social strata, though they were sadly mistaken, said Rosa. The noble families from centuries past were much more well-off than the families of the serfs who had toiled farming their lands. The Bernaldans were simply in denial. The class system was alive and well in their town.

I didn't know at the time, as I ate my spaghetti and sipped my wine, that all of this feudal history was another clue to the murder, staring me right in the face, like those faces on the cave wall in Matera. But like the cave stories, I couldn't quite see it yet, couldn't make it out.

I told Rosa about the bits and pieces I had gleaned about Vita and Francesco. I said that they were lowly farmers, and that Vita, a weaver, was maybe a concubine as well.

"Maybe she and her husband killed the landowner," Rosa suggested. I shrugged my Italian shrug.

"Maybe," I said. "But in my family they always said that Grieco helped Vita come to the United States."

"Well, I'm eager to find out the rest of your story," she said.

"So am I," I said laughing.

Rosa wished me luck: "In bocca al lupo," an Italian saying that translates as "In the mouth of the wolf." I wasn't sure if it was the equivalent of telling someone to break a leg, or if it referred to the mother wolf carrying her cub in her mouth in safety. Or maybe day-to-day life was so bad in Southern Italy years ago that getting eaten by a wolf was considered an improvement. Good luck. May you be eaten by a wolf.

BACK AT THE STATION I RECLAIMED MY BAGS, THEN TOOK THE MINI-elevator up to the main floor to the tracks. In the elevator, two young women, one with an infant in a BabyBjörn, asked me in Italian where the hospital was. I tried to tell her and her friend I had no idea. I explained that we were in a train station and as far as I knew, there were no hospitals here.

We all got off the elevator and I wished them luck. "In bocca al lupo!" I said, laughing, then walked to the newsstand to buy a bottle of water for the seven-hour train ride. But when I went to pay for it, I couldn't seem to find my wallet.

I squatted down to get a better look inside my bag and dug and dug like a woodland animal searching for some long-buried nut.

But the small beige wallet was gone. And I knew exactly where it was: with the woman with the baby. Her friend had unzipped my backpack while she was distracting me with her questions, had taken it out and had zipped it right back up without me even noticing. I spun around to see if she was anywhere in sight. But of course she wasn't.

I dumped the bag out onto the dirty cement floor of the station, while the guy with the water behind the counter nonchalantly placed the bottle back in the glassed-in refrigerator. He didn't even ask what was wrong. He'd probably seen this replayed dozens, maybe hundreds of times, over and over every single day. Some stupid American tourist who had gotten her wallet swiped.

"My wallet was stolen," I told him, in English. I was too panicked to remember the words in Italian. He shook his head and repeated over and over, "Zingare, zingare, zingare"—gypsies.

I had been swindled by gypsies, my New York sensibilities not strong enough to protect me in Rome.

I shoved my belongings back into my bag and tried to think but felt the panic slowly radiate from my head, my face, which I knew was bright red, down through my chest, and shoot out my arms and legs. My stomach lurched. Everything—except my train ticket and passport—was in that wallet. All my money, my credit cards, my cash card, my driver's license, without which I could not rent a car. That mule I dreamed of riding last night might not be a weird nightmare after all.

I tried to think clearly, then ran over to the station entrance to what looked like a golf cart with two cops lounging inside. They were both wearing sunglasses and were lazily watching the crowds stream past. In my most frantic voice, I shouted, "My wallet was just stolen," gesturing wildly with my hands, pulling at my hair while I stood there. They looked at me coolly, shrugged, and told me to go to the police station and file a report. I had fifteen minutes until my train left. That was impossible, wasn't it? I had no time to file a police report or to search for the woman with the baby.

But maybe this was another sign. Vita trying to stop me from heading south. Or the curse of Miserabila. I pictured her in her small stone house in Bernalda, laughing and sticking pins in a doll that looked just like me.

Go home, the voices in my head said. Turn around and just go home.

Go back to America and leave the dead in peace.

Evil happened in threes, even in Italy. Or maybe people just stopped counting after three. The saying here was "Non c'e due senza tre." There's no two without three. And this was my third strike: the explosive traces on my hands, the canceled flight, and now my stolen wallet.

Had I been able to think straight I might have laughed at the thought that I was no longer searching for a crime but was now the victim of one. But I wasn't thinking straight. All I knew was that I had a one-euro coin in my pocket.

With my mouth as dry as a passatella loser's, I walked to the restroom for a quick drink of water and to splash my face to calm myself down. But then I remembered you had to pay for the restrooms here. I didn't even have enough money to use the bathroom.

I texted my husband: "MY WALLET WAS JUST STOLEN." In all caps. I never texted in caps.

Wendell was used to handling reporters in crisis. So he calmly texted back, "Oh no. I'm so sorry. Just get on the train."

And just in case I had misunderstood the first time, he yelled in all-capital letters in a second text: "JUST GET ON THE TRAIN!!!!"

Chapter 15

GYPSIES, GYPSIES, GYPSIES

LEO WAS NOWHERE TO BE FOUND.

I looked around nervously at the darkened streets near the deserted Metaponto train station, every shadow a potential mugger or rapist. At least I had no wallet to steal.

I didn't know what the crime rate was in Basilicata, and right now, I didn't really want to know.

The five other passengers who had gotten off the train with me had quickly met their rides and were off. I briefly considered hopping in and hitching a ride to town. I hadn't slept in more than twenty-four hours. But I waited instead.

I looked up at the stars and tried to make out a few of the constellations, their Greek names swimming in my head, just to calm myself and pass the time. But there were just too many stars up there, all crowding together and confusing me and making me feel even more lost and insignificant. I craned my neck and looked down the dark and dusty road leading to the station.

No Leo.

I glanced over at the small station café, called Grofé, with its bar and couches and tables, but its lights were out and its glass door locked tight. I was alone. With no cash. No credit cards. There were no taxis. And once the train pulled away, no people. No stray dogs or cats. Not even any lizards. Just me. And the ghost of Vita, laughing in my ear.

I felt unmoored.

After about ten minutes of nail biting, I finally texted Leo. "I'm here!" I wrote, trying to sound upbeat and not too pushy. (I wanted to text, "Where the fuck are you?!" but I hardly even knew the guy and was grateful he had agreed to come and get me.) Southerners were notoriously late. And I knew it. But I was a tangle of frayed nerves.

"On my way," Leo wrote back, and within moments his compact car was rounding the curve to the station's pickup point, going so fast it practically screeched in on two wheels.

After a brief hello and a hug, I told him my wallet story.

Leo smacked the steering wheel with an open palm and chanted, "Zingare, zingare, zingare." He shook his head. "Don't worry," he said. "I will take you to dinner. You don't need money."

We headed to Bernalda for pizza and a beer, taking seats in an outdoor garden of the town's newest pizzeria. Though I hadn't eaten in more than eight hours, I had no appetite. The owner knew Leo and brought over a giant plate of appetizers: triangles of provolone, homemade circles of soppressata and soft mounds of ricotta, roasted red pepper strips, pickled artichokes, and some local peasant bread. It looked delicious, but I barely picked at it. I happily drank the beer, though, a local brew, served in what looked like a wine bottle. It was called Jazz Beer. The restaurant was packed with Bernaldans, including small children, though it was close to midnight. Leonardo knew everyone there. He chatted with some, waved to others, but greeted them all.

"Isn't today a holiday?" I asked Leo.

"Not so much down here," he said, shrugging. Leo's shrug said more than the volumes I had read back in New York about the history of Basilicata and the rest of the South. Centuries of domination had left the Southerner with a fatalistic view of the world—the Italian shrug, half-closed eyes, and melancholy outlook its main symptoms.

As Leo drove me to my apartment, my mind wandering in my delirium, I thought about the history of the dark fields we were passing. When I had first seen this landscape ten years ago, I had been struck by its simultaneous beauty and sadness. But since then, I had learned its history, which helped explain that sadness: decade upon decade of repression and the failed attempts, one after another, to remedy it.

A Neapolitan revolution, led by the Jacobins, broke out in the winter of 1799, with the invasion of revolutionary France. They promised reform for the peasants. But that summer, a Bourbon monarch took control, sentencing the Jacobins to death.

In 1806, Napoleon placed his brother, Joseph, on the throne in Naples, throwing the ruling Bourbons into exile. Serfdom was outlawed, with a plan to redistribute the lands among the peasants. But reform failed once again.

I thought of Garibaldi, and how he, too, had promised reform and a better life for the peasants. But the South suffered more at the hands of their northern brothers than they had at the hands of all those invaders.

Unification seemed to be the straw that broke the farmer's back. Brigands started to appear in the countryside, robbing the wealthy landowners, maybe not giving it over to the poor but nonetheless giving the peasants something to cheer about. Industrialization had taken hold in the New World. And so the peasants began to leave—streaming over to the Americas by the thousands.

From 1906 to 1915—the year Vita died—Basilicata lost nearly 40 percent of its population to emigration.

The government started to worry about the loss of its best and strongest, and finally made an effort to entice them to stay. After World War II, a series of identical white houses with arched doorways were built for the Metaponto-area farmers, which came with a small parcel of land.

Leo pointed the *colonica* houses out to me. It was like the American program of forty acres and a mule following the Civil War, but without the mule. In the 1950s and '60s, crops were diversified and true change started to take hold.

These days land was cheap and available to anyone who wanted to farm it, though it was hard work. Many of the young men in and around Bernalda wanted nothing to do with the agricultural life of their ancestors. They wanted instead to be rappers or videographers, chefs or bartenders.

Or beach bar owners.

Many of those small white houses, the ones set aside for the farmers, were now summer cottages. Some were rented out to tourists in the high season. In fact, Leo owned one of them. He pointed it out to me as we sped past, his small dog running out into the dark road to greet him. Leo nearly ran him over.

Chapter 16

MONDAY, TUESDAY, THURSDAY, WEDNESDAY

I MMA WAS TALL, WHICH WAS UNUSUAL FOR WOMEN IN THESE parts, or for anyone really. She had straight brown hair a shade lighter than mine and huge, curious eyes rimmed with dark eyeliner, though they were often covered in fashionable black sunglasses. With her bob and those sunglasses, she looked a bit like Anna Wintour, but always wore jeans, even in the hottest weather. She smoked Chesterfields and was cool but kind and smart and was always up for adventure, never saying no to a suggestion or request.

Like many of Bernalda's young adults, Imma lived at home with her parents. To make a living, she edited manuscripts and worked as a deejay in a bar, which she gave up for a month to devote herself solely to me and my research. She was going to be my Girl Friday, Monday, Tuesday, Thursday, Wednesday, and any other day of the week I needed her.

Her college thesis had been an analysis of the dialects of Pisticci and Bernalda. She had family in both towns and was a cousin

of the historian Dino D'Angella, Professor Tataranno's counter-
part in Pisticci. Imma also knew Tataranno very well, having had
his wife, Carmelina, as a teacher in school.

Giuseppe—my other researcher—was also unusually tall. He
was Hollywood handsome, with a wide, bright smile, downturned
black eyes that sparkled, dark, thick eyebrows, short, neat brown
hair, and a raspy voice. He was happily married to a beautiful
blond woman named Emanuela, who matched his good looks and
even raised them. She resembled a fairy-tale princess and was
just as sweet.

Her prince, Giuseppe, was at least a shade or two darker than
us all, with a deep tan from working his fields. Even though he was
a farmer, he had had a first-rate education because his family had
been landowners. His features and his speech were more refined
than most residents' but he moved easily between the locals he
had grown up with and the local landowners, who seemed more
sophisticated. Like me, he was caught between social classes and
the expectations that came with both. I had grown up working
class but had moved out of Jersey City long ago. I sometimes felt
adrift, without a real tribe to call my own.

Giuseppe was just a few years younger than I was. I noticed that
he popped the collar on his polo shirts straight up in a very 1980s
way like I had many years ago. (The popped collar was making a
comeback in Italy; Giuseppe was ahead of the trend.) His English
was impeccable and he was a gentleman, holding doors open for
me, explaining anything I was confused about—which was a lot—
and always arriving on time, a rare trait in the South. He was so
dependable and responsible that he wore a wristwatch, in a world
where most people simply checked their phones for the time, if
at all.

He was the one who drove me to the post office to pick up
money that was being wired by American Express my first afternoon back in Basilicata. We went to Marina di Ginosa, a small,

lively seaside village outside Pisticci where he had grown up. He knew everyone there but had moved out years ago to a private farmhouse in Marconia, nearby. It was difficult to live in Marina di Ginosa, he said, because some people resented him for coming from a long line of landowners.

Giuseppe was eager to find the murder, so eager that before I even arrived, he had found a local Grieco family with a *soprannome* that meant "murderer." After a few days of digging, he found out one of the ancestors in that Grieco family had simply been a very successful hunter and, because of his vast collection of animal heads, was jokingly called "the murderer."

Imma, meanwhile, had tried searching in the Bernalda archives but was rebuffed by the awful clerk there, who said she needed my written permission to look into my family records. Which was ridiculous.

The next morning, the three of us met with Professors Tataranno and Salfi in the scented garden at Francesco's Hotel Giamperduto. We all hugged and sat down at a long table overlooking the fertile Basento Valley. Twisted olive trees filled the property, making it look like the Garden of Gethsemane. Professor Tataranno looked nearly the same as he had ten years earlier, his face only slightly aged, his mind as sharp as ever. He was still chain-smoking. I worried his lungs didn't look quite as good as he did on the outside. I was happy to see that Professor Salfi was still alive. He didn't look much older, since he had looked so old to begin with, but he seemed much quieter this time around. I wondered if his hearing had gone.

We talked about the past ten years and about the murder. This time I was prepared. I had brought along copies of the birth certificates I had for Vita and her sons and also her death certificate and handed them around the table, as if shuffling cards in a game of passatella. They agreed to make some inquiries in town and we said our goodbyes, promising to reunite later in the week. But before we scattered, I handed out the baseball hats with "NYC" written on the front. Everyone laughed and put them on, looking like a ragtag team of players with me as their nervous coach. "Team Helene," Giuseppe said with a laugh.

GIUSEPPE WAS THE ONE WHO DID MOST OF THE DRIVING, SINCE I had a lousy sense of direction. Also, the streets in Bernalda and Pisticci had been built for mules, not for cars, and someone was always scraping the paint job off the side of their car. I didn't want it to be me. It was also possible I would get a ticket if caught driving without a license, even though I had a Bernalda police report explaining what had happened, safe in my backpack, which I now carried in front of me, like a baby in a BabyBjörn, like the one worn by the gypsy who had stolen my wallet. I hadn't eaten a proper meal for days. Maybe I would lose weight this trip, a first for a visit to Italy.

The rental car company was named Stigliano Motors, the same last name as Vita's mother. I wondered if we were related, too, and asked the car rental guy about the murder. He had no idea what I was talking about and shrugged. Luckily, he ignored the fact that I had no driver's license and simply handed me the keys to my boxy brown Lancia. I wouldn't have to ride a mule after all.

With my Lancia—lance—Giuseppe and I headed out like Don Quixote and Sancho Panza in search of enlightenment. (I wasn't sure who was who.)

Giuseppe turned to me and thanked me for hiring him. "It's not just the money that's important," he said. "Trying to find your family murder is kind of like therapy for me."

"Really?" I asked. "How?"

"It's helping me to forget my own family story for a little while."

"What story?"

"My sister, Sabrina, was murdered a couple of years ago," he said, very matter-of-fact. I stared at him.

"Oh my God," was all I could muster.

"She was killed by a stalker who was in love with her. She left behind two kids. Our whole family is still a little bit in shock."

I gasped. I didn't gasp often. It took a lot to make me gasp. I hardly knew Giuseppe and wasn't even sure how to respond to such an awful story. "Jesus," I said, finally, shaking my head in disbelief. "Did they catch the man who did it?"

"He killed himself," Giuseppe calmly explained as he drove.

"Oh my God, how awful. I'm so sorry," I said. I felt like he should pull over. But he lived with this horror story every day. It was only new to me.

"I know," he said. "It's a terrible story. But your family murder is helping me to forget my family murder. At least for a little while." He shrugged and tried to smile.

The murder—Sabrina's murder—had been big news in Cesena in northern Italy, where it had happened in the spring of 2012. Sabrina was forty-five years old, Giuseppe's big sister. She was scheduled to take her real estate agent's exam in a few weeks but was mostly a full-time mother of two. The kind of mother who still sang lullabies to her eight-year-old son.

Her biggest fault, said Giuseppe, was that she was too friendly and kind to those who didn't deserve her kindness.

She had complained to the police only weeks earlier about the sixty-year-old man from Bari who had become obsessed with her. He was the father of one of her friends.

The stalker had confessed his obsession and desire to kill Sabrina to a doctor, who then told the Bari police. But they did nothing.

The morning of the murder, Sabrina had just dropped her son off at school and was waiting outside her friend's house to meet her. The stalker, meanwhile, had driven up to Cesena with a pistol, his rental car full of scribbled rantings. He saw Sabrina outside his daughter's house and walked up to her car from the passenger side, leaning into the window and shooting her twice in the chest.

He sped away to the nearby seaside town of Cervia, where he took refuge in the cathedral there, taking two hostages, including the priest. After hours of negotiations with the police, Sabrina's killer shot himself in the chest upon the altar. Some said it was suicide. But the police chief told Giuseppe the killer was in the middle of a sentence when the gun went off, that it was an accident. Giuseppe thinks he was too much of a coward to deliberately take his own life.

Sabrina was one of fifty-five Italian women killed that year by men who claimed to love them—husbands, boyfriends, stalkers.

"Most days I wake up and I think it's some bad dream, some nightmare," said Giuseppe. "But it's real."

Giuseppe seemed like one of those good people to whom bad things happened, like a modern-day Job. Sabrina's death was the worst. But then his farmhouse had recently been ransacked and robbed while he and his wife were out. He had had cancer, though he was cured. And now he was having financial troubles with his farm in Marconia, which was why he had taken the job helping me.

Part of his apricot harvest was finished, but he still had to harvest his wheat, and the man who was supposed to come with the harvesting machine—the *mietitrebbia*—kept putting him off day after day after day. Giuseppe was worried the wheat would burn as the June days grew longer and hotter. After a week, he decided to hire another man, but when he arrived, the machine was not big enough. He told me all this as we drove, and not in a complaining way, but in order to let me know his story before we searched for mine.

Giuseppe was the first one to say out loud that maybe there was some sort of curse not just on his head, but on mine. Right after I arrived, Imma dropped her phone in the toilet and had to travel over an hour to Potenza to visit the only Apple Store in the region for repair. It wouldn't be ready for several days, making it difficult for us to contact one another.

"There is some spirit that does not want you to tell this story maybe," Giuseppe said. "Do you believe this is true?"

"I've been thinking the same thing," I said, trying to laugh about it.

"But we will overcome it," he said, patting my hand on the car seat. "We will be strong and we will find your murder. You will see."

Chapter 17

THINKING ON YOUR FEET

VITA'S PARENTS KNEW THAT ONE DAY THEY'D GIVE THEIR daughter a beautiful wedding. Simple, but beautiful.

And they had no doubt they would make the right match—the *bashad*.

When Vita was coming of age in the late 1860s, her mother would say to her "Non hai peli sulla lingua"—an idiomatic expression that meant literally, "You don't have hair on your tongue." It actually meant, "You always speak your mind." And Vita always did.

It's what made her attractive to the boys in the village, that edge she had over them. She was smarter than they were, quicker, more direct, and they were in awe of Vita.

By puberty, she was forbidden to speak to a boy without being accompanied by a guardian, but she would simply give them the look. The other girls—and women—looked away when a man looked at them, lowered their eyes in the usual submissive way.

But not Vita.

She stared right back at you, no matter who you were. The *sindaco,* or mayor, the *pezzi grossi,* the big shots, even the padroni. She stared you right down and seemed to say, "What the fuck are you looking at?" It wasn't the *malocchio* she gave them. No. It was even stronger than that. It was an inner strength and confidence.

It was moxie.

Vita wasn't beautiful, but she was sexy, the curve of her neck and the way she tilted her head when she listened. She was smart and wise all at the same time—what the Italians like to call "veramente in gamba." The Italian version of thinking on your feet. But it meant more than that. Liveliness and love of life was hard to find in a place as miserable as nineteenth-century Bernalda. And Vita had it. Vita had it in spades—to quote an American idiom.

She was so bold and so full of life that some of the other girls jealously called her a *puttana,* starting rumors.

On top of it all, Vita was funny. All the women in our family were comedians. People often called Vita *macchietta,* which meant "entertaining little person." She could turn a phrase. Tell a joke using a play on words, a favorite of Italian comedians. As the much hated tax man made his way down Via Cavour, Vita did a mean imitation of the man walking down the street—her legs bowed, her back hunched, her teeth bucked and eyes crossed. Vita was a skilled impersonator and mimic, like most of my great-aunts. The comedy gene had to come from somewhere.

THOUGH THERE WAS NO SUITOR JUST YET, TERESINA SET ABOUT HER mother's duty: gathering the girl's linens, bit by bit, piece by piece. Even the poorest mothers provided a trousseau for their daughters. A bedspread was cut and fringed. Teresina made and gathered the pillowcases, the wool blanket, a mattress of straw, secondhand dishcloths and napkins, which she lovingly embroidered with tiny flowers and patterns.

All Teresina's spare linen from her own marriage was recycled and made to look like new. The embroidery was beautiful, because Teresina was a talented seamstress and weaver. She would pass her skills on to her daughter, teaching her the complicated pedals and strings of the wooden loom, which looked like the inside of a piano.

In addition to the linen, Teresina and Domenico had to provide Vita with a chest for the linen and a chest of drawers, a board for kneading pasta, and one for carrying bread on her head to and from the communal oven.

Her father, Domenico, an old man by now at fifty-five, made them all himself with his still-strong hands, from the wood he chopped from the public land, the few parcels of land that didn't belong to the padroni yet.

Before the wedding, the parents of the bride and groom agreed in an unwritten contract as to what linens, furniture, dishes, clothes, and glasses would be given away with the daughter. Richer families discussed an actual dowry—money and lands that would be transferred from one family to the other.

And finally, the *bashad* was made. The love match. From the word "to kiss," *baciare*. Vita Gallitelli would be engaged to marry a neighbor, Francesco Vena, seven years her senior.

Who knows if Vita and Francesco were in love? Probably not. Few in Vita's day had the luxury of marrying someone they'd fallen in love with. Marriage was for convenience, for survival, for having babies to help work the farm.

Francesco knew Vita because he was friends with her brother, Leonardantonio, who was four years older than she was. Francesco had worked with him on the farms surrounding Bernalda and so he knew, from chatting every day with Leonardantonio, that Vita was not engaged to anyone. He liked the way she looked, her dark, thick hair, her long, lovely neck, and though she was small, her strong shoulders and hips.

Before the proposal, he floated the idea of marrying Vita past Leonardantonio, who was almost as enthusiastic as Francesco was. His sister was getting old, entering spinster territory. His parents were starting to worry.

She was nineteen.

Chapter 18

FAITHFUL HOME

PISTICCI HAD A CERTAIN LIGHTNESS AND AIRINESS ABOUT IT, since it was high up on a hill, within the clouds somedays. It felt so different from Bernalda. To get to the center, you had to drive around and around the hill at a pretty steep incline. Driving stick was especially challenging. But because the town was so vertical, many of the houses had views of the countryside. Bernalda was flat and laid out in a simple grid: you had to be at the very edge of town, at the town walls, to see the landscape.

I took an apartment in Pisticci this time around: maybe it would be luckier for me. The people here were generally friendlier and more open. And as far as I knew, Pisticci was the last place Vita had lived before coming to America. So maybe the murder had happened here.

Though it had a slightly bigger population, seventeen thousand, Pisticci was quieter than Bernalda. The men were gentlemen and the women were the prettiest in the region, I thought, although some of the older ones had mustaches.

Some think the name Pisticci comes from the Greek phrase *pistos spiti,* which means faithful home. Pisticci always offered the Greeks a place to stay. And so I decided to make it my faithful home.

My apartment was near the top of the town but was on the ground floor. It was clean and whitewashed on the outside, like all the buildings in Pisticci, with tall shutters and high ceilings that kept it cool most days. The place was simple but comfortable and decorated with framed paintings of Jesus and the Blessed Mother, and was fully stocked with pots and pans, sheets and towels, and everything I needed.

Vita's son, Leonardo, my great-grandfather, was born in 1879 in a house a short walk away. His house had a marble step outside, green wooden double doors, a second-story window, and a curved, red terra-cotta roof. It was much bigger than the one his brother, Valente, had been born in in Bernalda, and in a much fancier neighborhood. I wondered what had brought them here.

Down the street from Leonardo's birthplace at 34 Via Loreto was now a sign that told the history of the *rione.* "In this district there were: the homes of the Mayors, who were armed by the local squire, the houses of the priests, of the lawyers, of the doctors and the palatial residences that belonged to the noblest and wealthiest. . . ."

On Leonardo's birth certificate, it said the family had moved there for "work reasons" and that Francesco Vena was not present. At work, I figured. Maybe this time in the fields surrounding Pisticci.

Leonardo's birthplace and my apartment were near the center of town. I noticed a half-dozen churches nearby, twice as many as I had seen in Bernalda. The sound of church bells constantly filled Pisticci's air, which smelled of fresh baked focaccia from the local bakeries. The fragrant breezes were cooler than in Bernalda, especially at night.

I wasted no time in my local research, buying groceries on the main street, Corso Margherita, and asking everyone I met—the butcher, the baker, the vegetable seller, the gelato guy—about my family murder.

The main corso was hopping with residents out taking their evening *passeggiata,* chatting, laughing, enjoying the cool evening weather. I thought about America and how everyone was shut up tight in their houses most nights, watching television.

The corso in Pisticci was much shorter than the one in Bernalda and was made of shiny, long beige paving stones that reflected the lights on the street at night. It looked more like a dance floor than a street. And the crowds waltzed along it all evening, stopping every so often to chat and gossip. The crowd in Pisticci was much different than Bernalda's. Most of the residents of Pisticci were either very old or very young. It lent more of an innocence to the population.

The Bernaldans really didn't like the Pisticcesi and thought their town was boring, with far fewer bars and restaurants than Bernalda. They called Pisticcesi *cafone*—uncouth farmers (pronounced "ga-VONE" in dialect). The Bernaldans considered their town a city—even though they had no library, movie theater, or mass transit. The Pisticcesi knew they were a small town and were proud of it. I thought maybe the Bernaldans were just jealous.

But their feud actually went back several generations, to the Fascist years in Basilicata. Professor Tataranno had told me the story years ago, the one involving Pascquale Gallitelli, who was dragged out from under his bed and beaten and then shot in the head. That day of bloodshed had started because the Pisticcesi had come to Bernalda looking for a political enemy. A riot broke out, and three people wound up dead. The Bernaldans were still angry at the Pisticcesi over it.

The antagonism only grew in 1933 when Mussolini took some Metapontan land under Pisticci rule and gave it instead to Bernalda. When you go to the beach in Metaponto now, the signs say it falls under the comune of Bernalda. Which still pisses off the Pisticcesi.

THE PEOPLE IN PISTICCI SHOOK THEIR HEADS IN MUCH THE SAME way the Bernaldans had when I asked them about the murder. They had never heard of it. No was no, no matter how polite you were or how pretty the view was.

At the butcher shop, though, the face of the woman behind the counter brightened when I told her my story and that my family name was Vena. Finally, I thought, someone who knows the story. She held up an index finger and ran to the back of the shop. I closed my eyes and imagined her returning with a picture or a letter or some family memento.

Instead she emerged with a look of satisfaction on her face and a bottle of Amaro Lucano in her hands.

It wasn't the first time this had happened to me.

Whenever I mentioned the name Vena here, someone inevitably pulled out a bottle of this local bitter liqueur, manufactured by a family here with the same name. The factory was on the outskirts of town, protected by a sliding yellow gate that had VENA written across it in giant blue letters.

Vena was written on the bottle's label as well, next to a picture of the *pacchiana,* a woman dressed in the local costume of the region. She had a colorful skirt, a white puffy blouse, and a red vest, with her hand on her hip and her head tilted in a very saucy pose. The founder of Amaro Lucano, Pasquale Vena, was born in 1871, around the same time as Leonardo and Valentin, Vita's sons. Pasquale had gone to Naples with his brothers and had watched them sail for America. But he stayed behind and got a job and eventually invented Amaro Lucano.

Three brothers in Naples. Two sailing away to America. All named Vena.

On my more optimistic days, I liked to think it was our family and that Pasquale was the "lost" son of Vita. Maybe she was even the model for the *pacchiana* on the label, posing before she left for America.

I had written letters to the Amaro Lucano clan and told them the few facts I knew, hoping they could shed some light. They never wrote back. I even tried visiting the factory, but they said all the family members were at a family reunion. Without me. Which was all right, since they were probably drinking Amaro Lucano, which I couldn't stand. It tasted like Vicks Formula 44 cough syrup. Pisticci's generous residents, hearing my family name was Vena, offered me shot after shot of free Amaro Lucano. And to stay in their good graces, I obliged for the first twenty times or so. But I really hated the stuff.

Every time I passed the factory, I shuddered because a huge sign, a replica of the bottle, lay on its roof. The thought of that much Amaro Lucano made me queasy. All the bars, cafés, and restaurants carried it, and one café in particular—Bar Vena—had an enormous dusty bottle on its top shelf.

I told the lady butcher thank you, that I knew all about the Amaro Lucano–Vena connection, and declined her gracious offer of a free shot. I ordered a half pound of pork chops and headed home.

VENA WAS A MORE COMMON NAME IN PISTICCI THAN IT WAS IN Bernalda. I wondered if my great-great-grandfather Francesco was from Pisticci originally. The next day, Giuseppe and I searched through the Pisticci records to see if we could find a birth certificate for a Francesco Vena several years older than Vita, born in the 1840s or '50s. But there were several Francesco Venas around that age. It was hard to tell which one—if any—was our man.

Imma spent the day in Bernalda wrangling with the clerk there, trying to find some family records. The next day she planned to travel to Matera with Francesco, the lawyer to whom Leo had introduced me. I had thoroughly searched those Matera files years ago but I wanted Imma to take a second look to make sure I hadn't missed anything.

Giuseppe and I visited my great-grandfather's at 34 Via Loreto, hoping to turn up a clue to Vita and Francesco's story. An old woman down the street—Mrs. DiBello—had the key to the place. But the landlords, who lived in Turin, had told her not to let anyone in. We thought maybe we could sweet-talk her.

Mrs. DiBello was sitting outside her house with her husband, Rocco, perched quietly on small wooden chairs topped with square pillows covered in white floral pillowcases. They were in their nineties and spoke only in dialect. Giuseppe introduced me and quickly, though smoothly, explained my quest, moving back and forth between dialect and proper Italian—with lapses into English—so we could all understand.

Rocco was even shorter than I was, with red, ruddy skin, a long nose and chin, and big ears that had apparently kept growing after the rest of him had stopped. He was like a happy Italian elf. His wife, who was even smaller, looked a lot like my mother, with a round, flawless face, but with eyeglasses.

The DiBellos refused to give up the key, despite some gentle prodding from Giuseppe, but they were happy to tell us what it was like for their parents to live here years ago. They remembered living in the house with their animals, their chickens, a pig, and a mule, just like in the books I'd read. These people were like a time machine, taking me on a personal tour of the life my ancestors had led.

"I named all my animals when I was a boy," said Rocco. His

mule was called Ciccio ("CHEECH-o," short for Francesco). "Their ears would prick up when I called their names." I laughed and then asked if naming your pigs and chickens made it harder to kill them around slaughter time.

Rocco shook his head. "It wasn't sad when the time came to kill them," he said. "Besides, we only had meat three times a year, festival time—Christmas, Easter, or the feast of St. Rocco in summer. It was just a part of life."

His family was rich enough to own Ciccio, he said, who was kept in the back part of the house and whom his father rode to the farm before the sun rose each day. A manger with straw in it for Ciccio to eat stood beside the bed.

"There were no bathrooms or outhouses in those days," he said. "Just a pot—a *zio pepe*—and then a barrel in which you put that waste, which was then rolled down to a spot close to the cemetery and dumped." He pointed in the distance with his wrinkled, stubby finger.

Mrs. DiBello went inside and came back out with her mother-in-law's *pacchiana* costume, the same kind worn by the woman on the Amaro Lucano label. I had never seen one of the actual costumes, only photographs and drawings. Until the 1950s, all the women in Pisticci, Bernalda, and the surrounding villages wore the same outfit day in and day out.

This outfit looked like it was brand-new but Rocco insisted it was a hundred years old. Mrs. DiBello held up each part of the intricate costume, pronouncing the name of each piece in dialect. The long colorful skirt was called *a stuan*, which came all the way down to the feet. This one was green, a color meant to bring luck, with pleats and a single line of lace about three-quarters of the way down. Underneath that women wore a petticoat, called *u suttanin*. The white blouse, *a cammis*, had puffy short sleeves and was worn over *a lanetta*, the undershirt. The black apron, *u s'nal*, with a strip of black lace near the bottom, was worn on top of all the layers. The most colorful piece was a red velvet vest—*u sciupp,* bordered with a blue edge and decorated with gold braids on either side. Accessories included a belt and a scarf of white lace, like a handkerchief, called *a sciarpett* and also *a fazoletto,* a kerchief or veil worn over the head. This one was sheer purple.

Men's clothing was much simpler, a pair of black corduroy pants and a black velvet jacket, with a white, collarless linen shirt and a wide-brimmed hat to keep the rain and sun off your face. The jacket had four pockets, usually used for cigarettes and for a white cotton handkerchief, a much more utilitarian version of the lady's *sciarpett,* with which to blow your nose, wipe your sweaty brow, wave in surrender, filter dirty water, lend to your girlfriend in her time of need, cover your mouth when there was smoke, or tie as a tourniquet. You name it, the handkerchief did it.

Boys wore knee pants until they were around thirteen or fourteen and girls a simple blouse and floor-length skirt until they reached puberty and were allowed to wear the incredibly complicated *pacchiana* outfit.

Giuseppe said the intricate costume, worn by all classes of women, helped promote a sense of community among them, but I knew that the real reason they all wore such a complex getup was to make it difficult to get undressed quickly. You couldn't easily fool around or have a fling when you had to take all that clothing off and then put it back on again, though I didn't mention this to the DiBellos or to Giuseppe. I thought about how I would have hated wearing all those layers. I was always hot. In fact, I was sweating right now. I thought early June would be better than August, but, naturally, my luck, Basilicata was in the midst of a pre-summer heat wave.

The DiBellos apologized for not letting us into Leonardo's house and seemed genuinely sorry. But they were loyal to the absentee landlords and wouldn't budge about the key, as much as we tried to convince them. As a consolation, and to give us shelter from the punishing sun as noon approached, they invited us into their own home. They said it wasn't that much different than Leonardo's place.

The house had brick-arched doorways and a red-brick barreled ceiling, at least twenty feet high, which kept it cool in summer but also helped the warm air circulate in winter. Floors were either dirt or rough stone or brick. Back in the old days, on especially cold days, the family used a *braciere* (brazier), a large round metal stand with a space in the center where you placed hot coals. The family gathered around and propped their feet up along the edges to warm them. A large brick hearth, used for cooking, now held a modern toaster oven.

I had seen the house where Vita had lived in Bernalda and it was so small, three of them would fit inside here. Moving to Pisticci was definitely a move up.

For both of us.

Chapter 19

CUPA CUPA

W HAT VITA LOVED MOST ABOUT FRANCESCO WERE HIS SAD eyes. Big brown eyes that sloped downward and made her want to take care of him and make him happy.

She had seen Francesco most days with her brother and had admired him from afar. He was short, but handsome, with coarse, strong workingman's hands and a boldness to match Vita's. He had served in the army, like all young men did these days, and she had seen him a few times in uniform, with his dark blue jacket and the matching dark hat with its single plume.

He cut quite a figure, but I imagine he wasn't quite as smart as Vita was. Usually the men weren't as smart or as strong as their wives in Bernalda, though they liked to think they were and sometimes beat their women, even in public, to convince them of it. But there was a sweetness beneath Francesco's strength.

Nineteen-year-old Vita told him she loved him, with her own eyes, without having to actually say it. Francesco got the silent message and so proposed marriage, in front of Vita's father Domenico, in front of her brother, in their small hovel of a house in the old part of town. Teresina was there as well. And they all consented. Maybe they even toasted the occasion with a glass of homemade wine.

Vita tried to hide her excitement from her parents. But when they weren't looking, she stared hard at Francesco and wondered what it would be like to kiss him, to touch him, and to have his babies. She smiled at him and flirted with her black olive eyes and called him by his nickname, Ciccio, like most of his friends did, but never even touched his arm or hand. It was forbidden.

On the Thursday before the ceremony, a member of Francesco's side of the family came to inspect the linens and furniture that Vita's parents had made and collected. Then it was paraded through the village, carried on each family member's head. A celebration followed outside the house, a dance where all the young people came and flirted, one of the few occasions where they could.

Couples moved across the cobblestones to the music of the local band: the accordion, bagpipes, tambourine, and *cupa cupa,* a ceramic percussion instrument with sheepskin on top, and which made a noise when you moved a stick in and out of it. *Cupa cupa, cupa cupa.* (The word *cupa* meant dark, but it was a happy sound.)

The dances were like square dances, with partners changing it up and moving in circles, hand over hand over hand, spinning and laughing and touching, for once.

The night before the wedding, on Saturday, Vita wore a green skirt as part of her *pacchiana* outfit, a color meant to bring luck for the rest of the coming marriage.

Then on Sunday—the actual wedding day, November 20, 1870—Vita put on her white wedding dress, which her mother had finished sewing for her just that morning, a final stitch saved for right before the wedding, for good luck. Teresina helped Vita with her white veil, similar to the veils of the bridesmaids, her sisters, and friends. The matching veils were to confuse the evil spirits, so they wouldn't put a curse on the bride.

Vita and Francesco, without touching or holding hands, walked to the church together, the one built centuries ago by Bernardino de Bernaudo. The bell in the tall ginger-colored tower rang out, signaling to the town that a wedding and mass were about to take place.

In the street on the way to the mother church, townspeople placed obstacles in Vita and Francesco's way, a broom, a crying baby. It was an Italian tradition, to represent the challenges that lie ahead. Housework. The colicky kid.

Once they safely reached the church, they ascended the three worn stone steps and went inside. The interior of the church was simple and whitewashed, except for its exposed wooden roof beams. An old wooden statue of San Bernardino stood guarding one corner, and in another, a mural of St. John the Baptist looked over the baptismal font. A cemetery for children in Bernalda who died before the age of seven lay beneath this spot, underground.

Vita and Francesco approached the white marble eighteenth-century altar, one of three altars, this one decorated with a medieval mural of Jesus being crucified, with Mary Magdalene flanking the cross. Jesus had his eyes closed, his ribs showing, his golden halo faded over time. His mother looked on as he died his slow, painful death.

The small wedding crowd celebrated a long mass in Latin, at the center of which Vita and Francesco would say their vows. The priest, one of the few literate people in town, would read the vows line by line and they would repeat after him. With the Blessed Mother, Jesus, Rocco, Bernardino, and all the saints watching, Vita agreed to love and honor Francesco until she died. And he agreed to do the same.

Nella gioia e nel dolore (In joy and in pain)
Nella salute e nella malattia (In health and in sickness)
E di amarti e onorarti (And to love you and honor you)
Tutti i giorni della (all the days of)
Mia vita.

Francesco smiled and even laughed a little when he said those last words.

Mia vita. Mia Vita.

My life. My Vita. They were now one and the same.

And then, with his callused farmer's hands, he touched his Vita for the first time, taking her tiny and strong weaver's hands and placing a simple metal ring onto the third finger of her left hand. (The left hand, the cursed side, to ward off evil spirits. That finger was also connected to the vein that led to the heart.)

Francesco placed his rough palm onto her face and lifted her chin. Her skin was surprisingly soft, he thought. He gently tilted her face up toward his and kissed her thin lips for the first time. It was Vita's first kiss ever, though Francesco had probably had some practice with the local *puttane*. It was a short kiss, but Vita would sink into it, as if drowning in the Ionian Sea, which she had only ever glimpsed from a distance but could smell on the windiest days, when the hot North African sirocco was especially strong.

The couple left the church after the ceremony and hopped over a long red ribbon that stretched a few inches off the ground. It symbolized their crossing over together into a new life. Then Vita threw sugared almond "confetti" onto the cobblestones, a Roman tradition that symbolized fertility in the marriage. The neighborhood kids, waiting for just this moment, dropped to their scabby knees and scarfed up the white candied nuts.

The relative with the largest house hosted a small party afterward, with lunch for the closest family members. Only the rich held a big banquet for friends and extended family.

Everyone sat at one long table and ate a special, long wedding pasta called *macaroni a fierr*—which means macaroni by iron, since the pasta dough was wrapped around an iron poker or metal knitting needle. When it was pulled off, the pasta looked like a long curl of dough-colored hair. Long pasta for a long life together. Served over the *fierr* was a tomato ragout with meat in it, cooked for several hours ahead of time by the women in the family. Your daughter's wedding day was one of the only other times you ate meat.

Vita handed out more candied almonds for the children, an uneven number (since that was good luck). The band of local bagpipers and accordion players and *cupa cupa* players and a guy with a giant tambourine—so big it nearly blocked out the sun—played into the night. Vita danced, and danced and danced, spinning wildly and laughing. The guests then presented their gifts to the couple: simple offerings: liquor, sugar, a chicken, some eggs.

At the end of the night, Vita's father placed a vase on the floor in front of the new, young couple, who had to stomp on it as hard as they could and break it to pieces. According to tradition, the shards would be counted and would stand for the number of years they would be happily married. But Francesco stomped so hard there were only crumbs and dust left. Everyone laughed at his passionate attack of the vase.

But the fact that there were no actual shards worried Vita. It was a bad sign.

Chapter 20

WITH SNOW YOU GET BREAD, WITH RAIN YOU GET HUNGER

And you, ugly, obscure cloud
Why have you come? . . .
No! Go away to your obscure places
Where the cock doesn't crow
And there are no horse hoof prints

I BROWSED THROUGH MY BOOK ON MAGIC IN THE SOUTH DURING Pisticci's five-hour siesta and came across a whole chapter just about storms. Specific spells could undo an approaching storm that threatened the harvest. After the chant, a circle would be drawn on the ground with a sickle, which was then raised in the direction of the threatening clouds. It was the opposite of a rain dance.

I thought about Giuseppe's grain harvest and wondered if it would turn out all right. His wheat was standing tall somewhere out there in the distance. And I knew a hard rain could destroy it. "There is an Italian saying about the wheat my mother used to say," Giuseppe had told me. "With snow you get bread, with rain you get hunger."

Just as I was thinking this, I heard thunder. I thought I was imagining it. It had been sunny and stiflingly hot just an hour ago. But the clouds had since gathered and the humidity was about to break. It hadn't rained since I'd arrived.

Thunder cracked again, this time louder, and closer. I realized I should go out and witness the real thing and maybe throw a chant or two Giuseppe's way. So I put down the book, grabbed my small umbrella, the thunderclaps getting closer and closer, and headed to my favorite spot in Pisticci.

It overlooked the Dirupo, the part of town on the edge of Pisticci that had fallen off many times in landslides. The most famous was the landslide of 1688 and the most recent, 1976. There was a scientific explanation for why this land kept sliding off the cliff—the erosion of the Pliocene clay that made up the *calanchi*. But some superstitious townspeople still blamed the devil.

Grillaio falcons and *rondini,* small black swallows with white breasts, were here each and every afternoon flying in manic circles around and around as the sun set. Horses galloped on the farms below, proud roosters crowed, and sheep bleated like crying babies in the distance. I wondered if Vita had stood here as well, staring down with her two sons. I wondered if she felt more free here than she had in Bernalda. And more peaceful.

It wasn't raining yet. But the rain was on its way. In the distance was a huge black mass of clouds with a white shaft—the falling rain. It looked like a mushroom cloud and was heading straight toward Pisticci and eventually Marconia, toward Giuseppe's farm. The lightning was maybe a mile away, and every thirty seconds or so I would see its jagged jolt rip through the sky, over the small farmhouses and olive trees in the distance. The falcons and *rondini* were flying in mad circles over the Dirupo, just like they did during sunset.

I silently said an Our Father and asked that the storm by-pass Giuseppe's farm. Suddenly the wind seemed to change and the storm looked like it might veer out toward the sea and away from us. "Thank you, Jesus," I said, laughing and looking up at the brightening sky. I decided to take a walk up to the Chiesa Madre, the sixteenth-century mother church where I was sure Vita had gone to Mass. I would say a longer and more formal prayer there, not just for Giuseppe and his family but for myself, that I would find Vita's story.

The Chiesa Madre, also called St. Peter and Paul, was at the very top of the town. With its tall beige bell tower in my sights, I climbed the steep hill. Up here the streets were bordered by red brick steps, but the center path was smooth and made up of a collection of actual stones of different shapes and colors. The street resembled a riverbed.

I had been up to Chiesa Madre years ago and knew that its main building, tall bell tower, and rounded cupola had been built by brothers who had fled to Pisticci from their hometown of Mantua after being accused of murder. Just another Italian murder story for which I didn't have the details.

Halfway up the hill, with the cathedral in sight, the storm veered back toward Pisticci. I felt the first tentative raindrops. "Oh Jesus," I said, opening my umbrella. It was so hot out that the drops were like flames falling from the sky. I sprinted on up the hill, but the storm was moving much faster than I was. The sky grew even darker, the rain grew thicker, and hail started to fall, ice balls the size of lemon drops. So much for my prayers.

The umbrella couldn't handle the onslaught, so I made a break for the church, which was locked tight. With the ice balls stinging my skin, I knocked on the giant arched door. No answer. Etched images of Sts. Peter and Paul stared back at me from the metal door panels. I pulled hard at the handles but they wouldn't budge.

I looked at the handle and thought of jimmying the lock with a credit card—something I'd learned years ago in Jersey City from some of my more notorious friends. But I had no credit cards. The replacements from the stolen wallet still hadn't arrived. I considered picking the lock and wondered what I might have in my backpack that would do the trick. But Peter and Paul stared back at me and seemed to scold: "Don't even think about it." Besides, these locks were ancient and likely beyond picking.

The rain fell even harder now, and faster. I scurried around to the back of the church and cowered under my now-battered umbrella and waited for it to slow down. But it just kept falling. As the cloud settled over Pisticci, I started to think more seriously about the lightning. Worried the metal umbrella frame would attract a bolt and that would be the end of me—fried to bits at the top of Pisticci—I closed it and tossed it on the smooth stones at my feet. I could just see the headline now: STUPID AMERICAN ELECTROCUTED BY LIGHTNING NEAR CHIESA MADRE. I imagined my family back home getting the bad news. I found an archway and settled under it. And waited. And waited. *Aspet. Aspet.*

That cloud, like the church door, would not budge.

I peeked my head around the corner and saw that the stone path I'd just climbed to the top of the hill was now a wide waterfall, the rain flowing in a steady pour down its indented center. The street was a true riverbed now. The torrent swirled around to the next level below and then shot out through ancient gutters that dropped the water down, down to the next level and the next, where it circled around and then deposited itself farther down into town and finally down the side of the clay mountain and into the valley below. The power of the storm, and of nature, was overwhelming and for a minute I pictured myself swept away by the water, hurled down the mountain in a giant landslide.

But Pisticci was built to withstand the rain. The engineering was simple but effective. The church had a very deep foundation to stop it from slipping down the mountain.

So I just relaxed and began to enjoy the downpour. It was exhilarating. All the Pisticcesi were locked safe inside their homes, away from the elements, napping or eating a big lunch. But I was out here, soaking wet, and a part of the storm.

When the rain slowed down, I took out my phone and texted Giuseppe to see if the hail had hit his farm. "No," he answered. "We are fine here. No hail. I finally have some luck."

I headed back down the hill, drenched to the skin, but feeling clean and wide awake, as if newly baptized.

Chapter 21

DON'T SPIT IN THE PLATE
WHERE YOU EAT

VITA FORGOT ALL ABOUT THE PULVERIZED VASE, ALONE WITH Francesco on their wedding night in their tiny house. Francesco's naked back and shoulders were strong and tan, his muscles tight from his time in the army and all the work he did on the farm. She kissed Francesco again, this time longer and deeper, sinking further and further down as if happily drowning.

Francesco placed his rough hands on her face and slowly moved them down to start undressing his new bride. Vita felt an electric tingle move through her entire body.

Then, a sharp knock at the door.

It jarred Vita and brought her back to the surface, her eyes open, her heart quickening. The knock wasn't unexpected, but was still a shock. Vita and Francesco had hoped they would be spared this one tradition on their wedding night, that they would be somehow passed over.

It was the padrone, Grieco.

He was well dressed and well groomed, in a suit, with a hat over his recently cut hair He took off the hat, stepped into the middle of the room, and said simply, "Buona notte." The padrone didn't need to say much more since there was no doubt why he was here. He wasn't here to collect the rent or to see if Francesco was available for some last-minute farm work.

He was here for Vita.

Francesco obediently put his shirt back on, his shoes and his jacket, and without saying a word, without looking into the padrone's face, made his way toward the door.

Before he slipped out into the cool November night, leaving his young virgin wife to his boss, Francesco tipped his hat to him but looked into Vita's teary eyes with his own sad eyes. In that fleeting moment, Francesco silently told her so many things: how he loved her, how he hated this man, and how he hated this life they had to live.

Francesco wouldn't fight. There was no point. Though he refused his consolation prize, his lamb dinner, in protest. Besides, he was sick to his stomach.

Vita thought about fighting back, punching Grieco in his face and making a run for it, chasing Francesco into the dark night. But it would only end in disaster. She and her family and Francesco and his family would be punished and barred from working the farm. They would starve. In Italy, the saying was "Don't spit in the plate where you eat."

So she closed her eyes and imagined Francesco in the padrone's place as he put his hands on her, his mouth on her mouth, goose bumps of revulsion covering her arms. Vita let his tongue past her teeth, and allowed his big hands to move across her young, soft skin, skin that would be passed down in her genetic code to her granddaughters, great-granddaughters, and even to her great-great-granddaughter a century later.

Chapter 22

PINECONES FOR BRAINS

"THERE'S A MARRIAGE CERTIFICATE," GIUSEPPE SAID, LOOK-ing over at me. He had just gotten a text from Imma, who was in the Matera archives with Francesco, the lawyer. Giuseppe had arrived to pick me up in the morning for our day of interviews and research.

"I'll tell Imma we'll meet her in Matera this afternoon," I said, taking out my phone, while Giuseppe put the Lancia in gear. I wanted to drive straight to Matera to see what Imma had found, but Giuseppe and I had to make another stop before that. We had to take a ride to the nearby town of Valsinni to visit a mutual friend named Carla, the woman who had introduced us over the Internet. I hated making social calls, but Italy was all about the social calls. Without them I would never meet the people I needed to meet, or find the information I wanted. I needed to be patient, more Italian. I had to keep reminding myself.

Carla, an Italian American woman from New Jersey, happened

to have arrived here in Basilicata from America the same week as I had to visit her sick and dying ninety-four-year-old mother.

When she was young, Carla's father had moved to America to make money for the family. Carla was sent there to live with him in the 1970s because of her headstrong, independent ways. She gladly left and permanently settled in New Jersey, where I had met her about ten years ago at the Italian cultural center that she ran. But now she was back, at her mother's deathbed.

Carla was older than we were, and out of respect we agreed to meet her to thank her for introducing us—but mostly to provide her some relief from her deathwatch. As soon as Carla's sister arrived to take over deathbed duty, the three of us headed out to see the town.

Carla spoke in well-enunciated accented English, slowly drawing out every vowel and sound with perfectly lipsticked lips, with her hands folded in front of her as if she were an opera singer. She was well put together at all times, her highlighted, well-coiffed hair just so, her faux pearl necklace matching her outfit. Like a determined, highly organized tour guide, she led us up the mountain of Valsinni to its most treasured building.

At the top was a rocky medieval castle, where a poet named Isabella di Morra had once lived. We climbed up and up until we were greeted by a large man named Rosario, who was the actual tour guide, and whose job it was to meet infrequent tourists here whenever they might show up. Rosario sported a day's worth of dark stubble and looked like he had just woken up from some long slumber, surprised by the visitors who had suddenly arrived at his bear cave.

His large eyes, with long eyelashes, shot open beneath his thick glasses. He launched quickly and effortlessly into his story of Isabella di Morra with such force and affection that you could tell he had been silently, patiently waiting for days, maybe even weeks, to share his information with someone. He confessed that he was deeply in love with Isabella, or at least her legend. And like Isabella before him, Rosario was a sort of prisoner of this castle.

Rosario explained that Isabella di Morra was Italy's first feminist, one of its most famous writers of all time, a fifteenth-century poetess and scholar whose father had taught her to read Dante and Plutarch by the time she was six. Unfortunately, she had a bunch of ignorant, awful brothers who—as the Italians liked to say—had pinecones for brains ("avere le pigne in testa"). They resented all the time their father spent with Isabella. When he wasn't listening, they used to tell Isabella she was worthless, less than stone. "With stone," they said, "you can at least build something. With a woman, you can do nothing."

When her father was exiled by Basilicata's Aragonese rulers to Paris, she was left sad and lonely in her beautiful prison with the lush countryside and, on the clearest days, the Ionian Sea to gaze upon. On a really clear day you could even see Pisticci. Rosario recited Isabella's description from memory.

> From a high mountaintop, where one can see
> The waves, I, your sad daughter Isabella,
> Gaze out for sight of any polished ship
> Coming to bring me news of you, my father.
> But my adverse and cruel destiny
> Permits no solace for my aching heart,
> But, enemy to any thought of pity,
> Turns all my firmest hopes into laments.
> For I see neither oar cutting the sea,
> Nor any sail that billows in the wind,
> So solitary is this dismal shore. . . .

Carla was riveted by Rosario's words even though she had already been to this castle many times and knew the story by heart.

With unusual emotion in her own voice, she translated Rosario's words for me because he was talking so quickly.

When she was twenty-five years old, Isabella befriended a neighbor, the wife of a local Spanish baron. Eventually Isabella met the baron and fell in love. Isabella and the baron began exchanging love letters and poems. The relationship was never consummated, not even with a kiss.

Three of Isabella's brothers found her love letters and became enraged. One night they climbed the castle stairs to her room and stabbed her repeatedly in the heart, then hurled her body over the castle wall. I thought of Sabrina, Giuseppe's sister, and looked over at him to see if Isabella's killing dredged up his own memories. But he seemed all right, caught up in yet another Italian murder story, one of the country's most notorious.

An Italian family had recently bought this castle for a real bargain—for five thousand euro—and were excavating to find not only the original medieval rooms but Isabella's bones. It seemed everyone was looking for bones of the past. They hadn't turned up yet, but it was only a matter of time.

Rosario said that on the windiest days, the ghost of Isabella— his love—passes through the castle. Because she was a ghost, she was now free to roam wherever she pleased. Into the mountains, down to the sea. But most days, he felt her here, inside this castle.

I thought how tragic Rosario was, almost as tragic a character as Isabella. What was it like to be in love with someone who had been dead for five centuries? To be so obsessed with the dead? Why were Italians so consumed with murder stories and death? Maybe because there was just so much death and suffering years ago, they had been forced to build a culture around it.

And then it hit me that I wasn't all that different than the Italians, or Rosario. I thought about my being here and my own obsession with Vita. Wasn't that just as obsessive, chasing the ghost of Vita for the past ten years? I was also obsessed with the dead.

When Rosario was done telling us about Isabella, I felt bad leaving him here all alone. There were no other tourists and probably wouldn't be until July. But at least he had the ghost of Isabella to keep him company.

ON OUR DRIVE HOME, WE PASSED A SIGN THAT SAID "COLOBRARO." Giuseppe told me to never say the name out loud because it was the most cursed town in Italy. "Even just saying the name can bring terrible luck," he told me. "And your luck has been bad enough." Giuseppe smiled when he said it, and was laughing, but I could tell he was kind of serious. He said that when men passed that town, they scratched their private parts to guard against the curse.

The town's name came from a Latin word that meant serpent—*coluber* (visions of Adam and Eve again). But it wasn't clear what came first, the town's name or the curse. It's said to have originated many years ago after the villagers killed a woman they believed to be a *strega*—or a witch. Before she died, she put a curse on the town. More recently, a lawyer trying a case there announced in court, "If I'm lying, may this chandelier come down." The chandelier fell. Since then, the curse is believed to have become even stronger.

According to legend, babies there are often born with two hearts. Landslides and car accidents are all too common. But every summer, the town holds a festival celebrating the curse and the sorcery attached to it. Tourists have been pouring in, despite the possibility of bad luck and having a chandelier fall on their heads. Policemen there won't even give tickets to cars speeding through the town for fear they will be cursed.

Giuseppe, knowing this, drove as quickly as he could and headed toward Matera. As soon as we reached our exit, he received a text from Imma. He pulled over to read it. He smiled his bright white movie star smile.

"Francesco found some crime listing involving both a Gallitelli and a Vena man," he said, excitedly. He read on and frowned. "But the archives are closing early today. They didn't have time to dig out the actual file. We'll have to come back tomorrow."

I stuck out my bottom lip and shrugged, Italian-style. I knew it had to be a false alarm. I had only been here for a few days. And with our rotten luck, there was no way this was the murder.

Chapter 23

ECCOLO

I TOOK THE WIDE, SHALLOW STONE STAIRS TWO AT A TIME, Giuseppe and Imma beside me, to the research room in Matera. The stuffy, warm air smelled of dust and ancient, crumbling paper, just as it had ten years ago.

The room contained long white-topped tables made of pressed wood, with a wall of windows that were never opened very wide, maybe to prevent the wind from blowing the papers around. Imma started to sneeze as soon as we walked in. "God bless you," I said after the first few sneezes. But after four or five, I gave up. "I'm allergic to dust," she whispered.

"Oh no," I whispered back. "Maybe you shouldn't be here then. I can look with Giuseppe."

"No, no, no," she said, waving me off. "If it's the right murder, I want to be here. I don't want to miss this."

Two young Italian women searching for something together were the only ones here besides the middle-aged, bespectacled female clerk who approved all requests. She sat at a desk like a schoolteacher at the front of the room, vigilantly watching the visitors to make sure they didn't do any damage to the antique files. She spent most of her time simply sitting there, staring into space, or glancing out the window. I wondered if it was against the rules for her to read a book or a newspaper or her iPhone. I would have been desperately bored. But she seemed content and perfectly happy.

Ten years ago, I had leafed through arrest report after arrest report here, through yellowed piles of court records and criminal files. Imma told me that they had every birth, death, and marriage record for all the towns in the province, which either was something new or something I hadn't known before. Searching in Pisticci was easy, but Bernalda's bureaucrats made it nearly impossible to find anything in the comune there. People in Bernalda had nicknamed the woman in charge of the archives there "the demon." We could search here in Matera for everything we needed instead, even though it was forty-five minutes away.

Imma filled in a written request on a small slip of white paper to call up the case file for the listing Francesco had come across. File 644. She handed it to the clerk at the desk and a moment later another file clerk, a very efficient, serious man in dress pants and a collared shirt, came to collect the requests. Ten minutes passed in silence. Unless you whispered, it seemed wrong to talk inside the archives. The male clerk returned, rolling a squeaky metal cart into the room, breaking the hushed silence. The cart's two shelves contained several stacks of files, not just for us but for the other women here.

With his strong arms, he lifted from the top shelf a giant bundle in blue cardboard that was more than a foot thick. It was our bundle. He placed it right in front of me on the long research table. Inside were seven different case files, all tied together with a thin ribbon of white cotton, as if it were a big, dusty gift from the gods. I untied the ribbon with trembling hands, fumbling with its tightly knotted cloth, and realized it may not have been opened in more than a century. I wondered if moths would fly out. Part of me wanted to get it open as quickly as possible. But part of me was worried I'd just be disappointed again.

Then I thought: it might actually be the right file.

I paused for a few seconds. Once opened, the contents—like in Pandora's box—would come pouring out and would be impossible to push back in. I took a deep breath and turned back the blue cardboard.

Staring back at me from the top of the pile was a yellow page, with cracked and crumbling edges, issued from the Corte d'Assise, which was stamped at the top in bold black letters. The Italian Court of Assizes handled the most serious of crimes: murder, enslavement, terrorism, those offenses that could result in a sentence of twenty-four years or more.

Underneath were the names of the defendants.

Francesco Vena and Leonardantonio Gallitelli. Their names were written in elaborate, slanted cursive. It was one of seven files in the pile and the biggest in the bunch, as thick as an old New York City phone book, with more than six hundred yellowing, cracking pages inside. I carefully took it off the pile with both hands as if lifting a newborn baby and gently placed it on the table.

The court document was from 1873 and described a murder committed the year before. This was twenty years before Vita had left for America. I had always assumed the murder had happened right before Vita left in 1892, that she had run away to America because of it. The timing seemed off, but the ages of the men seemed right. Francesco Vena, age twenty-nine. And twenty-seven-year-old Leonardantonio Gallitelli, the same name as the man who had yelled at me ten years ago on the street with Miserabila to go back to America and leave the dead in peace. He was definitely a relative. He knew this murder story, whether it was mine or not. I knew all along that he knew something.

I read through that first page and saw that a third man was arrested along with Francesco and Leonardantonio, a man named Francesco Miraldi, age thirty-one.

With Imma looking over my shoulder, her hands on the back of my chair, and Giuseppe sitting beside me, I flipped through several pages of witness lists, jury records, and depositions, all written in fancy Italian calligraphy.

I leafed through a few more pages and found Francesco Vena's deposition, in which he states his name, his father's name, Donato, and his birthplace and residence, Bernalda. He states that he is a farmer, and gives his wife's name.

Vita Gallitelli.

I stopped breathing. I blinked once. Twice.

I read it silently again, to make sure I wasn't hallucinating. And took a breath.

Vita Gallitelli.

Goose bumps crawled up my arms, forcing the hair to stand straight up.

I read once more, this time aloud, my voice high and trembling, slicing through the silence of the room, "Vita Gallitelli. It says his wife's name is Vita Gallitelli."

"Eccolo," Imma said, towering behind me and nodding. Here it is.

"I told you that we would find it," Giuseppe said, smiling widely and wiping the sweaty front of his face with the palm of his hand. I turned and hugged Imma and then him.

"But I didn't believe you," I said.

"I know you didn't," he said, nodding, his eyes closed. I put my hand to my forehead and stared at the document.

After ten years, here it was, my family murder, right in front of me. I couldn't believe it. I wouldn't believe it. Not yet anyway.

Maybe it was a different Francesco Vena and Vita Gallitelli.

They were fairly common names. I had to make sure they were the right ones.

Francesco goes on to say in his deposition that he is not guilty and that Leonardantonio is his brother-in-law. Next are Francesco's and Leonardantonio's birth certificates. I scanned Leonardantonio's. His mother's name was Teresina.

"He has the same mother as Vita!" I shouted, pointing at the birth certificate, which set him as four years older than Vita. Vita's big brother.

Imma put in a request for the marriage certificates for that decade and moments later, she again had the one she had found yesterday for Francesco Vena, born November 8, 1844—same as on this birth certificate—and Vita Gallitelli, born August 22, 1851, same as on Vita's birth certificate. Now there was no doubt this was it. This was the same Francesco.

And this was our Vita.

This was our murder.

Chapter 24

GO TO COOL

FRANCESCO AND LEONARDANTONIO LEFT BERNALDA FOR work just past dawn. They drove their horse and wagon, which belonged to their padrone, through nearby Ferrandina, past a piece of land called Contrada Avella, not far from Pisticci's western border. A *contrada* was a piece of land on which several farms were located, as many as ten or twenty. Avella was the name of a small stream and bridge nearby.

This land was much like the land in Pisticci, mostly clay based, with a few patches of green sewn in, *calanchi* rising nearby. Livestock grazed here and there, cowbells tinkling in the distance, and the occasional blond Italian Maremma sheepdog, mangy and covered with flies, wandered about with a spiked collar to protect it from wolves. The dogs paid Francesco and Leonardantonio no mind.

The two men often passed this way and were familiar not only with the dogs but with the women, dressed in their long *pacchiana* outfits, already out on the farm by the roadside. It was November

4, 1872, a pleasantly crisp 50-degree Monday in Ferrandina, the orchards overflowing with fruit, ripe for the picking.

Ciccio and Leo, as they called each other, stopped and chatted with the young women and asked to taste some of the small pears—*perastre,* a particularly sweet variety from the region—lying in their big baskets. The perastre were green with a deep red blush. The women, blushing like the pears, obliged. Leo flirted with them and told them how much he loved their sweet pears. Leo nudged Ciccio, winked, and snickered at his joke. Ciccio rolled his big brown eyes.

Most towns in Matera province wouldn't allow their women to work the farms for this very reason, strange men approaching them and asking to taste their sweet pears. But some towns, like Ferrandina, encouraged their women to work. The women of Ferrandina were very attractive, taller than most of the women in the rest of the area. Maybe their active life on the farm, all that exercise, had something to do with how tall they grew.

Leo and Francesco, juice running down their chins, liked the pears so much they bundled some together under a freshly picked tree. They spoke sweetly to the women and asked them politely to leave the pears there. "Ladies," Francesco said, bowing, removing his cap, "would you do us the favor of leaving the pears here? They are so delicious and almost as lovely as all of you."

The women giggled and nodded. Francesco explained that they'd return the next day to take these pears and maybe even a few more home with them. The women shrugged and agreed. "Va ben, va ben," they said. They had no allegiance to the padrone. Peasants never ratted on one another, but shared a strong bond no matter what town in Basilicata they came from. They were *paesani.* And besides, it wasn't that many pears. The padrone would never even miss them.

A thirty-three-year-old miller by the name of Paolo Doraio met Francesco and Leo on the road that morning. They told him about the small, round pears that were especially sweet and deli-cious this fall—and their plans to bring them home to their fam-ilies.

Doraio told them that returning tomorrow was a bad idea, since the landowner was very vigilant, that he had a gun and was not afraid to use it. "You should stay away," Doraio said, wagging a finger at them. He even offered to give them some of the pears from his own padrone's land.

"No grazie," they said, shaking their stubborn heads. No thanks.

THE SUN HAD ALREADY SET, THE SHADOWS LONG AND DEEP ON THE Ferrandina farm road when Leonardantonio and Francesco re-turned to Contrada Avella late on Tuesday. It was best to steal at night because no one could see you, and even if they did, it was harder for them to make out the details of your face. Though they had never been arrested, they had, like most poor Lucani, done their share of harmless fruit swiping.

These early days of November, the sun set at 5 P.M. A skinny waxing crescent moon shaped like a toenail clipping barely lit the night sky. But the brilliant stars from the Andromeda galaxy, the giant W of Cassiopeia, and the sparkling broad stroke of the Milky Way—and all the thousands of stars in between—provided enough light for them to find their stash.

They brought a friend, Francesco Miraldi, a bricklayer. He didn't work with the other two men but was along for the ride, his large bricklayer hands and arms there for support in haul-ing away the delicious, hidden pears. Miraldi was not a handsome man, like the other two. He had marks on his face from smallpox and had grown a beard to cover his scars.

They found the pears and quietly, gently—so as not to bruise them or to make any noise—placed them in a large sack, filling it to the top with about twenty kilos, or forty-five pounds, of pears. Francesco Vena's twenty-eighth birthday was only three days away and these ripe, round pears were a little gift to himself and his hungry family back in Bernalda.

But before they could get to the horse cart, they heard a man's deep voice yelling for them to stop, piercing the silence of the country night. The voice was coming from the farm and when they squinted, they could see the thin man attached to that voice approaching from the direction of the whitewashed masseria glowing in the distance. He yelled at them to leave the pears and go away. But the voice only made them work faster, Miraldi and Francesco nervously laughing and lifting the sack together, Leo anxiously readying the horse. "Come on," Leo said, sotto voce. "Hurry up, you bastards." They laughed, dropping a few pears, then reached to pick them up and place them in the sack again.

But the voice from the farm rang out once more. "Put the pears down and go away," the man said again. "I have a gun." And as he drew closer, they could see now—their eyes adjusting to the darkness—that he was carrying a shotgun, the kind that you had to load from the front with every shot. Though they didn't know it yet, the man's name was Camardo. Antonio Camardo.

Camardo's mother, Carmina Albani, was with him, and they both shouted once again, in the dark, for Francesco and his friends to put down the pears and just go.

With so many years—generations really—of pent-up hatred between farmer and padrone, there was no way Leo or Francesco would have backed down. Stealing these pears was revenge for the meager pay, the kickbacks, and mostly, for Francesco, the humiliating rite of *prima notte*. Francesco and Leo considered themselves *furbo* and would outwit and outmaneuver this padrone. Maybe they even dared him to take a shot. It was so dark, he would never hit them.

So Camardo did. He fired a single shot.

It sounded like a cannon in the dusky silence, causing the horse to rear up and whinny, waking the sleeping Maremma sheepdogs. The shot hit Leo in the finger. He let out a loud roar, like an injured lion. Leo was stunned and surprised that Camardo had actually fired at him. He stared for a second at his bleeding, nearly missing finger in disbelief, then pulled out his dirty white handkerchief to wrap it and stanch the bleeding. Francesco looked at his brother-in-law, his mouth hanging open.

When he turned around, he saw that their horse was wounded as well. "Vaffanculo!" Francesco shouted, more angry about the horse than his brother-in-law's finger. His padrone would have him beaten for the wounded horse.

Francesco could see in the dark that Camardo was on the ground now, probably reloading his gun, so—without even thinking—he picked up a wooden stick, a branch from one of the pear trees, and ran straight at Camardo before he could reload. Miraldi cheered him on from the sidelines, watching the scuffle, the two men wrestling with one another on the dusty ground, the gun lying to the side now.

Leo ran over and grabbed the shotgun with his good hand as Francesco stood and backed away, Camardo bleeding at his feet. With the mother screaming like a madwoman and Camardo bleeding out on the fertile Ferrandina soil, the three men jumped into their cart and fled to Bernalda, their wounded horse slowly pulling them.

And their big sack of pears.

Even after they were out of sight from Contrada Avella, they could still hear shouting and commotion echoing from there, the mother wailing, several men's voices joining hers, along with the barks of the sheepdogs.

The sun had set farther past the horizon by now, so they drove into Bernalda under a heavy black veil, like widows *in lutto*. They hid out at a friend's stone house for a while, at first laughing about their haul, but then slowly realizing it was a mistake to bring the stolen goods home after beating that man. They still had the shotgun Leo had taken from Camardo. Why had they kept the shotgun and taken the pears with them? It was evidence against them if the padrone followed up the robbery and pressed charges. "Stunad," Francesco would say, insulting himself and his friends.

A neighbor, Giovanni Campagna, a friend of Leo's, noticed that night that the horse was injured. As well as his friend.

Hiding like a wounded animal, Leo spoke with Campagna and told him the whole stupid story. Campagna urged him to turn himself in. "It's no use," Campagna said. "The carabinieri will come for you eventually."

Leo considered his friend's advice, his head lowered, but said nothing. "All you will be charged with is stealing those pears. You didn't even hit the guy. And he shot at you first, remember. If you confess, they will have some mercy. Your sentence won't be so long."

So that night, Vita's big brother turned himself in at the small carabinieri station on the other side of town.

His surrender caused a commotion in the neighborhood. The women wept on the cobblestone streets, tearing at their hair and their patched and ragged clothes over the tragedy that was unfolding among them. Their sons and husbands were only trying to feed them, and now look. The women would starve even more. "Andare al fresco" was the saying. Go to cool. Which meant go to jail. That's where Leonardantonio was headed.

There was no justice. No fairness in this world. The hungry would suffer. And the padrone would grow fat on his pears, the pears that their sons and daughters planted with their own dirty hands, tended for him, watered and nurtured, and finally picked, only to hand them back over to the padrone and his family. *Bastardo.* He should choke on those pears.

Late that night, around 4 A.M., while most of Bernalda slept,

Camardo died from his head wounds in his home in Pisticci, his blood staining his pillow and fine linens.

A few hours later, the police came for Francesco and Miraldi. They were placed, with Leonardantonio, in the cold, damp Bernalda jail with the big clock and the small bells, and paraded past that third-story window for all to see, including young Vita, dressed in her *pacchiana* outfit.

I can see her now, her long skirts blowing in the autumn wind, her veil pulled tight over her dark hair, her kalamata olive eyes looking up toward that window, the rims red now from crying all morning, her face smudged with dirty tears, wondering what would become of her if her husband and brother were convicted of murder and sent to prison.

Chapter 25

DON'T TELL THE FARMER
HOW GOOD CHEESE IS WITH PEARS

M Y ANCESTORS REALLY WERE MURDERERS.
It was no longer family legend or mythology. But
reality. In black and white. Or black and yellow, really.
And it was nothing to be happy about, now that I had actually
found it and thought about it. In my bathroom that night, I heaved
a sudden sob, and continued to sob into the sink for the next few
minutes, tears of relief mixed with disbelief but also a certain
grief for having actually found what I was looking for. I wondered
how hard you had to hit someone to actually kill them. Maybe they
had stomped on the padrone's head when he was down, like a wedding vase placed on the ground. I cringed at the thought.

But Vita was innocent. After all those years of thinking she
was a murderess, I realized she was innocent. Those pictures
I had of her in my head, with a gun or a knife, killing and then
fleeing to America with her hair and eyes wild, were just wrong.
Grandpa Beansie had been wrong. Vita was not a killer.

Though Francesco was.

I thought about all the clues I had stumbled across. The cave wall with Adam and Eve stealing that fruit. The history of the strained relationship between the padroni and the farmers. It all played a part in my story.

I blew my nose and called my mother to tell her. I hadn't spoken to her since landing. My mother still lived in Jersey City, up the hill from where Vita and her teenage sons had settled in 1892.

When she heard my voice, she smiled. I could hear it in her voice, which was very much like my own voice. People always confused us on the phone. It was one of the many things I had inherited from my mother.

"How's it going?" she asked.

"Good, good," I said. I had decided not to mention the stolen wallet. She would only worry. "Everyone here sends their regards," I said. My mother had made many friends in her month in Bernalda and Pisticci with me.

"I have some news," I said. "I found the murder."

"What? Oh my God!" she shrieked. "Already? I can't believe it. But I knew you would."

"I wasn't so sure," I said.

"What did you find?"

I told her about Francesco and Vita's brother stealing those pears from the farm in Ferrandina, and then beating the landowner. I told her about the giant crime file and how we were still deciphering its nineteenth-century calligraphy.

"So it turns out Vita was innocent," I said. "She didn't commit the murder."

My mother started sobbing on the other end of the line, as if a member of some crying-jag tag team. I waited for her to calm down. Like me, my mother had wanted to know the details of the murder. But she, too, had a fondness and attachment to Vita and hoped, in her heart of hearts, that it wasn't true.

When she finally stopped crying, she told me, "You know, the other night, I put a picture of us in Bernalda next to my bed and I started praying for you and for her. I was praying for Vita. That she would be redeemed." She started crying all over again. "And she has been. I can't believe it. She has been. She didn't do it. Vita didn't do it."

IN BED THAT NIGHT, TOSSING AND STARING UP AT THE CEILING, I thought about that mural in the Crypt of the Original Sin and laughed at how I had missed the sign. It had been right there. The family's original sin was the same as Adam and Eve's. It all started with stolen fruit.

The story of original sin in the Bible involved what was probably the first crime committed in most societies. A crime that involved hunger. Stealing fruit was not a metaphor, but probably the first crime committed by most men and women on earth.

Before greed, there was hunger. And before possessions, there was fruit. Stealing from your neighbor's harvest. It was primeval. And hardly a crime, really.

Stealing food in my family had been raised to an art form. Grandpa Beansie had his stolen crate of beans. And Chubby his stolen roast for his heroin. And my dad stole every day from work to feed us at home: frozen turkeys, frozen steaks, shrimp, lobster tails. Your family needed to eat, so you took what you could and ran. Francesco was no exception.

Just like in Genesis, the first crime—stealing fruit—was followed by the second, more serious crime, murder. The sin of Cain and Abel. As in the first family on earth, the original sins in my family would beget future generations of sinners. Generation after generation.

Though most people associated original sin with the apple, its true origins lay in the stolen pear. St. Augustine, who developed the church's doctrine on original sin, had written about stealing pears when he was a teenager growing up in Africa in what is now Algeria.

In Book 2 of his *Confessions,* the first spiritual memoir ever written, Augustine told about how he and his buddies had stolen pears from a neighborhood orchard when he was sixteen years old—just for the hell of it. He asked himself why, when there was plenty of food at home, would he steal someone else's pears, which he didn't even bother to eat.

The pear incident, and his sexual escapades, including his keeping a concubine, led to Augustine's soul-searching and his eventual conversion to Christianity, his belief that man needs God in his life in order to avoid wrongdoing. His fourth-century musings on those pears led to his theory on the origin of sin itself.

> A pear tree there was near our vineyard, laden with fruit, tempting neither for colour nor taste. To shake and rob this, some lewd young fellows of us went, late one night (having according to our pestilent custom prolonged our sports in the streets till then), and took huge loads, not for our eating, but to fling to the very hogs, having only tasted them. And this, but to do what we liked only, because it was misliked. . . . A man hath murdered another; why? he loved his wife or his estate; or would rob for his own livelihood; or feared to lose some such things by him; or, wronged, was on fire to be revenged. Would any commit murder upon no cause, delighted simply in murdering?

I had never thought much about pears. But now my whole family history hinged on them. There had been no card game. No passatella. Only the stolen pears.

My brother-in-law, Will, had told me years ago that when he was a kid back in the 1960s in New Jersey, he and his friends stole dozens of pears from a neighbor. Just like St. Augustine. They hid them in Will's garage, but when his father found them, he made Will eat them all. Every last one. Sixty years later, Will still couldn't eat a pear.

In most places, pears were considered a rare blessing. Only the rich ate them in ancient China. In medieval Japan, a pear tree was planted on the northeast corner of properties—considered the cursed corner—to ward off evil spirits. And in Greece, the pear was considered the gift of the gods and was written about for the first time ever in *The Odyssey*. On the island of Scheria, his last stop on his ten-year journey, Odysseus encounters a beautiful garden in the king's palace, a virtual paradise.

> Of these the fruit perishes not nor falls in winter or in summer, but lasts throughout the year; and ever does the west wind, as it blows, quicken to life some fruits, and ripen others; pear upon pear waxes ripe. . . .

Seven centuries later, Basilicata's own Horace would write:

> . . . when crowned with a garland of ripened fruit,
> In the fields, Autumn rears its head,
> How he takes delight in picking the grafted pears.

A good pear, a truly good pear, was hard to find. So when you found a juicy one you ate your fill or gave one to the person you loved. There's the partridge in a pear tree, naturally, the very first gift in the Twelve Days of Christmas.

It wasn't until I met the man I would marry that I ate a good, ripe pear for the first time. On the first day of Christmas, 1990, his mother served a salad with blue cheese and ripe, sweet pears that she'd gotten from the Harry & David catalog. Those pears cost a small fortune. And I still remember biting into a slice of one of them, with a bit of blue cheese speared on my fork. It tasted so, so good. There was actually an Italian proverb that went, Don't tell the farmer how good cheese is with pears.

When I moved to Brooklyn to live with Wendell, I saw pear trees for the first time, Callery pear trees growing around the corner from our apartment, their white blossoms pungent and smelling of dead fish in springtime.

We had a painting of a pear in our living room, a picture that Wendell's stepfather, a still-life painter named Bob Kulicke, had given him as a gift for his college graduation. The pear was Bob's signature still-life fruit. Bob had started as a framer, mounting Morandi still lifes, which led to his own still lifes. He had started painting pears around the time Wendell and I were born and had become obsessed with them over the years.

"St. Pear," he called his subjects, placing each one in an elaborate frame of his own making, the type usually reserved for religious paintings, with Gothic arches and gold-leafed surfaces.

A Wallace Stevens poem from 1942, "Study of Two Pears," starts with Latin, "Opusculum paedagogum"—a little work that teaches. And it sums up why artists like Bob loved painting pears.

> The pears are not viols,
> nudes or bottles.
> They resemble nothing else.

Pears did resemble the female figure, particularly the shape of the earth mother. Along with figs and apples, they were considered sacred fruit in Christianity and were often used in paintings of the Madonna and Child, with Mary offering the fruit to baby Jesus.

The Spanish had an idiomatic expression "to be healthier than a pear," which was similar to our own "fit as a fiddle." The heart, in medieval times, was thought to be pear shaped. Diamonds were pear shaped, as were certain people.

The very same year Vita left for America, 1892, Lizzie Borden was charged with murdering her parents, and used pears as part of her alibi. While her father was being axed to death, she was in her barn, eating three pears, she claimed. Her pear defense was a success. Borden was found not guilty.

"Sweet Pear" was the title of one of my favorite Elvis Costello songs—a love song with a double entendre (sweet pair) and which my husband had put on a mixtape for me once when we were still just dating:

> Sweet pear, sweet pear
> Those who say they love you would never dare
> I'll watch out for you. I'll always be there
> In the hour of your distress, you need not fear.

Chapter 26

EMPTY CRIB

THE MALE CLERK WITH THE STRONG ARMS—HERCULES, I NICK-named him—pushed the squeaking metal cart through the open doorway with more gifts for me: bundles of records tied in white ribbon. He lifted several big piles onto our table. The three of us silently untied the ribbons and started searching again, this time not for a death, but for a life. Not for the murder, but for Vita's missing child.

We were back in Matera—Giuseppe, Imma, and I—searching through birth records for the years after Leonardo and Valente were born. Eighteen eighty and 1881.

For the past ten years, I had thought of Vita's "lost" child and often wondered if maybe he wasn't lost at all, but had simply died. In my family, when a child died, everyone said the family had "lost" a child, to soften the blow. You never used "child" and "died" in the same sentence. Children were lost. As if they had simply drifted away when no one was looking.

I came across a son "born to Vita Gallitelli, wife of Francesco

Vena" in 1881, two years after my great-grandfather was born. When I saw their names, Vita and Francesco, my heart started beating fast. The child was a boy and was named Domenico, after Vita's father. Little Mimmo!

Like Valente's and Leonardo's birth certificates, it said here that Francesco was not present for the birth and that he was "far from town." *Lontano dalla paese.* At work again, no doubt.

But this boy was not lost on the way over to America. Domenico was stillborn.

Maybe this was the third son, the "lost son" of family legend? Or was there another son, one whom Vita had taken on her long voyage to America?

Working backward now, I kept searching. Filling in one request slip after another, I untied bundle after bundle and flipped through birth certificates for the years right after Vita and Francesco were married. After several hours, I came across another son born to Vita and Francesco. This one was born in 1872, a few months before the murder. The boy was born in Bernalda on April 1. April Fool's Day. It was known in Italy as Pesce d'April, when boys would cut out a paper fish and pin it on another boy's back, leading him to be ridiculed by his friends. It was a day of pranks and jokes.

This baby was born "to Francesco and his wife, Vita Gallitelli." Francesco was present this time around. And the boy's name was Rocco.

No one in my family had ever mentioned this kid. There were no Roccos in our family. Had he been the one who was lost on the way over?

"You have the magic touch," Giuseppe said, coming over to look at the birth certificate. I searched the years earlier but came across no other children born to Vita.

So Rocco was the firstborn to twenty-one-year-old Vita, a year and a half after she married Francesco. He would be five years older than his brother Valente and seven years older than my great-grandfather Leonardo.

Rocco was not the product of *prima notte,* since he was born much too long after the wedding night. He was Francesco's son. Not the padrone's.

Rocco was born on Via Metaponto—later renamed Corso Italia, the main road in the historic district. The statue of St. Rocco stood guard at the entrance to this street. It was also where the jail and Our Lady of Mount Carmel church were located. The address listed for Rocco's birth was a tavern. Was he born during a particularly long game of passatella? Had Vita come running there to tell Francesco her water had broken, and then gone into labor on the tavern table?

Since I had never heard of a son named Rocco, I checked the death certificates for the years following his birth. I looked through the list of files for Bernalda and found the corresponding file numbers for five years following, then filled out the small white slips of paper. Hercules wheeled out the death certificates, a world of sorrow placed at my fingertips. Stacks and stacks of pages filled with the names of the dead, old men, old women, babies, children, teenagers, all of them long, long gone, murder victims, malaria victims, typhoid cases.

And sure enough, within minutes, I came across our Rocco. Rocco Vena, son of Vita and Francesco, dead at the age of four. Rocco had died three years after the murder. His patron saint, that statue down on the corner, had failed to protect him.

I had hardly gotten used to Rocco being alive, and now he was dead and buried.

Rocco died at the same age Dean was the first time we came to Basilicata. I thought about Dean that night ten years ago lying in bed, his fever raging, as I brushed the hair from his sweaty forehead and tried to get him to sleep, steps from where Rocco had lived and died.

Young Rocco would have had a big head full of brown hair like my son's, his eyes as big, but the sockets deeper and sadder from hunger. His ribs showing through his skin, just like all the statues and paintings I had seen of the martyr, St. Rocco.

Rocco's death certificate didn't say how he died. He could have died of any number of diseases, made susceptible because he had no father to provide for him and was likely malnourished.

And so was Vita. Malnourished physically and emotionally and every other way a person could possibly be. She held Rocco's skinny body as he lay dying, maybe wiping it with a cool cloth like I had wiped Dean's head the night he had that fever and no medicine. Rocco died in the middle of July in the afternoon, around what the Lucani called "the hot hour." When mothers called their kids inside and told them the marawall was coming to get them.

I had seen countless pietàs in my time in Italy, Michelangelo's in St. Peter's, medieval versions in Siena, and the one in the Chiesa Madre in Pisticci. That one was especially dramatic, Mary's robe a bright red and her veil a vivid blue, her son's lifeless head lying in her lap, his body bleeding from his wrists, torso, and knees. She was tenderly looking down into his face, cradling it in her hands, trying to coax him awake. But his body was pale, like the color of the stone houses. He wasn't coming back. Her baby wasn't coming back.

I thought of Vita holding Rocco's head in her hands, that big, round head like my son's, and her crying and crying, shaking and not being able to stop, her tears falling on his small, lifeless, skinny body. How did she survive it? I wondered. How did you survive the death of a child, especially when you had no other children to live for? When he was your only son?

When your husband was in jail and not there to comfort you?

The book on Southern Italian magic explained that many women in Basilicata suffered from *attasamento,* a common state that renders the victim immobile and is brought on by intense psychic trauma. Back then, people thought *attasamento* was brought on by a spell. But it was just a defense against daily life in Basilicata.

The *attasata* doesn't remember the death of a loved one and doesn't recognize anyone around her, not even her closest friends and family. When asked questions, she either doesn't answer or answers in nonsense phrases. *Attasamento* was a coping mechanism in a place where the horrors of life were constant and just too much to handle. A place where your children died, one after another.

When she comes to a few hours later, the mother cries out, remembering the horror suddenly. Then the opposite of *attasamento* happens. The woman flies into an explosive fit, throwing herself on the ground, banging her head against the wall, tearing her clothes, scratching her cheeks, howling and pulling at her hair—much like I did the day my wallet was stolen. But what was a lost wallet compared to a lost son, your firstborn?

Once her son was dead and the reality set in, Vita thrashed and pounded her head against the wall. She fell to the floor and tore at her blouse and scratched at her soft skin and cried like a wolf until her voice was gone. Vita cried and cried until she was empty and there were no tears left to cry. Only then would she lift herself up off the dirty floor and take care of business like she always did.

She arranged for Rocco's small body to be laid in a simple wooden coffin—the *caschedette*—to be carried by the family just a few blocks in a short funeral procession to the mother church, the same one built by Bernardino de Bernaudo, the same one where she and Francesco had been married. Inside the church, underground near the baptismal font, Rocco was laid to rest, in the small cemetery just for children who were under seven years of age when they died.

It was a wonder there was room for them all.

BACK IN MY APARTMENT IN PISTICCI THAT NIGHT, I NOTICED AN OLD bamboo crib on the tall bureau facing my bed. I had never noticed it before. But now it was all I could see as I tried to fall asleep.

I thought of the *succobi* and the *monacelli* I had read about in my book on magic, the unbaptized babies that came back from the dead and haunted people. I thought of Vita's dead children, my dead ancestors. Four-year-old Rocco and the stillborn Domenico. I got up and turned on the lights and grabbed a magazine to distract myself, but all I could see was that empty crib up there. I tried turning the lights off again and closing my eyes tight, but that was even worse.

Because he was stillborn, Domenico was not baptized. I thought of him appearing to me here, a ghostly presence of a baby in a long white gown as white as his blood-drained face, as white as the walls of Pisticci, eyes black like Vita's and boring right through me. I even imagined a creepy baby voice, high-pitched and frightening in that quiet room in Pisticci, telling me to leave the memory of his poor mother alone. "Please," I imagined a baby voice crying, "leave my mommy alone. It's not Mommy's fault I'm dead."

With eyes wide open, then eyes tightly shut, I waited and waited for a *monacello,* or one of Vita's babies, to visit me. I got up and tried to pull the crib down to move it. But it was too heavy and too high up. If I dropped it, I'd likely end up with a concussion, Vita's final revenge against me digging up the past.

I collapsed back into bed and finally somehow fell asleep, my dreams turning to nightmares of dead babies and tiny murderous spirits.

The next morning I asked Giuseppe to take the crib down and move it into the living room, where I would cover it with a sheet. He didn't even need to ask why.

III

TRIAL

Chapter 27

PUTTANA

M Y PHONE RANG ON THE WAY TO THE ARCHIVES. IT WAS A
call from America, but I wasn't sure of the number.

"Pronto," I answered, forgetting the person on the
other end probably wasn't Italian.

"Hi, Helene?" the woman said. "This is Dr. Pytlak."

My children's pediatrician.

"What's wrong?" I asked.

"I just wanted to let you know the strep test came back positive
for Paulina."

"What strep test?"

For the past few weeks, Wendell had been trying to keep me
in the dark about anything negative happening at home so I could
concentrate on my family research. But the strep had slipped past
the goalie.

I gave Wendell regular updates and news flashes and he sent
me short bursts of encouragement. Not once did he bother me
with any of the small dramas unfolding in Brooklyn.

Wi-Fi (which the Italians pronounced "WEE-fee") was spotty at best in Basilicata and nonexistent in my apartment. So communication was at a minimum anyway. My children, like most American teenagers, were allergic to phone conversations.

I tried texting them but only got one-word answers. Often Paulina responded with a single letter, "K." If they missed me, they weren't showing signs of it. Maybe they had no time to text because they were too busy getting into trouble without me there. I tried not to think of all the bad things I had done at Dean's age: standing watch while my friends shoplifted, the forty-ouncers in the school yard after dark, the joint passed around before the school dance.

On nights when Imma and Giuseppe spent time with their own families I just stayed in and read or watched bad television, the crib with the sheet over it in my peripheral view. It was then that I became homesick and missed my family. As long as I stayed busy, I was okay. So I watched a dubbed version of the movie *Casino*, with Joe Pesci yelling at Robert De Niro in Italian, and music videos from the 1980s, including Flock of Seagulls and one by Men Without Hats set during medieval times.

I watched several episodes of the children's Claymation show *Shaun the Sheep*, which was deeply satisfying since there was no talking in it and so I didn't need to translate anything. But there was really only so much children's programming I could take.

A few evenings, to escape both that crib and my homesickness, I went out with my long-lost cousin, Leo, the beach bar owner from Bernalda, whom Wendell started referring to as my "Italian boyfriend." Leo was always at least an hour late. He couldn't understand why I was staying in Pisticci and offered to put me up in his empty beach house. "It's so boring here," he said, giving dirty looks to the Pisticcesi as they walked by.

One night he took me for pizza at a place called Ruota—the Wheel—in a town named Tinchi, population 472. If you sneezed while driving through Tinchi, you could easily miss the entire town. Even its name sounded small: Tinchi (pronounced "TIN-ki").

The pizza place was run by an old mother and her son, who looked like a cross between Salvador Dalí and Larry from *The Three Stooges*. He had long curly hair and a fancy mustache and mostly just looked on as his old, gray-haired mama cooked. Her pizza was terrific, though not as good as the miracle pie at a place called Padre Pio, in the nearby town of Scanzano.

One night Leo took me to dinner at the masseria resort Torre Fiore—Flower Tower. Basilicata was littered with abandoned and renovated masserias, the large country estates where the padroni had lived and the workers had toiled. One in Scanzano had been turned into a music academy. One of my favorite masserias, Recoleta, was built in the seventeenth century from a fortified medieval monastery.

The palazzo had tall, arching windows and two gun towers on the corners of the building to guard against brigands and other invaders, and a giant metal armored door leading into the open courtyard, with a hole for a key that must have been as big as my head. The rusty, puckered metal door was several hundred years old. Recoleta had been taken over by local squatters, who kept animals like Vita's family did in the old days, goats and chickens.

Several masserias in the area had been turned into luxury hotels. They had heated swimming pools and lush gardens scented with jasmine and citrus trees, gourmet meals with fresh seafood caught on the beaches of Metaponto and Taranto, and rooms decorated with antiques from around Vita's time, spinning wheels, irons, and locks and keys. One still had its gun towers, which were now just part of the luxury "tower suite" that looked down on the rest of the palm-tree-dotted property. Something was slightly obscene about staying in such luxury in a place where workers had suffered and gone hungry, particularly when they were your ancestors.

At Torre Fiore, Leo knew the chef, who served us seafood pasta with shrimp, baby clams, and tiny scallops, all caught by the fishermen in nearby Taranto. Our main course was seared tuna with local greens, all served in an open-air dining room overlooking the countryside, the stars glowing overhead and the lights of Taranto twinkling on the horizon like a distant galaxy.

Leo invited me to a dinner party at his beach club with his entire family, and then back another night to celebrate a local filmmaker who had won a Donatello Award—the Oscars of Italy. He introduced me around to one character after another who spoke at me in rapid-fire Italian. I felt like I was trapped in some Fellini film. They spoke so fast, I had no idea what anyone was saying. A television journalist interviewed me for RAI—the state-owned, twenty-four-hour, all-news station. I started out all right, answering his questions about the search for my family crime, but I'm not exactly sure what he said after that or what I said back. I just smiled and nodded and said, "Sì. Sì," over and over again as he babbled on. I hoped he and the other people here weren't asking me to perform root canal on one of their relatives. "Sì, sì," I said, smiling and nodding like an idiot.

My last night with Leo was in the café outside Coppola's hotel in Bernalda, where he had introduced me to Francesco, the lawyer, back in October. Leo knew the whole white-jacketed staff and chatted them up as we drank Spritzes—Campari, prosecco, and soda with a slice of orange—which glowed fluorescent pink in the Bernaldan streetlights.

I have to admit that after being married for twenty-one years, I was enjoying the flirting that was going on here, the attention I was being paid. And so were the residents of Bernalda.

The locals passed in their steady *passeggiata* and craned their necks to get a good look at us. I was no longer the only American in Bernalda. But they all knew who I was and probably clucked their tongues when they saw me alone in the café with Leo, one of the town's most eligible bachelors. "Vergogna, vergogna," they were probably mumbling under their breath. Shame, shame. I had a wedding ring on my finger. And they all knew Leo was not my husband.

My husband was "far from town," just like Francesco had been when Vita gave birth.

And though I didn't hear anyone say it, I could hear them think it when they looked at me.

Puttana.

Chapter 28

TAKE THIS BODY, TAKE THIS BLOOD

EVARISTO WALKED FASTER THAN ANYONE ELSE IN BASILI-cata. He was from Rome, which explained why he operated in a higher gear, much closer to my New York speed. He was a policeman in Pisticci whom I'd met while doing research here ten years ago. Evaristo now had a gray beard and wore a tan cargo vest with lots of pockets. He looked like Ernest Hemingway, but I recognized him right away under all that facial growth as he hurried past me on the street one morning.

As he zipped by, I shouted his name. Evaristo!

He abruptly stopped, turned, looked up, and recognized me, a broad smile spreading beneath his shaggy beard.

We hugged and I told him that I had tried emailing him about this most recent visit, that I was living just a few blocks from here. He said that he—like many of the older Italians here—rarely checked his email.

I introduced Giuseppe when he arrived and told Evaristo we were doing research in the archives in Pisticci.

"I am now in charge of the police records!" Evaristo exclaimed, his still-dark eyebrows rising high on his forehead. "I can help you."

"It looks like we found the murder," I said, and told him about the stolen pears, and the shotgun and Antonio Camardo dying in the attack. "I want to look up the victim today. He was from Pisticci. Probably the landowner. I want to see if we can find his death certificate."

"That's easy," said Evaristo, leading us toward the comune. Minutes later he was perched on a ladder, reaching for the fourth level of a metal shelf seven feet off the ground. He put on his glasses, craning his neck to read the spines of the two-foot-tall books that were so big and heavy they had caused the metal shelves to sag. After a minute or so, he located the right book, a large brown marbled volume with the words "Registro Dei Morti Di Pisticci" written on the beige spine. Below that was the year, 1872.

Evaristo twisted around and handed the unwieldy book to me, then climbed down. He took the book back and placed it on a nearby desk. I came and stood next to him as he flipped through the yellowed pages and suddenly, there he was—our man, Antonio Vincenzo Camardo. Evaristo gave me a fist bump.

I leaned over and read the death certificate along with Evaristo. I read it once, and then read it twice. Because I thought I was reading it wrong. Then I read it a third time. It said Camardo was only fourteen years old when he died. How could that be? How could the padrone have been only fourteen? But there it was, in the book.

"Is this right?" I asked Evaristo, still thinking I was reading it wrong. "It says he was only fourteen years old." Giuseppe read over our shoulders.

"Yes," said Evaristo, looking again at the death certificate. "He was fourteen. A boy." Giuseppe nodded solemnly.

It also said that Camardo lived right down the street at 56 Via Cirillo. "This was not a rich neighborhood back then," Giuseppe said, pointing to the address in the book.

Antonio Camardo, the victim of my family crime, was not the padrone after all. He wasn't even the son of the padrone, judging by this address. This kid was a peasant, just like Francesco and Vita.

He was just a boy left to guard the land. A boy who had been hired and put there by the padrone to do his dirty work. It suddenly made sense why his mother was with him.

I thought about Francesco brutally beating a boy nearly the same age as my own son. In front of his mother. I wondered how hard Camardo had fought back, how he was surely no match for twenty-seven-year-old Francesco and his friends. It was no longer a story of a poor farmer in battle with an evil landowner unwilling to share his fruit, but a story of some violent, awful men punching and kicking a kid to death.

And those awful men were my relatives.

We checked Camardo's birth certificate, located in another big book, on another bent shelf, just to be sure of his age. And sure enough, in the yellowing book of birth certificates, there he was, born to Carmina Albani and Donato Camardo, a farmer, both age thirty, on September 12, 1858, at 1 P.M. here in this neighborhood in Pisticci.

We walked over to the address—a small white house with a brown wooden door—and rang the bell. We waited and then rang again. But no one was home. I was relieved. What would I say? My ancestor killed your ancestor? How do you do?

I tried to imagine what Antonio Camardo looked like but could only conjure pictures of my own son. A big head of coarse brown hair, big pools of dark chocolate-brown eyes, the stubble of his first mustache pushing its way to the surface of his upper lip. Maybe he had just started shaving with his father's razor like

Dean had. His voice had probably just recently changed, deep and more manly than the body that gave it life.

His body would be tall and tan and skinny, the lanky arms and legs of a still-growing, awkward adolescent, his mother hopeful he would grow into a handsome, graceful man one day. I wondered if Carmina looked at him like I looked at Dean, stealing glances at the dark, wiry hair just beginning to sprout under his armpits, the few hairs poking through on his chest and skinny legs. Did she project what those adolescent features would look like once they were finished changing and evolving, once they were set on the face of the man who was once her baby? Except her baby, this boy, Antonio Camardo, would not grow into a man. Francesco would see to that.

He would die, surrounded by his mother and father and his extended family, in that small house on Via Cirillo, his head wound bleeding not onto fancy sheets and a pillow, but on the straw-stuffed, lumpy mattress of a peasant.

I thought about this fourteen-year-old boy learning to shoot his gun. Dean had shot a gun once on a family trip to Wyoming. We were with a friend who knew about guns and we had all gone target shooting out on the prairie, an exotic outing for a kid from New York City, where playing with guns was not considered cool.

But here, in Southern Italy, boys on farms were taught to shoot rifles, to defend against poachers and brigands. And my relatives.

Any relief I had felt this week for having found the murder was now replaced by a feeling of sick sorrow for this unknown kid who wasn't even related to me. The murder was worse than I had imagined.

I thought about having fist-bumped Evaristo just now and winced. This kid dying was nothing to celebrate.

Maybe Miserabila was right. I should leave the dead in peace. Knowledge had led me to despair, just like Adam and Eve. Maybe I was better off being ignorant, happier not knowing. But there was no turning back now. The paradise of happy ignorance was lost.

I thanked Evaristo for his help, kissed him and Giuseppe on both cheeks, and told them I was heading home for lunch. But I wasn't hungry. My appetite was gone again.

I HAD GIVEN UP ON THE ROMAN CATHOLIC CHURCH LONG AGO, BUT I suddenly felt the need to inhale the familiar smell of incense and be surrounded by a comforting crowd of silent, penitent strangers. Hearing the church bells ring in the late afternoon, I got dressed and headed around the corner to the Convent of San Antonio.

I took a seat in the back. San Antonio—the same name as the victim—was filled with lifelike statues in bold colors and paintings of the saints done in the dramatic Neapolitan style. A painting of San Bernardino, in his monk outfit, was to my left, as was St. Margherita, St. Bonaventure, and St. Giacomo in a bright red cape. Over near the wall was the Blessed Mother with a luminous crown of real lights floating around her head.

The church was also filled with real people, on a weeknight, which would never be the case in the United States, men, kids, but mostly older women, more than one hundred of them, silently perched in the pews like statues themselves, patiently waiting for Mass to start. A painting of twenty-three Franciscan martyred monks being crucified in a row floated over the altar. The ultra-vibrant colors of the paintings and statues had a supernatural quality to them, almost paganistic, like something you'd see in your dreams or maybe a nightmare.

Mass began and I tried to follow along, sandwiched between two *anziane*. I knew the English mass by heart, but not the Italian. I worried the old women would notice I wasn't reciting all the prayers but was simply mumbling along with nonsense words.

Partly to avoid their stares, I did something sacrilegious. I went up to receive communion, which I hadn't done in years. I knew that you really needed to go to confession before receiving communion after a long absence from the church.

But there was no time for that. I went straight up to the priest, who was dressed in a white and gold cassock, my hands folded in front of me, lifted my chin up, and heard him say, "Corpo di Cristo." Body of Christ.

"Amen," I replied, pronouncing it the Italian way, with a soft "a." I stuck out my tongue and the priest placed the host into my mouth. I clamped my teeth down onto it and headed back to my pew, blessing myself quickly as I walked, bypassing the chalice of blessed wine, the "blood of Christ," which a deacon was handing out to those more faithful than I was. The nuns had taught us never to chew the host, to instead gently let it melt in our mouths. But I was no longer a schoolgirl.

We had been taught in Catholic school that Jesus had died for our sins—for that original sin committed in the Garden of Eden and all the millions of sins that had followed. Receiving communion, we were told, was our way of welcoming Jesus into our hearts, admitting our wrongdoing, and asking forgiveness, sinners bound by a sacrificial lamb.

I had never understood the idea of Jesus dying for our sins, but suddenly, looking up at the crucifix over the altar, I understood all at once. It was finally clear to me after all these years. Maybe it was because I couldn't understand the Italian mass and was left time to reflect for once, looking at him bleeding up there on the cross.

Jesus had been tortured and murdered in front of his mother and all his friends and everyone he had ever known, for no good reason really. But before he died, he forgave his murderers. He didn't just *say* love your enemies. He *did* love his enemies, even the worst of them. He forgave them for killing him. While his mother watched. That was about as bad as it got, killing someone

for no good reason in front of his mother. And he forgave them
for it.

I thought back again to my visit to the Crypt of the Original
Sin, where I had seen that mural of Adam and Eve for the first
time, the flowers blooming all around them, symbolizing rebirth
and regeneration.

Our sins were not a black mark against us, but our way of
learning and teaching ourselves a lesson. Maybe my search was a
search for redemption, not just for Vita and Francesco, but for my
whole family, a way to get back to paradise and put the past behind
us once and for all. It wasn't just about being stubborn, or worrying about my children's future sins, or wanting to get revenge
against Miserabila.

It was about forgiveness.

The *anziani* gave me a welcoming smile as I returned to my
pew and knelt down to begin my prayer. But I wasn't sure what I
was praying for exactly. My list of intercessions was quickly growing and at this rate, I would have to say a whole Rosary to cover all
my bases.

I had started my search thinking the murder was over a simple card game, one man and maybe a woman losing their tempers
and killing another in a moment of passion. But this was something else. I couldn't get the image out of my head of Francesco
kicking a fourteen-year-old boy in the head again and again while
the kid's mother watched.

Maybe I was praying for the strength to walk away. Or was
I praying for the strength to stick around? I was praying for
Giuseppe's harvest, that's for sure. And for his sister Sabrina and
the children she'd left behind. And for the man who killed her.
I was giving thanks for having found my murder and for having
found Imma and Giuseppe to help me. I was praying for my husband and mother back home, and for my children, that Paulina's
strep would go away without any complications. I was praying for

the souls of Vita's dead sons, Rocco and stillborn Domenico, who never made it over to America. And to ask forgiveness for my relatives, for Beansie and cousin Chubby and Mike, and Francesco and Leonardantonio, who had killed an innocent teenager. I was praying for young Antonio Camardo, killed for no good reason, in front of his mother—just like Jesus. I asked forgiveness for that stupid fist bump I had given Evaristo today. But mostly, I was praying for Vita, whose life was about to change because her husband was surely, rightfully headed to prison.

Chapter 29

FAR FROM TOWN

FRANCESCO AND LEONARDANTONIO WERE MANACLED THE whole bumpy ride through the mountains using a *bagno* handcuff. Rather than two separate cuffs, the *bagno* consisted of one forged piece of iron shaped like a McDonald's letter *M* with two spaces for hands and a vertical metal screw bar with a wing nut beneath the wrists that would be cranked up tightly so that the hands couldn't move. A padlock kept the cuff in place.

They wore shackles on their ankles as well, thick, circular iron cuffs bound together with a short iron chain. Their ankles were linked to one another, like on a chain gang. Since it was November, it was starting to grow cold in the mountains during their three-day journey. They stared out the carriage window at the countryside, the olive trees still green but the lush valleys now a golden-yellow stubble.

That little bastard—that tough guy Camardo with his gun— would have to up and die, Francesco thought. Just my luck. But what was Francesco supposed to do, just let him shoot at them again? He couldn't let him reload. He had had to attack him. It was his family duty. Leonardantonio was his brother-in-law and had been injured. And Camardo surely would have fired again.

But had they really punched and kicked him hard enough to kill him? Until he was on top of the guy, Francesco hadn't realized he was just a kid. But he was just a boy. Maybe it didn't take much to break him.

Francesco shuddered, thinking of his own son, Rocco, back home, replaying the scene over and over again in his head, the teenager and his mother shouting at them, Camardo aiming that gun. Loading it from the front and firing. He could see him on the ground reloading the gun, and picture himself running toward him with the stick to stop him. A few punches and kicks and the boy lying there with so much blood pouring out of his head. And then running. Running. And the long, drawn-out drive back to Bernalda with the injured horse.

He and Leonardantonio couldn't discuss the murder or their side of the story, not with the carabinieri right there in the carriage with them. But their slumped posture and their longing looks out at the countryside—their freedom suddenly taken from them—communicated all they needed to say to one another. They were headed to the regional capital of Potenza, where they would be tried. Over and over on that long, long ride, they replayed the murder. How could this have happened? What had they gotten themselves into? What would happen to Vita and young Rocco, only seven months old?

Francesco replayed his goodbye to them in his head, Vita holding the baby in her arms, like a sad Madonna and Child, both her and Rocco crying, sobbing, clinging to Francesco and not wanting him to go. Francesco told her not to worry, that everything would turn out all right. But he was lying. Nothing ever turned out all right in Bernalda in the nineteenth century.

He was worried this would be their last time together, that

he would never return, would never even see them again. They couldn't make the trip to Potenza to visit him in jail or to attend the trial. It was just not possible; they could barely survive life in Bernalda. And how would they survive without him now? Vita told him before he left, trying to look strong for him and swallow her tears, that she could move back in with her parents, with Teresina and Domenico. But they had their youngest still at home, and a small army of other grandchildren to take care of.

Francesco and Leonardantonio were tied up at night when the carriage driver and policemen rested in the countryside, darkness falling over the craggy mountains and straw-colored valleys below, like a dark velvet curtain falling on a tragic opera. The leg irons and the *bagno* cuffs—so named for the deep prisons that would flood, giving the prisoners a bath (or *bagno*)—were particularly uncomfortable. But for the sadistic carabinieri, that was part of their charm. Along with their worry, and the murder, replayed dozens of times, the cuffs made it hard for Francesco and Leonardantonio to sleep. Just as they drifted off, the sun rose and the carriage was off again, headed to Potenza.

Chapter 30

WAY OUT

ON SMOOTH ITALIAN HIGHWAYS, MY RIDE TO POTENZA WAS much shorter than Francesco and Leonardantonio's three-day journey. It was just ninety minutes, fully air-conditioned, though we no longer needed the AC by the time we arrived. The town was in the mountains and at least ten degrees cooler than the coast. I was actually a little chilly when I stepped out of the car, the first time I felt so that month. I thought of Francesco and how cold it would be at night in that prison in the middle of November.

Giuseppe couldn't come with us. His long-awaited wheat harvest was taking place that day. So Imma and I made the trip without him.

We wanted to see the prison, Santa Croce, where Francesco and Leonardantonio served time, and the old courthouse where they had been put on trial.

People from Matera still hadn't gotten over the fact that Potenza had replaced them as the capital of the region more than two centuries ago. But Potenza's 380,000 residents could not care less. Their city was more than six times larger.

Most of the town was modern and ugly. Earthquakes over the centuries had destroyed many of the old, beautiful historic buildings. Potenza was *brutta*. It couldn't compare to Matera's tragic beauty. When you told someone from Matera you were going to Potenza, they sneered and always made some snide comment. "Why would you want to go to Potenza?" "What does Potenza have that we haven't got?" "Have you been there? It's not worth the gas to get there."

The city's last major earthquake had been in 1980, so much of the architecture looked like it belonged in a drab office park in suburban America. Tall, featureless, boxy buildings were everywhere, eyesores compared to the charming medieval towns nearby.

Giuseppe put us in touch with someone he knew who worked in one of the new government buildings. He pointed us in the right direction. Imma had studied at the university here for a little while, so she was familiar with a few neighborhoods. After a few stops and what seemed like several miles walking up and down the steep hills of Potenza, we arrived at the state archive. My bunions were killing me.

We had to place all our belongings in a locker when we arrived. The building was very modern, even more modern than the archive in Matera, larger and more upscale, with polished wooden desks and wooden, cushioned chairs, tall ceilings and windows, and a shining tile floor. Framed posters covered the walls and glass cases displayed ancient texts. There didn't seem to be a speck of dust and the air was much cooler than in the stuffy archive in Matera.

It was nearly empty, with only one other person there doing research at one of the wooden desks. She shushed us when we spoke too loudly. The file clerks and librarians were dressed in long white lab coats and seemed especially official, more like scientists than librarians.

Imma told the clerk that we were searching for information on the Santa Croce prison. The lab-coated woman disappeared and emerged moments later with a cart full of large blueprints. Santa Croce—Holy Cross—was located on Strada Fuori near Porta San Luca.

Strada Fuori translated as Way Out. And this place was way the hell out there, at the very edge of town, surrounded by farmlands owned by Nicola Doti and someone named Decanto. According to the architectural drawings, a prison yard was surrounded by a series of cells. When we asked if the prison was still there, the clerk shrugged.

We headed out toward the historic district, one of the only places where old buildings were left standing and where the prison was supposed to have been. We found Via Pretoria, the Fifth Avenue of Potenza, with its fancy designer shops and Apple Store, where Imma had dropped off her waterlogged phone earlier this month. The neighborhood was quite beautiful and looked like a small town in France, houses made of large stones, with distressed wooden shutters and ornate metal balconies.

We found the street where the prison should have been, and the Porta San Luca—which was one of the three ancient gates into the walled city. Though the wall was long gone, the tall arched entryway was still standing. Down the block was a stone medieval tower—Torre Guevara—built by the Lombards in the ninth century as part of the city's battlements, the only part left standing. On the same property was a closed three-story school from the 1960s or '70s, judging by the architecture. The ugly beige school was boarded up and covered in graffiti. "I told my therapist about you," read one line in Magic Marker. Another read, "What does the fox say?"

Most of the buildings and the surrounding property were

closed off by a high iron fence. But through the bars you could see that the expansive space around the tower was covered in concrete, with clumps of grass, Queen Anne's lace and dandelions popping through. The property overlooked the lush, green countryside and was indeed the place where the prison had once been. It had been demolished sometime in the 1950s to make room for this school, which had itself closed in the last decade or so. The place was deserted. A sadness and seediness permeated the neighborhood and the spot, as if the awful things that had happened in the prison still somehow lingered.

We headed over to Piazza Prefeturra, where the courthouse—the Palazzo di Giustizia—was located, just a few blocks away in a much livelier, happy neighborhood. The courthouse was an orange three-story historic building with arched doorways, a center balcony, and windows topped with triangular Greek lintels. Though it was officially closed for renovation, I walked right in and pretended I belonged there, strolling past the few workers in the hallways, who greeted me with a simple "Buongiorno."

Old doors and entryways were plastered over, the skeletons of the original stone walls showing through in some places. From most windows, you could see the medieval church next door, which was practically pressed up against the courthouse.

The church was called San Francesco, naturally.

I thought of Francesco walking up these same worn, marble courthouse stairs I was climbing now, pausing for a moment, his hands in his rusty *bagno* cuffs, his body leaning against the smooth, wide wooden banister. I wondered if he stared out at the church that bore his name, saying a prayer under his breath to his patron saint that he did not get sentenced to a lifetime in prison. Or to death.

The church had a tall pointed tower, orange terra-cotta roof tiles, and a large circular window over its Romanesque rounded portal. It dated back to 1274 and held several treasures, including a faded fresco of San Francesco from the school of Giotto. It was said to be the first portrait of San Francesco in Southern Italy.

San Francesco was dressed in a friar's robe cinched with a rope, with a bald head ringed by a fringe of orange hair. His eyes were narrow as if he were concentrating and his chin was covered in an orange beard, a book under his left arm and his right hand raised. If you looked closely, you could see the stigmata wounds on his hand. He was wearing a golden halo. The painting was tucked away in a corner, near a Madonna and Child, and unless you were looking for it, it was nearly impossible to find. It was a hidden treasure that I'm sure my great-great-grandfather never glimpsed.

According to legend, the church was actually founded by San Francesco, Italy's national saint, who was passing through Potenza and laid the first stone for the building while on his way to Jerusalem.

The Franciscans owned and ran the church for centuries. The door, made from olive wood, was intricately carved with both saints and demons, including a devil rising up in an attempt to drag San Francesco down to hell. Griffins and gargoyles were everywhere. And I thought of Francesco, our Francesco, passing here day after day on his way from the prison a few blocks away, and staring at that terrible, beautiful door each time, his and his brother-in-law's fate growing closer and closer with each visit.

Chapter 31

RECOIL

F RANCESCO AND LEONARDANTONIO HAD TWO DEFENSE LAW-
yers who were the most celebrated lawyers of their day in
Basilicata. Their names were Nicola Branca and Giovanni
de Bonis.

When I asked how that was possible, how such poor farmers
would end up with such fantastic lawyers, Professor Tataranno
shrugged, took a drag from his cigarette, and said that many successful lawyers, like now, did pro bono work for those who couldn't
afford a decent attorney. Especially if it was a high-profile case.

We had given Tataranno an electronic copy of the criminal file
to help us decipher what was inside. Some things I could read for
myself, like the basic plot of the murder and the list of jurors and
alternates who were chosen for the case.

The twelve jurors were not exactly Francesco's peers: no farmers or day laborers, no stable hands or blacksmiths. No women, of
course. Twelve men were chosen from a pool of business owners,
lawyers, doctors, land surveyors, veterinarians, pharmacists,

and notaries—respectable citizens from as far away as Bella, Laurenzana, Maratea, and Lavello, towns all closer to Potenza than to Bernalda. None of the men were from Bernalda, Pisticci, Matera, or Ferrandina, to avoid a conflict of interest. Their accents were different than Francesco's, as were their customs and even some of the food they ate.

The subtle intricacies of the case I left up to Professor Tataranno. We visited him at his home in Bernalda on Via Karl Marx, which was fitting, since Tataranno had belonged to the Communist Party. His house was in the more modern part of town, his living room and dining room as neat as his memory. We sat at his long, polished dining room table and discussed what he had found.

Francesco had no property, according to the case documents. He had once been in the army, like all young men in Italy from 1865 on, but had been discharged. This was the first time he was ever arrested.

Miraldi, the bricklayer and third man involved in the crime, was not charged with murder, but with being an accomplice to the robbery. He was sentenced to three years in prison.

Two witnesses, Donato Mentessano and Bernardino Chiruzzi, testified that Camardo had attacked Francesco and Leonardantonio first, and that only after he tried to reload his shotgun did they run toward him to attack him. Francesco said that he never even hit the boy, that Camardo's gun backfired and he hit himself in the head. When he got to him, Camardo was already on the ground, bleeding.

An autopsy revealed that Camardo died from being hit in the head with a hard object. The defense argued during the trial that Camardo was not beaten to death, as was charged, but that the gun had recoiled. Since he was so young and inexperienced, he had been holding it wrong, on his neck rather than his shoulder. When it recoiled it slipped and hit the back of his skull, the fatal blow.

Tataranno said one of his teachers taught him to shoot one of those shotguns when he was young. It was entirely plausible, he said, that if you didn't hold it correctly you could really hurt yourself. With his cigarette still between his fingers he pretended to hold a shotgun up to his eye, lifting his right shoulder to show where the butt of the gun should be placed. With his other hand, he showed how the gun could have slipped off and hit the back of the boy's head. "The defense's claim was not so outrageous," he said, sticking his bottom lip out, the imaginary gun gone, both his palms turned up, cigarette still burning.

I was skeptical. Maybe Camardo died from a combination of hitting himself in the head with his own gun and a few blows from my great-great-grandfather. Francesco wasn't getting off the hook that easily.

Chapter 32

SONG OF THE PRISONER

ONLY FRANCESCO WAS CHARGED WITH MURDER. LEONARD-antonio was downgraded to simple robbery of the pears and served a short sentence at Santa Croce.

For Francesco, the entire process took five years. That happened to be an especially quick turnaround for Italy, where cases could take up to twenty years to wend through the system. But it was a long five years for Francesco inside that dungeon of a prison, that hellhole on the edge of Potenza, waiting every day for another earthquake to strike this godforsaken city and either crush him with falling stones or crack the place wide open and set him free.

He learned the "Song of the Prisoner"—"Canto di Carcerato"— from the others, some of whom had been there for decades. It was a slow dirge of a folk song that was all too popular in Southern Italy. It had many different versions, but was usually sung high and wavering like an Arabic song. Like the rap of its day, it was a defiant shout-out to a society that didn't prize its strong, young men, a country that didn't give them the opportunities they needed to succeed, which had pushed them to become criminals simply to survive. And it never had a happy ending.

> The dark, midnight air tolls
> And the birds sleep in silence
> Midnight in the cell tolls
> And he wakes up to the sound of the bell
> And God in heaven have mercy on me
> I am closed in this cell
> And I pray to you
> . . . The warden stares at me and asks
> Young, handsome man,
> What is your sentence?
> I was innocent
> And was condemned to life
> My life a disaster
> The pains I have suffered

Francesco's lawyers came to him one day after he'd been locked in Santa Croce for three years with terrible news: his son, his Rocco, had died. Maybe Francesco punched the wall over and over again until his knuckles bled and the guards escorted him, sobbing, back to his tiny cell. He hadn't even gotten to say a final farewell. He wondered if his son would have even remembered him. His only son. His only child. He was gone. He would never see the boy again.

He had a feeling when he had said goodbye to him in Bernalda that he would never see him again. But Francesco assumed he himself would be the one to die, not Rocco. With those hours and days and weeks and months in his lonely cell, Francesco thought of Rocco. Agonized over Rocco. About how Rocco would still be alive had he not gone to prison. He would give his life for Rocco's, be hung for this stupid murder just so Rocco could live. It was payback, he knew, for killing that boy, Antonio Camardo, God's way of punishing him for the murder. Rocco dying was much worse than any penalty the court could hand down.

Francesco heard rumors that now that Rocco was gone, Vita might be moving to Pisticci, for work reasons, but he didn't know for sure. Maybe her parents had grown tired of her crying, for her missing husband and now her missing son, and sent her off to the masseria.

Neither Francesco nor Vita could read or write. So there were no letters back and forth with news in them. No "I love you" or "I miss you terribly" or "I'll wait for you." And the telephone—the magical device, invented by a fellow Italian, that could transmit the voices of your loved ones over long distances—had only just been patented two months before Francesco's final sentence. There were no telephones yet at Santa Croce.

FRANCESCO STOOD IN THAT VERY SAME COURTHOUSE I HAD VIS-ited, when his sentence was handed down on March 16, 1877. He was much skinnier than that ride five years earlier on the way to Potenza. Dark circles half-mooned beneath his eyes; his skin was pale and mottled from a lack of sunlight. He was dressed in a new cheap black suit that his celebrated lawyers had bought for him. Those lawyers stood by him, at his side at the wide, wooden courthouse table, dressed in black robes over their more expensive suits, silver tassels on their shoulders. The medieval church of San Francesco stood tall outside the courtroom window, casting shade on the courthouse walls.

The courtroom was crowded—not with the relatives of those involved, for they were too poor to travel to Potenza, but with lawyers and reporters curious to hear the final judgment in this high-profile case. Even if she had somehow found the money to come to court, the victim's mother, Carmina, would never have been able to attend the sentencing of her son's killer: she had died a little over a year ago in January at the age of forty-eight. No cause is listed on her death certificate, but watching her son get killed was surely more than her heart could bear.

The judge, dressed in his long black robe with gold tassels on the shoulders, his frilly white dickey and small white bow tie, and cylindrical black hat, asked the jury if it had reached a final verdict.

The foreman rose. He was a business owner named Donato Schiró, from the town of Ripacandida, near the dead volcano of Mount Vulture, where the soil was rich and good for growing grapes. The town was known for its Great Forest of cedars and oaks, where brigands would often take shelter when hiding from the law. Schiró looked at the judge, then over at Francesco.

Francesco stared out the window at the church and said a final prayer to his patron saint. Please, please, San Francesco. Let me go. Please, I have suffered enough. Please, God. Send me back to my family in Bernalda. Back to my Vita. Back to my life.

And so Donato Schiró delivered the jury's verdict: Francesco Vena, guilty of manslaughter in the death of Antonio Camardo.

Not innocent. But not guilty of murder, either. Manslaughter was a lesser charge. It meant Francesco had unintentionally killed Camardo in a moment of passion. There would be no life sentence. No death penalty. But no freedom just yet. It was a purgatory, an in-between state that Francesco would have to endure.

Francesco was sentenced to six years in prison. Since he had already served five years while awaiting trial, he would be scheduled for release in one year, in late 1878.

But there was a hitch. Camardo's family members were suing Francesco in civil court for damages and expenses related to the killing. Seven people, including Camardo's father, Donato, his grandfather, and his mother, Carmina, while still alive, had filed the suit.

Francesco wouldn't be able to pay his damages and expenses, because he was a poor farmer, so he would have to pay off his debt by staying longer in prison. And that meant more than six years.

I ROLLED THESE DATES OVER IN MY HEAD AND THOUGHT ABOUT everything I knew about Francesco and his sons. Rocco was born in 1872, just before the murder; he died four years later. Valente, his second son, was born in 1877. Valente's brother, Leonardo, my great-grandfather, was born in February 1879. Domenico, who would have been the fourth son, was stillborn in 1881. His birth certificate—like Valente's and Leonardo's—said that Francesco was far from the town and could not be present for the birth.

The puzzle pieces were jigsawing themselves together in my head. A full picture finally presenting itself.

Francesco was not there for the birth of Valente or Leonardo or even Domenico. He was away but he was not working the farm.

He was in prison.

"Was Francesco in prison the whole time, from the time he was arrested?" I asked Professor Tataranno.

"Oh yes. No doubt," he said, tilting his head to the side.

"Did they have conjugal visits back then?"

Tataranno laughed out loud. "No, no, no," he answered. "Santa Croce was not a country club or even a hard-labor camp in the countryside. We're talking about a maximum-security, over-crowded dungeon." He counted out on his fingers, "With no heat, no lights, and no bathrooms."

Prisoners wore striped uniforms, he said, which were covered in filth. "Many of them committed suicide rather than live day after day in Santa Croce. It was notorious. A living hell, and once you were locked away, you weren't let out at all until your sentence was over. If you made it that long."

It dawned on me sitting there at Tataranno's dining room table that Francesco was not only absent for his sons' births.

He wasn't there for their conceptions, either.

Leonardo and Valente and Domenico were *all* illegitimate sons. When it said Francesco was far from the town, he was way up in that prison in the mountains of Potenza.

Francesco was not my great-great-grandfather.

He was no relation whatsoever. He had been in prison the entire time. His only son was Rocco, who died long ago and never had any offspring. The Vena name was not our name. We were not who we thought we were. I was not who I thought I was.

And the family murder was not my family murder at all.

Not only was Vita innocent, but this man, this Francesco, was not a relation. The ground felt like it was shifting under my feet, as if one of those countless earthquakes were hitting Basilicata.

It wasn't a sense of relief I was experiencing. Relief comes when you find that missing kid's sneaker you've been searching for for three days under the living room couch. Or when you finally get that long-awaited freelance check to pay your bills. It wasn't even the relief you get when the test for cancer comes back negative. I had gotten those results before. This, this was something else. This was some kind of realignment of being, an erasing and rewriting of history. And since I wasn't expecting it, since it had crept up on me, it took a few minutes to actually sink in. Disbelief and numbness, followed by a trickling of feeling that turned into a downpour, much like that hard rain I had experienced at the top of Pisticci. A soaking baptism.

I needed to lie down.

Beansie had not inherited a murderous gene, but had been an aberration, just like my mother had claimed, a product of a series of environmental forces, the lost twin, the cold mother, the car accident, being forced to write with his right hand. He was an archvillain in a family of petty crooks. The murder gene had not been passed down through the generations. My children, safely ensconced in Brooklyn this past month, had no trace of murderous Vena genes in their DNA. Because there was no trace of Vena blood in their veins.

I went back and checked the copies of the birth certificates for those three babies—Valente, Leonardo, and Domenico—and realized that it didn't say that Francesco was the father. It simply said that Vita was his wife. The babies were "born to Vita, wife of Francesco." That was all. He had never claimed those sons as his own. I had never even noticed that wording before. When I went back to look at Rocco's birth certificate, the wording was different. Rocco was "born to Francesco and his wife, Vita." That was a few months before the murder, before Francesco was sent away.

When I showed the birth certificates to Professor Tataranno, he nodded his head and said, "Yes, you are right. Francesco is not the father of those three sons. He would have several years to claim them as his own, which he never did."

It's as if my family had been pardoned after years of being falsely accused of murder. Vita didn't do it. She had been a loose woman. But that had saved us from those murderous genes. Vita was a hero. She had obviously slept with someone else and had delivered us all from evil. Her indiscretions had paved the way for our innocence.

This was the piece of the family story I had been searching for, even though I didn't know I was searching for it, the reason I had crossed the ocean multiple times and combed through these files. It was the knowledge I had inadvertently come all this way to find, the absolution, resolution, and piece of fruit that once bitten, would change our family history forever.

But it led to another question: who the hell was my great-great-grandfather?

Chapter 33

TO EVERY BIRD,
ITS OWN NEST IS BEAUTIFUL

V ITA HAD NOTHING TO LOSE.

She worked now each and every day in the white-washed masseria. Since Rocco was gone, and her husband was gone, and she had to eat somehow, she boldly knocked on Grieco's door. Just as he had knocked on hers years before on her wedding night.

The padrone had taken something from her and now she would take from him. She would offer herself up again in exchange for shelter, food, and protection.

Inside the safety of his giant palazzo on the masseria property, with its rounded gun turrets surrounded by tall palms, with cactus and pines and citrus groves that left their sweet smell in the air, Vita made the first move.

Maybe it was even a comfort for her, the idea of body pressed against body, a few moments of pleasure to forget the endless pain of losing your firstborn, your only son. And your husband.

When Rocco died, something snapped inside her, some switch was thrown, some fuse forever blown.

Because of her sass and her attitude, Vita was already known as a *puttana*. Now, it would be true. She was almost proud of it. Relieved, in a way. If they were going to call her a whore, she might as well reap the benefits.

It would cause a small scandal. Having sex with Grieco again, this time at her initiation. But the scandal would die out, and be replaced by someone else's scandal, another's misfortune. The woman carrying triplets out of wedlock. Or the people down the street who had to send their crazy mother to the insane asylum in Aversa because she tried to cook the baby. No shortage of pain and scandal to replace Vita's.

Vita knew, from watching and listening to the neighbors' gossip in past sex scandals, that her father would be rewarded for her actions by being given regular work. In most concubine setups, the woman's father would move from *bracciante* to *mezzadro*—or sharecropper, where he would be given a small plot of land to rent and farm, with seeds, supplies, fertilizer, and a house provided by the landowner. Maybe he would even be bumped up to *fattore*, or steward, representing Grieco and overseeing the day-to-day business of one of his *latifondi*, getting the best parcel of land for himself.

Her mother no longer had to scrounge in the fields for a few bits of wheat to make into bread, for a stray tomato or *babadool* (dialect for pepper). Their suffering would end. Or at least be diminished.

So when Grieco touched Vita, she didn't recoil. And when he kissed her, she kissed him back. Tongue and all. She had learned how from Francesco. When Grieco told her he wanted her, she told him she wanted him back. She touched Grieco as Francesco had taught her to touch him, gently, but firmly, without fear, and with confidence. So different than Grieco's proper wife.

In this way, my great-great-grandmother, Vita Gallitelli, became a concubine.

With Vita's help, Grieco slowly peeled away the layers of her ragged *pacchiana* outfit until she stood defiantly naked before him, her dark and wiry hair pulled out of its usual bun and draped down past her shoulders, her wild, black pubic hair like the weeds she pulled in his front yard, daring him to come closer. That's how I liked to think of Vita. Not cowering in some corner, afraid of his advances. But meeting him halfway. With nothing to lose. Nothing to lose. Looking like that portrait of Eve inside the cave near Matera, defying her husband, defying God. And even the devil.

Have a taste, she would say. "Just one bite."

Vita's virginity was long gone. Grieco had taken it years ago. She never had much honor to begin with in a place like Bernalda. She didn't have a lira in her pocket. All she had was her body. And that face, that *faccia di Gallitelli*. It was a pretty face. Not beautiful. But pretty enough. Its skin still pliant and soft.

She was only twenty-four, after all. No longer a girl but a woman, a young woman in her physical prime with full hips and breasts. And a sharp mind, as sharp as the knife the farmhands used to kill the pigs.

Vita was *furba*—the female equivalent of *furbo,* feisty and wily and able and willing to take advantage of a bad situation, using whatever was at her disposal to get ahead, tricking the person who thought he was tricking you. Like a fox.

She wasn't shy. Vita was never shy. In fact, she liked being naked. It was much cooler and less confining. Why didn't people get naked more often around here, like in the Garden of Eden, she wondered. It was only natural. What was the true point of clothing? she thought, as Grieco climbed on top of her.

While she lay there, she admired his room: its clean, whitewashed walls and the intricate molding up near the ceiling, and his big, expansive wooden bed, with its carved headboard, with not only blankets but sheets. She had never lain on sheets before. Only itchy, woolen, dirty blankets.

Grieco was married, she knew. But so was she. It wasn't marriage she was after, but a foot up. A better life for her and her parents and brothers and sisters. And a few minutes of pleasure. In a life so hard and deprived all the time, in a place where you went hungry and sometimes thirsty for days, where your children died starving in your arms, what was the harm? Sex, she discovered, was one of the few pleasures. And it was free. Most of the time, anyway.

From now on, in exchange for work, rent, and meat more than just two times a year, Grieco would visit Vita whenever he pleased, in her small house on Via Cavour.

AFTER VALENTE, THEIR FIRST SON, WAS CONCEIVED AND BORN IN Bernalda, Grieco would place Vita in a house in Pisticci, away from her family, away from the gossipers. It would be easier to visit her there and she wouldn't feel the stares of the other women, at least not right away.

Though it helped the family financially to become a concubine, socially it was suicide. Immorality was thought to be passed down from one generation of women to another, so the misdeeds of one wife cast a shadow on all her female relatives. It was best to move to Pisticci.

It was only a matter of time before news of Vita's new lover and her sons reached the prison cells of Santa Croce. Maybe a new inmate from Bernalda who had heard of the scandal delivered the news to another inmate, who passed it along to another and another and then to a guard who menacingly, hurtfully told Francesco with a laugh, "Hey, Ciccio. I hear your wife is fucking another man."

Francesco was so angry, he wanted to bend open the iron bars, climb out, and first kill the guard and then travel over the mountains for three days to find Grieco and kill him with his bare hands. Kill them both. Vita, too. Vita must have known this, but what could she do? How would she survive without her husband?

Since Grieco was a landowner who employed not only her family but Francesco's, there was really nothing Francesco could do. Padroni could do as they pleased with the wives of their workers and their workers' families. And Francesco, sitting alone with all those hours to think in that lonely prison high up in the mountains, eventually realized it was all his fault. Vita never would have strayed had he not stolen those pears and gone to prison. She had loved him. He knew it. But he was not there providing for her. What the hell did he expect?

But still, some nights Vita worried that Francesco would escape somehow, tunnel out of that terrible place, steal a horse, and ride all night, making his way in a blind rage back to Bernalda.

In Pisticci, she could hide from him. At least for a little while.

VITA'S LIFE BEGAN ANEW. SHE HAD VALENTE, BORN IN A TINY STONE house in Bernalda at the end of Via Cavour, where it turns and deposits you onto Corso Italia, the main street of the historic district, where the jail is and the old tavern where Rocco was born and Our Lady of Mount Carmel.

Valente was an unusual name in this part of Italy. It meant able-bodied and talented. An incredibly unorthodox and optimistic name to give your son in a place like this.

Before Valente could even walk, Vita was pregnant with the next, Leonardo, whom she named after her brother and her mother's father, her grandfather Leonardantonio Lupo. Lupo, they called him. The wolf. Because he was especially hairy.

A third, Domenico, was born two years later. She named him after her father, but he would die, stillborn. It wasn't like when Rocco had died, though, not as devastating, since she had the older boys to look after now. There was no long mourning period. No comatose state of denial.

For a time, life was good in Pisticci. Vita loved her new house, with its marble step outside, its wooden double doors, second-story window, and high barreled ceiling. It was her own. There was a saying in Italian, "To every bird, its own nest is beautiful." Some nights, on her way back from Mass, she stood over the Dirupo and watched the *grillaio* falcons and *rondini* circle at sunset. On a clear day, you could see the Ionian Sea from this high up. It would sparkle in the sun. She had never seen it close up. But like Isabella di Morra in her lonely castle in Valsinni, Vita looked at the sea from afar and dreamed. She didn't lament her fate like Morra, who waited in vain for sails to appear in the distance and come and save her. Vita dreamed of sailing away. On her own. Without a man.

She took walks up to the Chiesa Madre, even in the rain, and sometimes gazed at that sorry pietà and thought of Rocco. But now she had two new sons, from a rich man. They ate better. Slept better. The boys, as they grew, would not work in the fields as she and Francesco had, but would train with the local barber. A maestro. With the master. Their hands were soft, like hers once were and like Grieco's, not rough and calloused like Francesco's.

Barbers were respected. They sometimes performed minor surgeries, like pulling teeth or applying leeches to let the blood of those suffering a fever. They could read, and wrote letters for people to send to their loved ones in America. Valente and Leonardo would learn to read and write. Vita would make sure of that.

And on their nights together, when the boys were out and before Grieco gathered his things to head home to his wife and children, Vita asked him about going to America.

She tried to convince him that once Francesco was released from prison, he would find her, no matter where she was in Basilicata. He had killed before and he would kill again. He would surely kill her and maybe even Grieco and their sons. Though she didn't really believe that. It was unacceptable to kill an amorous landowner, even if he was sleeping with your wife. And Francesco wasn't all that bad. He was just trying to be a good provider, stealing those pears. Sometimes she even cried for him—her Ciccio—thinking of him all alone in that awful prison up in the mountains in Potenza.

But that's not what she told Grieco.

Night after night, she tried to convince him that Francesco would be coming for her. Maybe Grieco even fell in love with her. Not love at first sight, but the opposite.

Love over time.

After practically living with Vita for several years, Grieco was starting to fall in love with her. With her long, dark, thick hair and her stubborn streak, her soft hips and small hands, her crooked smile, round face, and black eyes that were so dark they caught any light in a room, no matter how small, and threw it back at you like the surface of a dark lake. Lagonegro, he thought. That was a town not too far from here, Lagonegro, where they said the model from the *Mona Lisa* was buried. Vita looked like Mona Lisa, in fact, except her hair was curlier. But she had that same uncertain smile, that same full face. That same confidence and, in Vita's case, false air of nobility.

Maybe Grieco liked the way Vita stared you down and never looked away first and how she sometimes had a bad temper. He laughed sometimes when she lost it, which made her even angrier. When she got that angry, he tried to hug her, hug it out of her. But she pushed him away, like an angry child. He laughed and laughed and walked away, leaving her in peace to cool off. And slowly she came back to him, in her own time.

He loved the way she smelled, too, a heady mix of the outdoors, the garlic she used to cook with and a natural musty smell, which he was pretty sure was coming from beneath that big head of hair. He loved how funny she was.

And maybe, just maybe, Vita fell in love with him.

Love over time. When he fell asleep in her bed and didn't rush off, Vita had a terrible desire to reach out and touch his receding hairline and his back and his face. To run her hand along its rough surface, feel the stubble smooth in one direction and prickly in the other, as she ran her hand back and forth. To trace her finger on his full lips, which her sons had inherited. And when he awoke, she would look him in his dark eyes, and not with her usual boldness, but with a tenderness she wasn't used to feeling or offering. A tenderness he wasn't used to seeing. And before she knew it, she was in love with this man. Though she wouldn't admit it at first, not even to herself. Certainly not to him. It would only complicate things.

These feelings made her angry for a while. Grieco noticed her bad mood and kept his distance. But the anger faded and was replaced with elation, every time he walked in the door, a quick flutter in her heart and stomach as if a small family of silk moths were living there.

We had nothing to go on, no love letters or diaries from Vita, so what wasn't passed down by mouth died in its own time. Love didn't last, except for the babies that were born from it.

Just because there were no love letters, didn't mean there was no love. So I imagine a love affair for Vita, not just sex for comfort. A love so deep she tried to convince him to let her leave for good, to give her and his sons the money to flee. To America. Because

Vita was like all the women in our family, always wanting something more for her kids, wanting a better life for them, no matter what the cost.

He would think about it, Grieco told her. But he had already thought about it, and had started putting money aside for their long, long journey.

Chapter 34

ONE FACE, ONE RACE

I T WAS NOT ONLY ACCEPTABLE IN SOUTHERN ITALY TO KILL A wife who cheated; it was expected. Professor Tataranno told me the night of *prima notte* was one thing, but to carry on a full-blown love affair was quite another. And when Francesco got out of prison, he would likely kill Vita, or at least beat her badly. It was also acceptable for him to kill the man who was sleeping with her. Unless, of course, he was the landowner.

Grieco.

When I thought about it, it all made sense, really. I told Tataranno that people had always mistaken me for Greek. When I was a kid, my mother would pick me up for lunch from school and take me to a diner across the street. It was a Greek diner and the people in there loved me. They told my mother they wanted to adopt me because I looked like them and because I loved their chicken orzo soup.

In college, my best friend, Nick, introduced me to his Greek family in the Bronx and they immediately took a liking to me, more so than Nick's other friends. His aunts would braid my long, thick hair and his mother taught me the right way to pronounce *spanakopita* and *taramasalata*. They told me I seemed like a Greek, like one of the family. "Are you sure you're not Greek?" they asked me, squinting.

They were the first ones to mention the Italian/Greek saying to me, "Same face, same race." In Greek it was "Mia fatsa, mia ratsa." And in Italian, "Una faccia, una razza." Their food, culture, and faces were so similar that they considered themselves brethren.

Now I wondered if I really was related to Nick's family. By Greek blood.

I was Grieco. I could feel it in my bones.

That afternoon I also reminded Professor Tataranno how Vita would later die, hit in the head with a sock full of rocks in Jersey City. His eyes narrowed. "You know that it's a very typical weapon in Basilicata. The shepherds often use a sock full of rocks to scare away predators. And the brigands, well, it was their first weapon of choice."

I told him killing someone with a sock full of rocks was not typical in America.

"Maybe," he said, "maybe Francesco did make his way to America finally and took his revenge."

That had never occurred to me before. And it seemed kind of drastic, for him to wait all those years and travel there to kill his philandering wife.

"Or maybe he hired someone in Jersey City to kill her," he said.

That seemed more plausible, since the area where Vita lived in Jersey City had a large community of Bernaldans. I thought of Francesco, stewing year after year, getting angrier and angrier that she had left with those bastard sons of hers, and working his way into a vengeful fury and hiring a friend in America to knock her off. Was it possible there were two Vena murders?

I VISITED THE ARCHIVES IN MATERA ONE MORE TIME, TO SEE IF I could find any other murders or any other children born to Vita. I went alone this time. Imma was busy reading through the tangled calligraphy of the criminal file and Giuseppe was enjoying a visit from his niece and nephew, the children of his late sister Sabrina.

He didn't see them very often but they were here for several days with their father, Sabrina's widower, staying in Giuseppe's farmhouse. They ate big meals and told family stories. Giuseppe's wife, Emanuela, made *pasta coi fagiolini,* spaghetti with long green beans that were now in season, a family favorite.

I wondered if the children looked like Sabrina and if it brought Giuseppe any comfort to see them. Or maybe it made him feel worse. I didn't have the heart to ask him. When I spoke to him on the phone, he used words that described how happy he was that they were visiting, but there seemed an underlying anxiety to those words. Giuseppe was always positive and cheerful, but today his voice sounded strained and full of sorrow, a way I had never heard it before.

By now the staff at the Matera archives knew me well, and brought my files quickly. They even stood by to see what new information I discovered.

Within minutes, flipping through the dusty book of birth certificates, I found another child of Vita. This time, a daughter.

Her name was Nunzia. Born 1883, this time in Bernalda on Via Eraclea—the Italian name for Hercules. The same street where Coppola's ancestors had lived.

A daughter! It's a girl, I nearly shouted into the archive room.

Her name was a holy one, which referred to the Annunciation, when the angel came to Mary to tell her she was going to give birth. And give birth she would.

This time to a little baby girl.

Someone I had grown to know and love—Vita—had given birth to a new baby girl. Her final, wonderful surprise. The last reveal in a series of reveals.

Vita, I felt, or the spirit of Vita, had tried to stop me from coming here and finding the story of her husband, Francesco. But I had persevered and she was revealing all to me now. You want it. Here it is, I heard her whisper to me.

In Italian, naturally.

Eccolo.

No one in my family had ever mentioned a daughter. I wondered if Nunzia looked like Vita, like me or the other girls in my family. As with the previous three sons, Francesco Vena was listed on the birth certificate only as Vita's husband, not the father, and was "away from the city." In prison. Still. As late as 1883.

A daughter. How about that? Vita had a daughter. Born in March, just like me. But why, I wondered, had no one ever mentioned her? And then it hit me.

Nunzia probably hadn't lived for very long.

I reluctantly requested the book of death certificates. And there, that very same year, only two months later, is Nunzia. Another dead baby. I thought of the crib in my Pisticci apartment and dreaded going back there alone.

I wondered if Vita's milk had dried up. Maybe she had tried to feed the baby tainted goat's milk or crushed-up solid food. Or maybe the baby simply caught one of the many diseases circulating through the neighborhood. Maybe Vita had given her a dose of poppies to calm her screaming and had given her too much. There were a hundred ways for a newborn to die in Basilicata in the 1880s.

I scrambled back to the birth certificates and continued to

search, in the hopes there would be another child. And sure enough, two years later, in 1885, another daughter was born, in February. Vita was thirty-three, the same age that her mother was when she had had her.

This second daughter of Vita was also named Nunzia, born on the same street—Eraclea. Vita's husband, Francesco, is again not present for the birth, being "far from the town."

I searched and searched but couldn't find a death certificate for this new Nunzia.

But there was one more surprise, the last one folded inside, waiting for me in that book of the dead. As I searched for Nunzia, I came across an unexpected death certificate. There, on the afternoon before I left Basilicata for the last time.

"Oh my God," I gasped, shaking my head. The clerk looked up from her daze and tilted her head as if to say, "What? What did you find now?"

"My great-great-grandfather, Francesco. His death certificate," I mumbled, still shaking my head. She smiled and went back to staring straight ahead. I'm sure she heard this kind of discovery every day. Of course I couldn't go into the whole explanation of how he wasn't really my great-great-grandfather, the story of the murder, which we had discovered in this very room, Contrada Avella, the courthouse, the prison sentence, Vita's life as a concubine, the dead babies. It was all too much.

I looked closer at the certificate and saw that he had died in 1887 at eight minutes past eight o'clock on the morning of November 28 in Bernalda. He was forty-three years old, fairly old for back then.

One of the witnesses to Francesco's death was a man named Filippo Grieco. Was this our Grieco? Our man? Age thirty-four? Could it be? I traced my finger over his name. Filippo Grieco. In slants and curlicues. Maybe he was my great-great-grandfather. Could he have been there, at his rival's deathbed?

No cause of death was listed. I wondered if heartbreak really could cause someone to die. Or maybe Grieco killed him. Or maybe he died in a card game. Maybe Vita killed him. Or maybe one of the brothers of Antonio Camardo had taken revenge, vendetta.

One thing was certain. This death certificate proved that Francesco did not kill Vita or have her killed in Jersey City.

I was finally ready to leave the dead in peace.

Chapter 35

DEPARTURE IS NOTHING MORE THAN THE BEGINNING OF THE HOMECOMING

NOW IT WAS TIME FOR MY REVENGE.

I headed back to Bernalda to find Miserabila and Leonardantonio, the two who had yelled at me on the street ten years earlier. I wanted to tell them the story they refused to share with me years ago, a story I was sure they knew all about. I had dreamed of this moment for years. It had helped propel me back across the ocean.

I bumped into Leonardantonio on Corso Italia and told him what I had found, the murder file involving Francesco Vena and Leonardantonio Gallitelli—his namesake. He flinched when I told him, but then tried to smile as if he were surprised and pleased. He had been right years ago. This was a Vena murder. Not a Gallitelli murder. He had known all along.

The feeling of revenge wasn't as satisfying as I had thought it would be. Revenge never was.

I went around the corner and easily found Miserabila, who

was sitting outside Maria Natale's house on their small chairs near the corner of Via Cavour. Miserabila's natural frown was turned down an extra notch when she saw me.

I told Maria—and, without acknowledging her, Miserabila—about what I had found, the file containing the murder, the other babies, the whole story. But Miserabila did not respond. Either she didn't understand my bad Italian or she didn't want to give me the satisfaction of seeing her upset. But suddenly I was the one who was upset. Not by her reaction or lack of a reaction. But when I looked at her out of the corner of my eye, I saw a sadness beneath the miserable frown that I had never noticed before. Maybe it had always been there.

This secret, not just the murder but the dishonor that came with Vita's infidelity, had no doubt swirled around her family for decades and brought them disgrace here in Bernalda, had made their lives miserable. My branch of the family had escaped the dishonor. But she and her relatives had to live with this legacy every single day. Why was I throwing it in her face? I wanted to tell her I was sorry, that she shouldn't be ashamed of Vita, that she had done nothing wrong. But I was afraid she would punch me.

Maria hugged me and congratulated me, and told me to return with my husband and family next time. She couldn't wait to see them again.

Neither could I.

I dropped in on Leo and said goodbye and thanked him for picking me up at the station, for all the meals and drinks he'd bought me and for introducing me to Francesco, without whom I might never have found the murder. He gave me a long hug and said, "Next time, don't stay in Pisticci. You stay at my beach house."

I said goodbye to Francesco as well and thanked him for finding the listing for the criminal file in Matera. "I am eternally indebted to you," I said. He smiled his embarrassed smile and looked down at his shoes. "Prego," he repeated over and over. "Prego. Prego." You're welcome.

My trip was almost through, and more than anything—more than gratitude or happiness or the need for revenge—I was feeling overwhelming relief that no more bad luck had befallen me this last week. I would soon be reunited with my own family. My real family. The one that still lived and breathed thousands of miles from here. They seemed like a dream to me now.

The departure is nothing more than the beginning of the homecoming. It was yet another Italian proverb. So true, I thought. So true.

I was going home.

AND SO WAS VITA.

Sometime in 1883 she and her two young sons pulled up in front of 102 Via Eraclea in Bernalda, their mountain of belongings transported by a horse cart belonging to Grieco. The address was just one block away from Miserabila and the apartment where I had lived ten years before this trip.

Vita moved back from Pisticci a conquering hero, with beds for each of the boys and herself to sleep in, with armchairs and tables and shining pots and pans. She was no longer the lowest of the peasants, but now was somebody. The women still gossiped, but they made sure they did it quietly.

The house was bigger than that other house on Via Cavour, even bigger than the one in Pisticci. It was two houses joined, with a second-story window and two steps up, like in Pisticci. The place was on the very edge of town, with a view of the Basento Valley below. A home with a view. She would give birth to her two daughters here.

The street was named for Hercules—Eraclea—which was fitting. Hercules was a hero, but also a God, since he had been born from Zeus and a mortal woman. Like Beansie, he had been a twin, born from a separate sack, from two separate conceptions. And like Beansie, he was not suckled by his own mother, but by another woman.

Hera, Zeus's wife, was tricked into breastfeeding him. Her super-goddess breast milk gave him his legendary strength. He is named after her. But Hercules pulled so hard when suckling that he hurt poor Hera, and when she pulled her nipple away, her breast milk sprayed into the sky and created the Milky Way. Hera later tried to kill Hercules by placing two snakes in his crib. But badass baby Hercules strangled them.

Hercules, part hero, part god, had a life of trial and pain. And I wondered if people in Bernalda knew the stories of the gods and heroes—the same ones that their streets were named after—and if they told them to their children, like I had told them to Dean. Vita probably had no idea that at the climax of Book XI of *The Odyssey*, Odysseus runs into Hercules in Hades. He's the final ghost to speak to Odysseus in hell before he sails away, for home:

> Are you too leading some wretched destiny
> such as I too pursued when I went still in the sunlight?
> For I was son of Kronian Zeus, But I had an endless
> Spell of misery. . . .

I thought of Vita and her endless trials and *miseria* and that final Herculean task of traveling across the ocean, not unlike Odysseus. She would live on Via Eraclea for only a short time, until she would make that final, fateful jump across the Atlantic. Vita was our family heroine, life giver to us all. Like all immigrant families, her pain and vice paved the way for our comfort and virtue. But like most Americans, we had also inherited the restlessness and discontent that had propelled nations across the sea.

A few verses after meeting Hercules, Odysseus sets sail.

And quickly they went aboard the ship. . . .
And the swell of the current carried her down the Ocean
    river
With rowing at first, but after that on a fair wind following.

Chapter 36

LAST SUPPER

EVERYONE IN TOWN KNEW THAT IMMA'S PARENTS, MIMMO and Virginia, were wonderful cooks. Mimmo had a large, round belly, a drooping mustache, and the typical big, brown downturned eyes of Basilicata. Virginia was fit and pretty, with a slight overbite and dark circles under her eyes, probably from all the housework and cooking. With their six-hectare farm in San Basilio, near Giuseppe, they grew many of their own ingredients, putting to shame many of the chefs at the local resorts and fine restaurants. They grew parsley, plums, olives, grain, figs, artichokes, and citrus.

My last night in town, they cooked a farewell dinner for me and invited Giuseppe and his wife, Emanuela, as well as Professor Tataranno and his wife, Carmelina. Imma's father, Mimmo—short for Domenico—was from Pisticci originally, but had settled in Bernalda because his wife, Virginia, was Bernaldese. Here a man usually settled in the hometown of his wife, since the wife's family provided help in raising the children.

Their house was in the newer, more modern quarter of Bernalda. It was three stories high with comfortably plush furniture and a fireplace, over which hung a hundred-year-old copper bed warmer, a *scardalet*, belonging to Mimmo's grandfather from Pisticci. During World War II, the family had had to hide it, since the government was confiscating all copper for the war effort.

Imma was Mimmo and Virginia's only child, and they had poured all their knowledge and every ounce of love and wisdom into her, including their love of food. It was as if Imma's family, and all of the families in Bernalda, were making up for all those meals that their ancestors had never eaten. They had gone hungry for centuries without access to their own land, which was divvied up among the ruling class—the 1.4 percent of the population.

But now things were different. On Christmas Eve, for instance, typical Lucani didn't just have the Feast of the Seven Fishes, like most Italians did. They had thirteen different kinds of fish. Food was abundant, and so they partook, happily, though not greedily, sharing it with whoever showed up on their doorstep.

I was lucky to be standing there.

MIMMO AND VIRGINIA SERVED THEIR OWN YOUNG, FRESH ASPARA-gus and pickled artichokes, which were from the first harvest—*spolverata*—so they were especially tender. I had no idea that fruit trees and vegetables had several flowerings and that the first was usually the best.

They made three kinds of focaccia (one with green onion, another with peppers, and one with tomatoes), an arugula salad with sliced veal and a tangy balsamic dressing, delicately fried zucchini and grilled eggplant, alongside cappacuolo slices laid out like a deck of cards, and six kinds of cheese (ricotta salata, scamorza, provolone, soft, sweet ricotta, salty burrata, and strong, sharp caciocavallo, aged two years). To accompany the cheese was fig jam, which Virginia had made from her own figs. Virginia served a green salad with a magical dressing that she claimed was simply vinegar and oil but couldn't have been just that, sausages that Imma had stuffed herself, and hearty, thick Pisticci bread to swipe our plates when we were done. The bread from Pisticci was better than Bernalda bread, made with a special, natural yeast and baked in a tall oven.

Many of the delicacies were served on beige pottery painted with tiny blue flowers, each like a child's version of a daisy, made of six indigo dots. It was the typical pottery of Basilicata. I had a platter just like it back at home, which I had somehow carried back on the plane with me after my first trip.

Lemon sorbet made by Virginia with lemons from the farm was rich and tangy and served in our prosecco glasses, with some prosecco poured on top. When it was all over, I had a small glass of acidic grappa with Mimmo, to destroy the contents of my stomach.

I toasted everyone during dinner and thanked them for their help and patience with my bad Italian and endless questions. I thanked Giuseppe's wife for lending me her husband, and Imma's parents for letting me spend so much time with their only daughter. And I hugged Professor Tataranno and thanked him for all his knowledge and wisdom.

I raised my glass once more. "To Vita," I said. And they all repeated, "To Vita," our crystal glasses cutting through the warm June air.

For dessert, Virginia made a gorgeous dome-shaped cake soaked in orange juice and covered in cream, paper-thin orange slices, and dark chocolate leaves.

We ate dried figs—*ficchi isechi*—which Virginia had made by picking the figs fresh last September, cutting them and placing them in the sun and covering them with a veil to keep the flies away. When they were ready, she would place an oven-baked almond inside each—like a pit—and then put the whole thing back in the oven. Giuseppe said they were so good "they make the angels cry."

The meal ended with giant fresh figs the size of baseballs, lovely fat apricots from Giuseppe's harvest, and finally perastre—the same kind of pears Francesco had stolen more than a century ago.

I STAYED AT IMMA'S HOUSE THAT NIGHT NOT ONLY BECAUSE I WAS too full to move, but because the two of us were leaving early the next morning on a train for Naples for the last of our research. Imma's mother had offered to drive us to the station, and I didn't want her to have to go all the way to Pisticci to fetch me in the morning. And besides, I didn't want to spend one more night alone with that empty crib, even if it was covered with a sheet.

We left for Naples right after sunrise, with a big paper bag filled with leftover focaccia and panini made from the cappacuolo and scamorza from last night's table, two giant bottles of water, and a half dozen of those sweet, small pears. Imma rolled her eyes when her mother handed her the heavy bag. "She thinks we're going to Madagascar," Imma joked. Our train ride was only three hours.

We traveled on the same train line that Vita and her children would have taken. The line from Naples to Potenza was laid down in 1882, and ten years later, just in time for Vita's voyage, the tracks from Metaponto to Potenza were complete.

When Vita left for America in 1892, Francesco was buried in the local cemetery and was no longer a threat. But Basilicata still was. By the time Vita left, the entire country was in the grips of a great depression.

That year, a quarter million Italians emigrated. And it wasn't even the peak. In 1913, nearly 900,000 left their homeland, each one with a story as sad and as incredible as my great-great-grandmother's.

Chapter 37

GET ON THE TRAIN!

V ALENTE WAS THE FIRST TO GO. HE BOOKED PASSAGE THAT
April on the *Burgundia,* a ten-year-old ship with three
masts and one funnel. It picked up its first load in Naples,
then stopped in Marseilles for its second, and more than a week
later, arrived in New York Harbor.

He set up a place for them to stay in the town of Giesity. That's
how he spelled it, this Jersey City, this far-off land of riches where
a *compare*—a family friend—lived. (In Jersey City we pronounced it
"gumba.") A whole community of Bernaldans had settled down-
town, many who probably knew the Vena-Gallitelli murder story,
who knew that Vita was a kept woman. Her reputation, no doubt,
preceded her to the New World.

Grieco, maybe this Filippo Grieco, gave them the money to
go, two lire each for the passport, and then two hundred to three
hundred lire each for passage, the cost of three or four houses, a
huge amount for a peasant family to scrape together.

Even those with the means to leave sold off all the family

jewelry to pay their way. Some were so desperate they traveled as stowaways.

That following September, five months after fifteen-year-old Valente sailed, Vita left Bernalda with thirteen-year-old Leonardo and Nunzia, who would have just turned seven. Nunzia, with missing front teeth and long, stringy, uncombed dark hair like mine at that age, was excited but a little scared of the voyage ahead.

It would be quite a journey for a little girl. For all of them, really. They had never been farther than Pisticci, so they had no idea what they were in for.

I like to think that Grieco gave them a ride to Metaponto and its brand-new train station in his horse and carriage so they didn't have to walk and drag their baggage to the coast.

Vita could smell it first, the salt settling in her nostrils. And then, there it was. After living so close to the sea for so long, Vita saw its sandy beaches and waves for the first time in her forty-one years on earth.

It seemed like the waves might hurt if you touched them, like jagged white teeth on some giant monster, churning and chomping angrily. Nunzia huddled against her mother in fear. How on earth would she ever be able to get on a ship?

The sea went on for what seemed like infinity, meeting and matching the cloudless blue Ionian sky in its enormity. So big, so powerful that it scared not only Nunzia, but Vita. It could easily suck them up and spit them out.

Grieco said goodbye at the station. But Vita decided suddenly that she didn't want to go after all. She was too frightened, too anxious. What if America wasn't what they said? What if it was a lie?

Grieco held her for a moment and kissed her gently and told her there was nothing to worry about, as the locomotive pulled up to the platform. "Just get on the train," he said. "Get on the train!"

And so she did. She got on the train, for the long ride to Naples.

THEY BOARDED THE THIRD-CLASS COMPARTMENT WITH A COUPLE of sacks, one with a bit of bread, maybe some small pears. Vita sat on the hard wooden seat by the window, with Nunzia on her soft lap, Leonardo by her side, and watched Grieco and the world they knew, the lonely landscape of home, slowly fall away.

The first stop on the train was Ferrandina, where the killing had happened. Vita was happy to see it pass by her window for good. *Vaffanculo,* Ferrandina, she probably thought. Good riddance.

Tiny, mumlike yellow wildflowers lined the tracks between the stations. Vita didn't realize that one day soon she'd miss them. And the sheep in the distance past the town of Baragiano, a pastoral scene she would never see in Jersey City. How could she know that mountains and fig trees and shepherds would be replaced with factories and smokestacks and cops walking the beat?

The sheer cliff face rose up near Bella-Muro, which meant Beautiful Wall. And it was, this cliff, it was beautiful, as was the stream that flowed at its base, filled with chalky rocks and boulders, a landscape Vita had taken for granted.

They watched the craggy Lucanian Dolomites rise like giants in the distance, and made their way past bare-faced hills and tall cypress trees. They passed through Eboli, the place where Christ had stopped in Carlo Levi's book, where civilization ended. But Levi hadn't even been born yet, much less passed through here and written his masterpiece. In Torricchio, the train snaked through pointed pine-covered mountains and dipped into low, green valleys. They sped through forests where brigands had once hid out and stashed their kidnapping victims. Where treasure was said to be buried.

After about ten hours, after what seemed like 1,001 stops at every coastal village along the way, Naples appeared in the distance, announced loudly by blue Vesuvio, its top covered in wispy white clouds. Was it smoking? she wondered, fearfully. But its clouded peak was quickly forgotten as she stepped off the train into the city.

What a circus. It was churning with madness, with toothless beggars begging and train conductors in blue uniforms shouting and carabinieri in capes and mustaches giving orders and the big, shining duomo in the distance and palm trees and the manicured park and the horses and buggies with their drivers in tall hats. It was too much to take in all at once, and Vita feared she would fall into one of those stress-induced states, where everything would go numb and she would cease to function. But she held it together. She squeezed Nunzia's hand so tight the girl cried out as they marched into the madness, my young great-grandfather Leonardo happily, bravely leading the charge.

This was their first lesson, a good lesson, to prepare them for the insanity of the New World.

She and the children asked the conductor which way, which way to the harbor and he pointed. But it wasn't necessary. Half the train's passengers scrambled to the same spot, through the grand arches of the train station, under its stone balconies and giant clock. Vita was just one of 61,631 Italian immigrants to travel to the United States that year.

They made their way like a river of bodies day after day through the crowded streets, past tall buildings, five, six, seven stories high, with French-style wrought-iron balconies covered in laundry, shirts and skirts and underwear strung across side streets where the buildings nearly touched one another. So much laundry. So many people. How could so many people live in one place? A half-million people.

Vita and her children walked the two and a half miles to the harbor, past Garibaldi Square, now with the big statue of the hero in his caped uniform, leaning on his sword. They made their way past the curved square known as the Four Palaces, whose build-ings were held up by giant men made of stone. Vita had never seen anything like them. They looked so real she expected them to break free and come down and speak to her, to point the way to the port. Most spectacular of all, though, was the newly built, 22 million lire Galleria Umberto I, the long glass and metal-ribbed wonder, with its huge dome and four offshoots, the whole building shaped like a giant cross. It ran 160 yards from Naples's main street—the Toledo—all the way to city hall. Massive angels, wings spread, floated just below the glass ceiling, five stories high. How did they not fall and come crashing down on their heads? How they floated up there, like real angels!

And just when Vita thought she could never glimpse anything more wonderful than that, they arrived at the port, the beauty so intense it caught her breath. Too beautiful to describe really, with the blue island of Capri floating like a big slipper in the distance, and the green island of Ischia, and the great rocky castle at the water's edge. At sunset, the islands turned purple and the houses at the foot of the mountains blazed orange in the dying light. It was so gorgeous, tough little Vita nearly cried.

Italy had been cruel to her and her family. To everyone she had ever known. But this, this was the cruelest of all, seeing the most beautiful scene ever before leaving it for good. See Naples and die, went the saying. And now she understood it.

Italy was like a lover who was so gorgeous, he could mistreat you whenever he liked. But a woman could take only so much. Vita would leave and not look back.

And now there was a new lover, America, more beautiful and much kinder. At least that's what she'd heard.

Though Vita had no idea what to expect, exciting things were happening in America that year. Not all of them good. Labor strikes had broken out that summer, including the Homestead Strike among Pennsylvania's steelworkers, in which ten men were killed. In Wyoming, farmers were going up against the big ranchers in the Johnson County War. And in Oklahoma, a hundred men—mostly Italian immigrants—would die in a mine explosion. When some black men tried to help rescue the survivors, they were threatened with rifles.

But in Vita's future home state of New Jersey, John Philip Sousa's band was making its debut with its patriotic marches. The first American-made car was taken out for a test drive. And the Pledge of Allegiance, written over the summer by a Baptist minister, was published for the first time and would be recited by millions of schoolchildren in a few weeks, that following Columbus Day, words that no one had memorized just yet. They were like the words to a new prayer that the immigrants wanted badly to believe were true.

> . . . One nation,
> Indivisible,
> With liberty and justice
> For all

Vita and her children spent one final night in Naples, sleeping on the cobblestones like most of the other emigrants set to leave the next day. The shipping companies wouldn't provide boardinghouses for emigrants until 1901, and then not because they cared about them, but because the hordes were spreading disease. The twelve companies were required to board the emigrants one day prior to shipping. If the ship was delayed, they had to house them until they sailed, and give them a forty-cent stipend for the day for food and drink.

But not yet. Not in 1892. Bed was the cobblestone street, just like in Bernalda each summer. Vita didn't mind.

A canteen near the harbor served food: soup, boiled meat, potatoes, bread, even beer for twenty-five cents each, though the prices varied depending on how rich you looked and how good you were at negotiating. But Vita was saving her money for America. She fed the children the scraps of bread that she had brought along in her bag on the train ride, and they drank the fresh water sprouting from the local fountains. So many fountains. So much fresh water for the taking.

Vita slept on top of their bags all night, with her daughter tucked under her arm for safekeeping. It was a fitful sleep. When Nunzia awoke, Vita lulled her back to sleep with the song her own mother used to sing to her when she was little, "Ninna Nanna."

> Oh, my little sheep
> What did you do
> When you saw yourself in the mouth of the wolf,
> Who ate the skin and who ate the wool?
> Poor little sheep how it screamed.
> Sleep, my sweet friend
> sleep for a long time
> and don't make me suffer.

Vita watched her daughter gently close her eyes but stayed up most of the night herself. She was worried they would miss their morning call at Molo dell'Immacolatella Vecchia, the slip from which their ship, the *Neustria*, was sailing.

The *Neustria* had room for only eighteen first-class passengers, since hardly anyone fancy ever took her to America. It had been built a decade earlier by the French Fabre Line with a total of 1,100 third-class berths, a workhorse of a ship, meant to accommodate poor emigrants like Vita. It was caught between two eras, with a single black funnel for its steam engine and two masts for sails. The bow was a straight line cutting the ocean, the stern a graceful curve. The *Neustria* would disappear somewhere in the Atlantic in 1908, going down with its crew and its human cargo, but for now it was seaworthy.

VITA AND HER CHILDREN WENT TO THE AGENT'S OFFICE FOR THE shipping company early the next morning to pay the balance of their fare. Vita gave their names, ages, jobs, country of origin, marital status (widow, said Vita), the address where they last lived in Basilicata, the address of where they were headed in America, the names of those waiting for them, the name and address of a relative left behind, the amount of money they were carrying, and whether they had been to America before. No one asked any questions about your past, your mental state, or your morals. The officials on this side of the Atlantic were anxious to be rid of Vita and her kind.

In order to embark, each traveler had to endure certain trials, most within the confines of the harbor compound, or *capitaneria*.

Vita and her children and what little baggage they had were loaded onto a small steam launch and taken across the harbor to the fumigation station, where they and everything they owned were deloused. Their bags, clothes, and any inanimate belongings were steamed at a high temperature, killing any bugs they might have met on the streets of Naples or that took the long ride with them from Metaponto.

They were then separated by sex, and made to strip and wash with a strong mix of soap and kerosene. If bugs were found, they were shaved of all hair—head, pubic, chest, and face—if there was any hair to be shaved. Both Italian and American officials did a final inspection to make sure all the bugs were gone and then issued certificates attesting to the fact.

At this point, no one was allowed to return to the streets of Naples. Vita and her children were transferred to the clean part of the *capitaneria*, to the medical center, where they formed two lines.

Doctors on one line checked heads and skin for scabies (infectious mites also known as the seven-year itch), seborrhea (a white scaly rash), eczema, ringworm, and favus, a widespread honeycombed scalp fungus. The doctor on the second line turned up eyelids for trachoma, the leading cause for being turned back. Trachoma, incredibly widespread at the time, was a highly contagious bacterial eye infection that could cause blindness if not treated.

Doctors prodded and poked any strange-looking parts of the emigrants' bodies for disease. Rejects were whisked from the *capitaneria*.

Rumor had it that the inspection ordeal on the other end—at newly opened Ellis Island—was much worse, and much more stringent, so much so that part of Vita dreaded landing in America, for fear she would be sent back home.

Those not eliminated from the line were vaccinated for smallpox at the expense of the shipping company. Passengers proudly bore a large scar marking each of their upper arms, the sign they had been admitted into the elite ranks of the *emigranti*.

If all went well in Naples—and even if it didn't, since bribes were common—documents were checked before boarding. Most emigrants didn't have passports, but rather a work book showing their employment history with a blurry seal. Vita nervously handed hers over. But she was waved through and permitted up the gangway, where there was one final check: one last trachoma and favus inspection. Healthy people had been known to stand in for the diseased, have their card stamped, and then pass it on to the sick person. But there were no substitutions with this final check right before boarding,

And last, but not least, this is the place where weapons—mostly knives—were taken from all those passengers who were carrying them. Vita argued that her knife was only used to cut pears and other fruit for the children but she finally relented and handed it over.

Chapter 38

COUNT YOUR NIGHTS
BY STARS, NOT SHADOWS

THE *NEUSTRIA* SLOWLY PULLED AWAY FROM THE PIER AND into the harbor. The red port buildings, Castel Nuovo, and the glass dome of the Galleria grew miniature in minutes, but the wind and the smell of the sea, the salt air, grew stronger. As the ship gained speed and passed the long black jetty, Vesuvio rose up, getting bigger and closer. Seagulls circled as they passed buoy after buoy, the red lighthouse, other ships riding at anchor.

Most of the passengers shoved their way to the upper deck to watch their country shrink in the distance. And so Vita went with her son and daughter to say a final goodbye to Italy's beautiful face. A final *vaffanculo*.

Capri began to fade. The water was a deep sapphire with whitecaps, the spray hitting the faces of those nearest the railing. Soon the houses on the mainland thinned out, replaced by rocky cliffs and patches of green. Eventually Vesuvio and the coast blended into one single mountainscape beyond the stern.

The *Neustria* slipped past the pastel houses of Procida Island

and the Palazzo d'Avalos; Ischia and its volcano, Mount Epomeo, with its silent crater up top; and small volcanic islands whose names Vita didn't know. Nunzia counted the castles hanging near the edges of earth, so many castles, Castel dell'Ovo, Castel Sant'Elmo, and Castello Aragonese, in front of Ischia. They had been built centuries ago to scare invaders. But now they were growing smaller, like toy castles in the distance, no longer large and imposing, no longer threatening.

The hills grew greener, the houses fewer and fewer until all Vita and her children could see was blue. Blue sea. Blue sky, a gentle blue like the color of Mary's veil at the Chiesa Madre. Everything Vita ever knew, fading, fading, not just the landscape, but the memory of it all. The murder, the lover, the dead babies, and Rocco cradled in her arms. All of it. Fading fast.

THE PASSENGERS RETREATED TO THEIR QUARTERS, WHICH WERE divided into three classes: women traveling alone, men traveling alone, and families. Vita was allowed to stay with Nunzia, but Leonardo was on his own since he was thirteen, already a man.

Men made up nearly 80 percent of the immigrant population coming from Italy. Women almost never traveled alone.

The sleeping quarters were barely lit and cramped, with as many as three hundred people to each. The six-by-two-foot berths, with two and a half feet of headroom, were packed tightly in two tiers. Each iron bed frame contained a lumpy mattress filled with either straw or seaweed, covered in coarse canvas, a life preserver for a pillow, and a small, thin blanket, which wasn't nearly enough for the chilly September nights at sea.

Vita and most of the other passengers went to bed fully clothed, sometimes wearing everything they'd brought, since there was no room in the berth for bags. You wore it or slept on top of it or hung your clothes like drapes from your berth, which was the wisest option since crew members came and went as they pleased, barging right through the women's bunk areas in the morning, just when the women were dressing or undressing. Washrooms were above deck and less open to shifty porters.

A law passed ten years earlier barred the crew from the passenger compartments, but no one really paid much attention to it, since many of the passengers couldn't read the postings placed on the walls. When a crewman entered the women's compartment, he would gawk at those dressing and undressing and sometimes even cop a feel. Some women fought back. But the commotion just blended into the general din of steerage.

The Italian men played lotto and shouted at one another. One man played his violin. Children laughed. Babies cried, their mothers pushing them toward withering breasts.

Passengers of different sexes could mingle by day, usually fighting for space above deck, trying to take in a few rays of the precious sun, the lovely sun that they had all abandoned in Southern Italy.

They sat amid all the machinery that crowded the deck, the cables, winches, spare masts, and curving air intakes, because there were no chairs or benches. Some were lucky to scam a coveted spot on the cover of the cargo hold, spreading a shawl or jacket to claim the space as their own. A steady snowfall of cinders from the black funnel floated down onto Vita's kerchiefed head and into her children's eyes.

The crew was allowed to mingle with passengers on deck, cursing and making inappropriate comments to the women, sometimes touching or fondling them. But if anyone tried to touch Vita or her daughter, she would not hesitate to punch him.

Women wouldn't dare venture out on deck at night, though some men, like Leonardo, did, to breathe the fresh salt air, and wonder at the phosphorescent wake, the sky salted with stars and the glowing Milky Way, that last vestige of Hera's squirting breast milk. "Count your nights by stars, not shadows," went the Italian saying. And Leonardo did. Though there were too many stars, really, to count.

The sea was a vast void of nothingness by night, until the moon rose. The voyage to America was so long, some watched the moon wax through a third of its cycle, growing like the belly of a pregnant woman. Its milky light was reflected on the ink-black water. At 10 P.M. the deck was hosed down, forcing everyone down for the night.

Vita was already inside, and sat with her youngest snuggled up against her, keeping her warm between her chest and her armpit, singing songs or telling her stories to pass the long hours. She told her all about Francesco and the murder, though Nunzia had heard this story dozens of times and could practically recite it. The stolen pears, the young man with the gun, the fight, the prison sentence. Vita sang to Nunzia. She sang a version of the song, "Canto di Carcerato," that she had learned years ago after the murder and would cry herself to sleep with on those long nights when Francesco first went away.

> See what in town they all are saying of me
> And see if my affair is growing quiet
> For then, if God so willing as I am praying
> My longing eye for freedom soon will spy it.

Vita would sing her daughter "Ninna Nanna" to put her to sleep on the rocking ship. And when she was sure Nunzia was asleep, when no one else in the world was watching, Vita would finally cry, those pent-up tears spilling out finally, tears for her three dead babies and for Grieco and for her long-lost love, Francesco.

WHEN THE SUN ROSE, BEFORE MOST OF THE OTHER PASSENGERS were awake, Vita would set Nunzia free, let her run around on deck so that she could stretch her young legs. Little children, even girls, were like young goats or sheep. They needed space to roam and grow.

When they first boarded the ship, Vita and her children were each handed a metal fork, a spoon, a cup, and one tin dish for all their meals, which they had to store in their berth somewhere and had to somehow clean in the scarce fresh water on board. Water here was nearly as rare as back home in Basilicata, and because of the new layout, much harder to find. It seemed ridiculous, with those miles and miles of rolling waves out there. No towels were provided. Passengers used clothing or their blankets to dry their dishes.

The wooden floors below deck were never washed on the voyage, only occasionally swept. No sick bags or buckets or trash cans for waste. Fruit pits, fish bones, nail clippings, eggshells, apple cores, wrappers, cigarette butts, orange peels, and other garbage sat for hours or sometimes days.

Vomit stayed on the floorboards for hours, soaking into the wood, the stench remaining the entire trip. Which led to more vomiting. A few conscientious crew members sprinkled a bit of sand on top.

When it rained, everyone stayed inside their berths, which were wet from the rainwater coming through the hatchways and leaking from the ceilings. With the roiling, rolling sea, seasickness was widespread, and without proper ventilation, those suffering didn't stand a chance to recover.

Only on the day the voyage ended were the toilets and washroom floors finally cleaned with disinfectant to pass inspection. But not before then.

The only good places to throw up were overboard and into the washbasins in the washroom. But those basins were also used to bathe, wash your dirty dishes and utensils, do your laundry, and shampoo your head, if you could stand it in that dirty, nasty basin.

There weren't enough basins for so many people, only ten basins per washroom.

Simple wooden benches were placed in the passageway between sleeping compartments to serve as a dining room. Passengers lined up in a single file in front of four stewards handing out rations. Breakfast at 7 A.M. was easiest, since it was only coffee and a few hard biscuits, keeping with Italian tradition. The other meals, served at noon and at 6 P.M., were slightly more elaborate.

When the bell rang, stewards ladled out the soup, limp vegetables, leathery, smelly meat, or pasta—often pasta, or what the steamship company liked to call pasta. Any fruit was of the poorest quality, the bruised, sad remnants from the bottom of the barrel, literally. Children and infants were served condensed milk.

The food was so bad that some of these people—these starving people who had gleaned in empty fields for wild roots and herbs—wound up throwing more than half their meal overboard. Most lived on coffee and bread, which was stale and sometimes moldy, but at least not rancid.

Some of the smarter passengers, with time and money to plan ahead, had brought their own rations—fruit, some fresh bread, scamorza, or homemade soppressata—the likes of which no Italian on board would see again for a very long time. Maybe a lifetime.

A bar served fruit for three cents apiece, candy, and drinks, though hardly anyone had any money for that.

Vita and her children learned to scramble for their food, as bad as it was, and as quickly as possible, since once it was gone, it was gone, just like back at home in Basilicata, with that big plate in the middle of the table. You had to be fast, or else you went hungry. You also had to hightail it to the washroom, to get a spot at the single warm spigot, to get your dishes clean. Leonardo simply licked his clean, then placed it under his pillow, his life preserver.

Chapter 39

COME HERE

VITA WAS ANNOYED. SHE CALLED THE GIRL AND SHE DIDN'T answer. "Nunzia," she bellowed, like she would in Bernalda just before dinner or at the start of the hot hour, when it was time for all children to come inside.

Nunzia had been playing on deck, but Vita lost sight of her. "Nunzia!"

She took a deep breath and yelled again, "Nunzia!" She searched the deck, calling, calling her daughter's name. She searched below deck. Calling, calling.

But after ten, fifteen, twenty minutes, which then turned into a half hour, the panic started to rise like high tide inside Vita's chest. "Nunzia!" she screamed, with more urgency, her throat becoming soar. "Nunzia, vena qua."

Vita again searched the upper deck, back down to steerage, in and around their berth, and back up again, pushing people out of the way as she called, "Nunzia, Nunzia!"

Vita tore at her clothes and her hair as she frantically searched, then wrapped her arms around her chest, rocking back and forth and feeling the imprint of Nunzia there between her chest and her armpit, where she had been, safe, only a few hours before. Vita would get lost herself, between decks, with her bad sense of direction, searching, searching for her daughter. She looked over into the waves, wanting, but not wanting at the same time, to find her daughter there, floating away from the ship. Could she have survived a fall? But she was not there.

Vita wrung her small, pretty hands, her dark eyes brimming over. Have you seen my daughter? Have you seen my Nunzia? The terror rising, rising in her chest.

Young Leonardo heard his mother's shouts and came running. He searched and searched for his little sister, too, running between decks, looking in the same crawl spaces, three, four, five times, the ship growing ever closer to its destination, him running his hand frantically through his thick black hair. Eventually crying, shouting through his tears, "Nunzia! Nunzia! Where are you?"

When I find her, he thought, she'll get the beating of her life. How could you worry Mama like that? How could you worry me? He imagined chastising her when he finally found her. If he finally found her. But he knew he would hug her first. He was a good big brother, an adoring big brother, a protective big brother. How could he have let this happen?

Vita grew more and more worried, and then hysterical, slipping into one of those immobile states, the trauma too much. Then the ship-wide search, halfheartedly done by the weary crew, as the *Neustria* pulled into New York Harbor, the Statue of Liberty not a welcoming face, but a sign that Vita would have to leave the ship finally without Nunzia beside her. Without her only daughter. Without her small hand in hers.

There's thirteen-year-old Leonardo crying, too, but lifting his mother up off the floorboards of the deck and dragging her away, onto the gangplank. But her resisting, screaming Nunzia's name, swearing it was all her fault, payback for what she had done back in Pisticci. Payback for her sins. For taking up with another man while her husband was in prison. It was her penance. The price she would pay. Another child, lost. Gone like Domenico and poor Rocco and the first Nunzia. The score etched on Vita's heart was no longer three dead and three living. There was only a 50 percent chance of survival before the age of five in Basilicata. Vita had thought she had beaten the odds with seven-year-old Nunzia. But now she was gone, too.

Vita's shrieks died down to sobs and eventually to moans and then silent heaving as Leonardo carried her from the *Neustria*.

Leonardo would whisper through his own tears. Quiet, Mama. You still have me. And Valente. Valente is waiting.

And so she would stop. Vita would stop screaming her daughter's name, a name not found on the passenger arrival list for 1892, a name completely forgotten by her family for the next century, until it was found again deep in the archives of the dusty province of Matera at the instep of Italy's boot.

Chapter 40

SEE NAPLES AND DIE

I HAD TRAVELED ALL OVER THE WORLD IN MY HALF CENTURY ON earth and had seen quite a few sights: Hong Kong's harbor with its roar of construction and thousands of man-made lights, the pyramids perched on the edge of the desert as the evening call to prayer was shouted from Cairo's minarets, the view of blue Diamond Head from Waikiki at dusk, Venice by night as an orchestra played in Piazza San Marco. I had watched the sun rise over the red rooftops in Vienna, climbed a castle to get a good view of the bullfight below in a small village in Spain, visited the Eiffel Tower with my two children, drank Mekhong whiskey at night on the beach in Ko Chang, Thailand, with my husband, danced on the frozen Bering Sea, and had driven clear across my own beautiful country, through its prairies, badlands, and mountains. I witnessed the wonder of New York City pretty much every day of my adult life; I walked most of its streets and had seen it from a blimp and a helicopter and from countless planes, trains, and cars. On this last trip, almost home, I would take a ride on the back of a friend's motorcycle through Rome. All thanks to Vita, who had come to America and had given me—and my family—the chance at a charmed life.

But all those things I had seen and done, they all paled in comparison to the Bay of Naples, the place where my great-great-grandmother had started over, for all of us.

That's how beautiful Naples was to me at sunset—its violet waters tranquil, Capri whispering, the thousands of tiny houses aflame with orange light, and Vesuvio calmly looking down on it all like a patient mother. See Naples and die, the saying went. But I would see Naples and live. And so would Vita.

I had written thousands of stories in my lifetime, as a newspaper reporter, magazine writer, and author. But none of those stories compared to Vita's life story. The *miseria,* the dead babies, the living babies, the murder, the trip to and then from Naples. She hadn't written about others' adventures, but had lived her own, which gave way to ours. She and all those millions of immigrants—your family included—who had come to make their lives and the lives of their children better.

The mothers, the grandmothers, the great-grandmothers, and the great-greats were the unsung champions who had cooked and cleaned and washed mountains of laundry and fed and taught and nursed us back to health decade after decade, pushing each generation forward, not out of self-interest or personal gratification, but out of love.

They were the true heroes. Not victims, but victors. Forget Odysseus and Hercules and the rest. Forget Zeus and Hera and the other gods and goddesses.

Vita had changed her destiny and ours. And I wondered suddenly if it mattered who my great-great-grandfather was and whether there had ever been a warrior gene in my family. Vita had helped make our lives what they would become, by sheer force of will.

IMMA AND I SPENT TWO DAYS SEARCHING NAPLES' ARCHIVES FOR newspapers from the time of the murder. But we had no luck. I decided, finally, that our research was done. It was time to have some fun.

We ate a wonderful dinner at a place in the Latin Quarter called Hosteria Toledo. I didn't feel guilty, like I usually would have, thinking of Vita's hard life. I knew if she had been here she would have toasted me with some *primitivo* wine and told me to enjoy every damn bite.

A family of four flew past us on a moped as we ate, mother, father, infant, and toddler, none of them wearing helmets. People had told me to avoid Naples, that I would hate it. But I loved it. The excitement of it, the charge in the air, the feeling of life swirling all around you and threatening to eat you alive. Maybe it was the wine. Or maybe it was me, Vita's spirit rising in me. I really adored it here. Though I guarded my wallet carefully.

The next morning we visited the veiled Christ, a delicate sculpture that seemed to be made of cloth, which was just down the street from our *pensione*. We ate pizza that was so good it was worth waiting ninety minutes in a cramped crowd, nearly getting run down by motorcycles. And drank pink Campari Spritzes as we sat outside in the neighborhood.

As we walked the narrow, crowded streets, we looked into the open living rooms of Naples's citizens, freely displaying the details of their lives like the characters in some dramatic play. More than once, I saw a mother and her teenage daughter, clearly pregnant, screaming and flailing arms and making obscene hand gestures at one another, all right in front of us, the gray-haired grandmother joining in with a curse every now and then.

We saw rats. And miles of laundry. And piles and piles of garbage. We watched women go by dressed in short-short black netted skirts barely covering their thongs, their breasts spilling out of their skintight tank tops, their heels spiked, their hair elabo-

278 - Helene Stapinski

rately teased, and their makeup bold and garish over unnatural orange salon tans.

"We call these coarse women of Naples *vrenzole*," Imma explained, like an anthropologist. "They're not prostitutes. It's just the way they dress. The male equivalent are called *cuozzi*." She pointed a few out to me. They wore their hair gelled or with their initials shaven into the backs of their heads, their jeans tight and riding low, and their shirts unbuttoned halfway down to their stomachs, silver chains adorning their orange-tanned chests. "Wow," was all I could muster as they loped past us, chewing gum and talking loudly.

On the way back to our *pensione*, I watched the city fly by from the taxi window, my head swimming from Campari and prosecco. Crowds of young people laughing, couples kissing, mopeds whizzing. Our driver, like most of Naples's drivers, was an older man, with white hair and a quick smile, happy to have two women in the backseat of his cab. Shouting over the loud chatter of the dispatcher on his radio, he made small talk with us, about what we'd seen and where we were headed.

We hopped out of the cab at our corner. After three or four beats, I felt for my cell phone and realized—with panic—that I had left it on the backseat of the taxi. "My phone!" I shouted to Imma and then promptly took off running after the small white cab, which was at the top of the block, stopping for traffic, its red taillights lit.

"Fermata! Fermata!" I shouted. "Stop! Stop! Mi telefono! My telephone is in that taxi!" People on the street stopped and looked at the crazy American woman speaking her own incomprehensible dialect.

I chased the cab several blocks, my flip-flops nearly flying off on the wet, grimy cobblestone streets. I wished I was wearing my sneakers. But it wouldn't have mattered. The cab was much too fast for me, its lights shrinking street by street. I heaved for breath, sorry I had smoked several Chesterfields that weekend with Imma.

Finally I stopped and put my hands on my thighs and bent over, gasping for air. I looked up and watched the taxi's distant taillights disappear around a corner into the chaos of Naples.

I was slightly dizzy, not just from lack of oxygen, but from the alcohol. I was tipsy, and had no one but myself to blame for my lost phone. Not the ghost of Vita or Miserabila. No *zingare*. There were no curses. Only bad luck we made for ourselves.

Imma was waiting for me on the street back near the *pensione*. She was talking to a police officer, who shrugged and said that aside from calling the phone, he could do nothing. Imma had been calling my number for the past ten minutes. The radio dispatcher was no doubt too loud for the driver to hear the incessant ring.

It rang and rang. Until, after about fifteen minutes, it didn't ring anymore. It was powered off. Someone had found it on the seat and had taken it, naturally. What did I expect from Naples?

But what was a lost phone compared with a lost child? How lucky was I to have only lost a phone?

I was experiencing perspective. The perspective of the blessed. I lived a blessed life. A charmed life, all because of Vita. I said a small prayer in my head, not to the saints or to Jesus or the Virgin Mary or the gods. But to Vita, to thank her for the life I had.

UPSTAIRS IN MY ROOM—MY MODERN, COMFORTABLE ROOM WITH ITS balcony and refrigerator and snacks and bottled water—I emailed my husband from my computer. I told him the phone was lost but that I would see him, and Dean and Paulina and my mother, the next day after my nine-hour flight. What was nine hours compared with ten days on a ship, throwing up without a bucket?

I realized not only that I had perspective, but that my perception of myself and my whole family and world had changed. I thought back on the story of the cave, not the ones here in Matera, or the Crypt of the Original Sin, but the one that Plato had written about. The Allegory of the Cave. I had been so young when I'd first read that. And so wrong.

The facts and the reality I thought I knew about myself and my family were, like those shadows on Plato's cave wall, all a substitute for the truth—the reality that I had dug up in Matera. The reality that was Vita and Francesco.

I had had it all wrong. The murder genes. The card game. The lost son, who had turned out to be a daughter. I wasn't even the person I thought I was, fighting off that defective DNA all these years. My perception was forever altered.

For decades I thought I had been outside the cave, one of the lucky ones, but I had been a prisoner—like Francesco—all along, gazing at the shadows of what I perceived to be the truth on the cave wall.

I was lucky to be at the mouth of the cave now, the darkness finally passed, squinting into the sunlight.

Epilogue

V ITA LAY DYING.

It was a stupid way to go, she must have thought, lying in that bed in Jersey City with a bandage on her head,
sixty-four years old, ancient by Basilicata standards. White hair,
prolapsed uterus, no teeth from malnutrition and too little den-
tal care. And all that hard Italian bread she'd eaten over the
years.

Vita Gallitelli, like all the women from Italy, would die with
her maiden name still intact. It was too hard to change your name
legally in Italy, too much bureaucracy and red tape, too much a
pain in the ass, so women simply kept their own names. It had
nothing to do with feminism or independence, only convenience.

So here she was, Vita Gallitelli, the life slowly draining from
her small, birdlike body. Tragic. Senseless, too, this death. There
was an American saying: What goes around comes around. And
maybe Vita thought it while she lay there for eleven days, linger-
ing, sleeping and then waking enough to remember it all. Not just

this tragedy, but the others, the ones that came before. Soon she'd be dead, just like all those bodies she left behind in Southern Italy.

You could run, but the past would catch you soon enough and kick you in the ass when you weren't looking. That wasn't a saying in America, but maybe it should be.

If only she hadn't lost her temper again, she wouldn't be lying here on the verge of extinction. And all because of her big friggin' mouth. You'd think after sixty-four years she would have learned her lesson. That big mouth, as big and wide open as a cave.

Vita could see the scene over and over, unable to go back and sweep it away. She could see the murder back in Italy in her head, though the facts were getting clouded, had been for the past twenty years, as if the sandy African sirocco wind that blew through her Italian town were blowing through her head right now. What she could see more clearly was her own death now, and the faces of her would-be killers, from just the other day.

It was Mischief Night, 1915, and the boys in the neighborhood had been nasty, swinging their flour-filled socks at each other, at the horses and their carts, at the poor rag man, that poor, pathetic rag man. What kind of holiday was Mischief Night? Just an excuse to be an idiot, that's all.

Mischief Night and what they called Halloween here in America were like Carnevale back in Italy—that springtime Bacchanalia when the pagan spirit of the land was resurrected, Christianity forgotten for a few hours, when people dressed up and went wild in the streets, when the *streghe*, or witches, came out, when the werewolves howled in the woods and really scared the hell out of you. Some people dressed as ghosts in white robes, brandishing sticks and threatening to hit anyone who got in their way. Vita did not miss it one bit. But now she had Mischief Night to contend with.

This year, Mischief Night was even more awful than usual,

since it fell on a Saturday night. They were all out late, even the good kids, the ones who hadn't dropped out of school.

To make things even worse, Mischief Night in America always coincided with election week. And in Jersey City, that meant trouble. The boys in the neighborhood would scavenge for wood for weeks beforehand to prepare for their big election night bonfire. They tore down wooden fences, pulled old doors off their hinges from brick row houses, stole people's chairs from in front of their clapboard homes and brownstone stoops, and swiped the brooms left in hallways. Some kids even went so far as to take the wooden wagons from the horse carts down at the castor oil company stables and throw them on the fire. They would steal Vita's broom and her chair but had no idea of the wrath that would follow.

Election night, they would pile all the wood up and set it ablaze in the center of Bay Street, right around the corner from Vita's twelve-dollar-a-month apartment on Grove Street, which she shared with her son, Valente, his sweet wife, Maria, and their big brood of kids. The bonfire was twenty feet high, easy, the dark smoke dancing up and meeting the dirty industrial air, which drifted down, down from the nearby coffee factory and cigarette factory and condom factory. All that dirt and ash mingling and making it hard to breathe.

No one said a word to these boys. They let them steal the chairs and the brooms and the horse carts and set fires and smack each other with their flour-filled socks. Some socks were filled with worse. Horseshit. Or coal. Or rocks. Yeah, rocks, even. Like the brigands used to brandish in the hills of Basilicata, swinging them over their heads during their raids.

At least no one was throwing eggs. People in Jersey City were too poor still for egg throwing on Mischief Night. Too hungry. A dozen eggs cost a quarter back then, a small fortune.

They let the boys waste that flour in those socks, though. The ones who could afford it. Ten cents a bag. What a waste. Vita would have shaken her head if it didn't hurt so much now. She could have made some nice Italian bread from that flour, not like the bread back in the old country, mixed with beans, chestnuts, or sawdust or whatever else you could scrape together. Bread like that would have fed her whole family at one time. Though no more. The family had grown too big, its tastes, like the flour, too refined.

So she said something to those kids. Those neighborhood kids. How could you not? If you're not gonna say something, I'm gonna say something. How many times had she said that to her husband, to her grown sons, her daughter-in-law? She couldn't just stand by and watch as they dirtied her street, her precious Grove Street. Not a grove in sight, barely a tree, but her part of pavement and cobblestone was immaculate. No matter how old and bent she was, she swept and washed it down every day with the water, the lovely water that flowed so freely from the American pipes.

Her failure to just turn around and ignore those boys was a family trait. This search for justice or whatever it was, this always looking for a fight, this temper, this would be passed down to her grandchildren and great-grandchildren and even her great-great-grandchildren, though at this point, she had no way of knowing that, no way of seeing that her pending extinction was not an extinction at all, no, not at all. Just a passing on—of family traits and mannerisms and lessons to the next generation.

So there she was, on Mischief Night, yelling at those kids. How could she not? A little old lady like her, suddenly standing, no longer sitting on her stolen wooden chair out there in the evening chill. It was a habit, this sitting outside each night and every day, a habit leftover from Southern Italy, from her town of Bernalda, where the women would bring their midget straw and wooden chairs outside each night and sit and sit and watch and wait. Wait for something exciting to happen.

She and Francesco had made something exciting happen,

forty years ago. They had given those big-mouth neighbors something to chat about, all right. A murder and its aftermath in a small town goes a long way, survives a hundred years of gossip. A hundred years or more. They would remember her—that Gallitelli woman and the Vena man and that murder. It's why this was happening to her now. Why she was dying before her time. Past her prime, maybe. But before her time.

She would have liked to have gone back home to die. To die with her lover, the one she left behind, the one who told her to go. But it was not to be. She wondered if he knew now that she was suffering. Could he feel it, her life slipping, from three thousand miles away? Probably not. Men weren't so good at those things. And he was probably dead by now anyway.

No one would take much notice at all when she died. It wouldn't even be recorded on the local obituary page. Old Italian ladies didn't make the obituary pages in 1915. Her death certificate would say, "Myocarditis." And it's true. Her heart would give out. She was sixty-four, old for those days. Ancient, really. Especially after all she'd been through.

She had her work as a weaver, and Rocco to take care of, and the housework, and the farm work, and then, of course, the murder. The murder. That had taken its toll. And that awful ride across the Atlantic. How many people do you know who would survive that? Three million Italians had done it between 1900 and 1915, mostly from the South. Your grandparents maybe, or great-grandparents. But how many women, alone with their kids, had done it? Not as many. No, not as many. But Vita had, and she had survived it, every last bit of it.

Until now.

Now Vita lay dying. All because she had yelled at those boys. They didn't take criticism well, teenage boys. It was part of their nature. She should have known that. She had had three sons of her own after all. At one time, she had had three. Four, really, if you counted Domenico. Though just two remained. She had had a daughter, too, the one that got away. And she wondered now where she was. If she was better off. The last time she had seen her she was just a girl. A tender seven years old. Vita talked to her, to Nunzia, sometimes and told her stories and sang her lullabies and hoped that she could hear her, wherever she was.

Vita didn't even mind dying so much when she thought of Nunzia. Maybe Nunzia was dead. And she would see her soon. Nunzia. And Rocco. And Domenico. And the baby Nunzia who had died so young. And Francesco. She would see them all.

But what a stupid way to die.

If it had been one or two boys on the Jersey City street, they would have shown the proper respect and apologized to her maybe for stealing her chair and her broom. But this was a crowd and crowds were never good. They were American boys, only one generation removed from Ireland or Poland or wherever their parents had come from, but already they were arrogant. Taller than Vita and much stronger.

She yelled, yelled at them in Italian to stop making such a mess of the street, her street, and to stop badgering the poor people. Give her back her chair. And her broom. That old witchy broom. But they laughed at her. And before she knew it, before Vita could see what was coming, that little bastard took one of the socks from his friend and hit her smack in the head with it. He thought he was being funny, probably. The little bastard. Or maybe he thought it was one of the flour-filled socks or the one with the horse manure in it. But it wasn't.

It was the one with the rocks.

So that was how it happened. How she wound up on this damn deathbed of hers. Tough little Vita Gallitelli, hit in the head with a sock full of rocks on Mischief Night, 1915, on the streets of Jersey City.

When she hit the pavement on Grove, crumpled into a large

pile of clothing—her long dress, underskirts, corset, apron, stockings, and high buttoned shoes—no one even noticed at first, since she was so small and made so little noise, just the slightest muffle. But someone, her sons, or one of her grandkids upstairs in their second-story apartment above the grocery store, must have noticed Nonna lying there. The family came running.

Then everyone in the neighborhood was there, in a circle: the guys drinking at Chiefy Green's tavern; the bookie, Jake the Jew, who operated out of the deli downstairs; Venutolo, the Italian grocer on Bay, where everybody bought their vegetables and pasta. The word went up and out through the neighborhood, so even people as far away as Jimmy the Greek's corner store on First Street came by, Conti's barbershop on Henderson, and Louie's Meat Market. They were all there to see what happened to Vita.

But who knew it was so bad, that smack in the head? Vita got up eventually, groggily—"Va ben, va ben," she would say, waving one hand and holding her head with the other—and went straight up to bed. But she never woke up again, not completely anyway. She would linger, and dream and think. Think about her sins. The priest would be called from Holy Rosary parish to give last rites. Not that she needed them. She had gotten last rites back in Italy years ago on the day she was born.

VITA DIDN'T DIE FOR ANOTHER WEEK AND A HALF. VITA'S SON, Leonardo, who lived right around the corner on Bay Street, read her the paper that week as she lay dying. He tried to elicit some sign of life from his mother, tried to make her laugh, even. He and his brother, Val, could read. She had made sure. And they were now successful barbers. Not criminals. Leonardo, whose hands were soft like his mother's and always manicured, shaved the heads of the local politicians, even the mayor, in his own shop right across from city hall. Imagine that. The mayor. They would never believe it back in Basilicata.

Leonardo took the afternoon off to visit his dying mother. He read aloud about the dockworker in Hoboken who got hit with a hog's head, which fell thirty feet from a ship and broke the poor guy's neck. What a way to go. Poor bastard. And the little five-year-old boy who was hit by a trolley on Grove Street, not far from Vita's door. So sad. And the sensational story, BOY KILLED BY POISON APPLE. A strychnine-laced apple. They found him dead on his steps, the partially eaten apple next to his body, his dog dead, too, at his side.

A bunch of Italians from Hoboken were poisoned that week as well, but none of them died. It seems they bought poison mushrooms from some peddler in Fort Lee and all got sick. So Vita was not alone in her *miseria*. No. Not at all.

So much life. So many stories:

BLAZE IN BUTCHER SHOP.

POLICEMAN FALLS FROM STOOP.

WOMAN SLIPS AND FALLS DOWN COAL CHUTE.

YOUTH TOSSED BY ANGRY BULL.

HORSE BITES OFF DRIVER'S FINGER.

CHARGE MILKMAN WAS OBSTREPEROUS.

It was business as usual in Jersey City: Five hundred phony names were found on the poll lists for the upcoming election. The suffragettes were out marching. A clergyman said a man in his Bayonne parish was offered two dollars for his vote.

To brighten things up, Leonardo moved to the movie listings. He would tell her that nine movie theater owners were arrested that week for opening their doors on Sunday. At the Orpheum they were showing a movie called *A Mother's Confession*. It was as if the theater owner were taunting poor Vita to come clean for the sins she had committed long ago. Over at the Strand, they were playing a movie called *The Bludgeon*.

Very funny, Vita thought, not awake enough to laugh.

The city's Young Socialists held a big dance. The vaudeville team of Potash & Perlmutter played the Majestic, and the Famous Hawaiian Sisters sang and danced at the Academy of Music, followed by a Taffy Pulling Contest. So much life still going on as she lay dying, it almost didn't seem right.

ON TUESDAY, ELECTION NIGHT, VITA COULD HEAR THE COMMOTION out on Bay Street as she lay there, semiconscious, the sound of wood being piled up, drifting in and out of her head. Celebrations erupted in the streets. The state would elect Republicans that year, but Hudson County would faithfully remain Democrat, filling the freeholder and assemblyman seats with old-school machine politicos.

Over at the Academy of Music, the election results were read from the stage and the news traveled like lightning down the street, igniting the bonfires as it struck. The boys piled the wood high that night, an effigy of the Republican losers up top. They lit a match, then hurled a jar of oil waste from the railroad cars onto the pile and watched the flames spread. The smoke made it hard to breathe.

Bonfires burned all over Jersey City. Like the one over on Cornelison Avenue, which got out of control and spread because of the strong wind that night. The fire department came and put it out and the police squad came to round up the kids who started it, but everyone—the twenty-five smoke-scented and soot-covered kids in the neighborhood—claimed they had nothing to do with it.

The bonfires were all over the city every year on election night. But none of them, not even the wildfires, were like the fire on Bay Street. That one was always the biggest. The firemen blamed it on all the Poles who lived in the neighborhood. Nobody could collect and hoard wood like those Polish kids, the Irish cops joked.

As the flames climbed higher and the fire grew hotter, the merchants ran out in their aprons, their hoses in their hands to spray their windows. But every year it was the same thing. The fire was always too hot. The shop windows on Bay Street always cracked.

The fire department would come and put the bonfire out, leaving a big black hole in the middle of the street. But as soon as Hague's men left, the kids would pull out more of their wood and spark it up again. And so it burned, as Vita lay dying, the orange glow falling on her windows, so much smoke it seemed the whole world were burning.

So much smoke that the smell lingered in Vita's bedroom for days after, lingered almost as long as she did. It took her ten days to die, as long as that ship ride over to America.

Until just like that, her light went out. She would die in November, two days after Francesco's birthday. It seemed so much in her life had happened in November. Her wedding anniversary. The murder. Francesco's death. And now she would join him.

Poor Vita, killed by a sock full of rocks on a Jersey City street. Her life, her story, everything she had ever known about the world, gone in a beat. She could see that long life now, below her as she floated, as if on a magic carpet: the yellow fields where she had gleaned with her mother; the cobblestones of Via Cavour, where she had hung her laundry; the ginger-colored Chiesa Madre, where she was married; Francesco's strong farmer hands taking her small hands into his; the girls working the farm in Ferrandina with those sweet little pears that would change her life; the jailhouse window in Bernalda where she looked up for a glimpse of her Ciccio; the small casket with her baby, Rocco, buried in the back of that church; the beautiful red rooftops of Pisticci and the birds flying over the Dirupo; those boys born one after another, running and playing with each other on the narrow streets; Grieco and the life he offered; the big house in Bernalda; the escape, the train to Naples pulling out of Metaponto with them on it, past tall cypress and toward mountains she could never have imagined; and the ride across that vast ocean, that long, terrible journey by ship, and her greatest tragedy and most awful secret, losing Nunzia. All of it about to be forgotten forever.

But Vita had survived it all. Somehow. Until now. Today in person, she thought, tomorrow in the grave. One last Italian proverb echoing through her head.

Author's Note

Vita was illiterate, so she left no diaries or letters, only stories passed down through the generations. Miraculously, the six-hundred-page criminal file exists, and provided me with vivid details of what transpired more than a century ago. My historical re-creations are based on those pages, on archival materials, interviews with historians, residents, and experts on the time period, in addition to the work of those writers who came and researched before me. In Vita's most intimate moments, I have used my own Gallitelli bones and blood to imagine how she would have acted and what she would have thought and said about the incredible events in her life.

Acknowledgments

Thank you to the people of Bernalda, Pisticci, and Matera for their help and generosity, particularly Angelo Tataranno, Francesco Montemurro, Imma Marzovilli, Giuseppe Blotti, Evaristo Ippoliti, Dino D'Angella, and Antonio Salfi, without whom there would be no book. Thanks to Olga and Antonio Braico and their family, to Leonardo Fuina, Natasa Coen, Maria Xenia Doria, Mariana Giannone, Rosanna Pastore, Alessio Ippoliti, Maria Gallitelli, Maria Natale, Dorothy Zinn, Antonio Panetta, Ferdinando, Mariangela and Flavia Forte, Rosaria Fabrizio, Domenico Marzovilli, Virginia Braico, Matteo Calciano, Antonio Santamaria, Emanuela Campa, Vincenzo Puntillo, Damiano Scalcione, Rocco Romano, Leonardo Leone, Antonio Biscaglia, Cynthia Karalla, Judith Edge, Mariateresa Cascino, Mariapia Ebreo, Graziella Sisto, Ersilia Troiano, Amy Weideman, Dr. Giuseppe Vena, Rosella DeFilippo, Rosario Mauro, Mr. and Mrs. DiBello, and Rosalba Corrado Delvecchio for their incredible hospitality and guidance. Thanks also to Rosa Parisi, Angelo Musco, Carmen Vicinanza, Stefano Luconi, Michael and Vivian Forte, Lisa Bauso, Bessie Jamieson, Walter and Kathy Jamieson, Barry Moreno, Jeffrey Dosik, Tom Pitoniak, and Carla Mastropierro. Special thanks to Tony Muia, for his research, interpreting skills, and laughter. To Dolores Stapinski and John and Anita Apruzzese for translating. To my mother, Irene Vena Stapinski, for her never-ending stories and enthusiasm. To Mary Beth Vena Mancuso and Jamie Vena Gotschall for their family research. To Jennifer Rudolph Walsh for lighting the fire. To Steve Reddicliffe for sending me back again. To Lisa DiMona for her faith and dedication, and to Nora Long for her early insights. To Julia Cheiffetz for her confidence and brilliant revisions. To Stan Stapinski and Paula Christen, for their terrific memories. To Lauren Spagnoletti, for inadvertently taking Grandma to meet the pope. And most of all, thanks to my husband, Wendell Jamieson, for his innumerable edits and for believing even when I didn't and to my wonderful talented, noncriminal offspring, Paulina and Dean. I love you guys.

Bibliography

Alliegro, Enzo. *Basilicata e Il Nuovo Mondo*. Potenza: Consiglio Regionale della Basilicata, 2001.

Ambrosano, Filippo. *Istoria Civica di Bernalda, 1798*. Matera: Antezza Tipografi, 1997.

Augustine. *The Confessions of Saint Augustine*. Project Gutenberg, 2002.

Baedeker, Karl. *Southern Italy and Sicily*. Leipzig: Karl Baedeker, 1887.

Biancha, Federica. Comune di Cesena press release, May 31, 2012.

Cornelisen, Ann. *Torregreca: Life, Death, and Miracles in a Southern Italian Village*. Boston: Little, Brown, 1969.

———. *Women of the Shadows: Wives and Mothers of Southern Italy*. Boston: Atlantic/Little, Brown, 1976.

D'Agostino, Peter. "Craniums, Criminals, and the 'Cursed Race': Italian Anthropology in American Racial Thought, 1861–1924." *Comparative Studies in Society and History* 44, no. 2 (April 2002): 319–43.

D'Angella, Dino. *Saggio Storico Sulla Citta di Pisticci*. Pisticci: I.M. D. Lucana, 1978.

Davis, J. "Honour and Politics in Pisticci." *Proceedings of the Royal Anthropological Institute* (1969): 69–81.

———. *Land and Family in Pisticci*. London: Athlone Press, 1973.

———. "Passatella: An Economic Game." *British Journal of Sociology* 15, no. 3 (September 1964): 191–206.

De Martino, Ernesto. *Magic: A Theory from the South*. Translated by Dorothy Zinn. 1959; reprint, Chicago: HAU Books, 2015.

Dickie, John. *Darkest Italy: The Nation and Stereotypes of the Mezzogiorno, 1860–1900*. London: Palgrave, 1999.

Dillingham, William Paul. *Emigration Conditions in Europe*. Vol. 4. Washington, DC: U.S. Government Printing Office, 1911.

Douglas, Norman. *Old Calabria*. Boston and New York: Houghton Mifflin, 1915.

Douglas, William A. *Emigration in a Southern Italian Town: An Anthropological History*. New Brunswick, NJ: Rutgers University Press, 1984.

Gissing, George. *By the Ionian Sea*. London: Richards Press, 1901.

Graham, John Maxtone. *Crossing & Cruising*. New York: Charles Scribner's Sons, 1992.

Gramsci, Antonio. *The Southern Question, 1921–26*. Trans. Pasqualie Verdiccio. West Lafayette, IN: Bordighera Press, 1995.

Gross, Feliks. *Il Paese: Values and Social Change in an Italian Village*. New York: New York University Press, 1973.

Hare, Augustus. *Cities of Southern Italy and Sicily*. London: G. Allen, 1891.

Herkner, Anna. *Steerage Conditions: United States Immigration Commission Report*. Vol. 37. Washington, DC: U.S. Government Printing Office, 1911.

Hobsbawm, E. J. *Social Bandits and Primitive Rebels: Studies of Archaic Forms of Social Movement in the 19th and 20th Centuries*. New York: Free Press, 1959.

Hogenboom, Melissa. "Two Genes Linked with Violent Crime." BBC News, October 28, 2014.

Homer. *The Odyssey*. Translated by Richmond Lattimore. New York: Harper Perennial, 1991.

Janik, Jules. "The Pear in History, Literature, Popular Culture, and Art." *Proceedings of the Eighth International Symposium on Pear*. Vol. 1. *Acta Horticulturae* 596. International Society for Horticultural Science, 2002.

Jersey Journal. October 31–November 15, 1915.

Kahn, Charles. *Pythagoras and the Pythagoreans: A Brief History*. Indianapolis: Hackett, 2001.

King, Russell. *The "Questione meridionale" in Southern Italy*. Durham, England: University of Durham, 1971.

Lear, Edward. *Journals of a Landscape Painter in Southern Calabria*. London: R. Bentley, 1852.

Levi, Carlo. *Christ Stopped at Eboli*. New York: Farrar, Straus, 1947.

Lomax, Alan. "Olive Pressing Song." *Italian Treasury: Folk Music and Song of Italy—A Sampler*. Rounder Records, 1999.

Lombroso, Cesare. "Why Homicide Has Increased in the United States." *North American Review,* December 1897.

Lombroso, Cesare, and Gina Lombroso Ferrero. *Criminal Man, According to the Classification of Cesare Lombroso.* New York and London. G. P. Putnam's Sons, 1911.

Lombroso, Cesare, and Guglielmo Ferrero. *Criminal Woman, the Prostitute, and the Normal Woman.* 1892; reprint, Durham, NC: Duke University Press, 2004.

Lopreato, Joseph. *Peasants No More: Social Class and Social Change in an Underdeveloped Society.* San Francisco: Chandler, 1967.

Maraspini, A. L. *Study of an Italian Village.* Athens: Publications of the Social Sciences Centre, 1968.

Milton, John. *Paradise Lost.* New York: Odyssey Press, 1962.

Molfese, Franco. *Storia del brigantaggio dopo l'unita.* Milan: Feltrinelli, 1966.

Morgan, Appleton. "What Shall We Do with the Dago?" *Popular Science Monthly,* December 1890.

Morton, H. V. *A Traveller in Southern Italy.* London: Methuen, 1969.

Parisi, Rosa. *Il Paese dei Signori: Rappresentazioni e pratiche della distinzione.* Naples: L'Ancora dei Mediterraneo, 2002.

Parks, Tim. *Italian Ways: On and Off the Rails from Milan to Palermo.* New York: Norton, 2013.

Petrillo, Giovanni, and Allesandro Mazza. "Uccide l'ex in Via Mameli." *Cesena Today,* May 31, 2012.

Peyrefitte, Roger. *South from Naples.* London: Thames & Hudson, 1954.

Pucci, Idanna. *The Trials of Maria Barbella.* New York: Vintage, 1996.

Randall, Frederika. "Basilicata, Rock Hard and Still Untamed." *New York Times,* September 3, 2000.

Rotella, Mark. *Stolen Figs: And Other Adventures in Calabria.* New York: North Point Press, 2003.

Russell, William Clark. *The Emigrant Ship.* London: Sampson Low, Marston, 1893.

Scott, Joan, and Louise Tilly. "Women's Work and the Family in Nineteenth Century Europe." *Comparative Studies in Society and History* 1 (1975): 26–64.

Scotti, Fred. "Canto di carcerato." *La Musica della Mafia.* Vol. 1, *Il Canto di Malavita.* Play It Again Sam, 2002.

Serafino della Salandra. *Adamo Caduto*. Cosenza: Gio. Battista Moio and Francesco Rodella, 1647.

Steiner, Edward Alfred. *The Immigrant Tide: Its Ebb and Flow*. New York: Revell, 1909.

Sturino, Franc. *Forging the Chain: Italian Migration to North America, 1880–1930*. Toronto: Multicultural History Society of Ontario, 1990.

Swinburne, Henry. *Travels in the Two Sicilies*. London: P. Elmsly, 1783.

Talese, Gay. *Unto the Sons*. New York: Knopf, 1992.

Tataranno, Angelo. *Vivurre: Bernalda, 8 Aprile, Fatti e documenti*. Matera: Pitagora Scolastica, 1992.

Villari, Luigi. *Italian Life in Town & Country*. New York and London: Putnam, 1902.

Walsh, Michael. *Butler's Lives of the Saints*. New York: HarperOne, 1991.

Yeadon, David. *Seasons in Basilicata*. New York: HarperCollins, 2004.

Zimmern, Helen. *The Italy of the Italians*. New York: Charles Scribner's Sons, 1906.

Zinn, Dorothy Louise. *La Raccomandazione: Clientelismo vecchio e nuovo*. Rome: Donzelli Editore, 2001.

Reading Group Guide

1. Author Helene Stapinski spent ten years searching in Basilicata for clues to her family crime. The people in Bernalda who seemed to know about the murder wouldn't share the information with her. Do you think they had a duty to tell her the family story? Or was she wrong to exploit them in her book?

2. Stapinski was fearful that her children would carry on the criminal gene. Is that something she should have been concerned with? Do you worry that your children will carry on unsavory characteristics in your own family?

3. Some flashbacks to the 1800s use fictional devices, like dialogue and interior thoughts of characters. Do you think this is effective? Is it wrong for a nonfiction writer to use fictional devices, even if she includes an author's note about it?

4. How does *Murder in Matera* speak to the controversies at the center of our present political climate—for instance, the persecution of unwanted immigrants and labeling whole populations as "criminals"—in America and across the globe?

5. What do you think of Stapinski's relationship with her mother? Was it something that guided Stapinski in her own child rearing with Dean and Paulina?

6. Do you think Vita's story of immigration is typical of those who came to America around the turn of the century? How does it compare to your family stories and those you have heard from other families?

7. Women are often not the protagonists in many Italian American stories or films. But in Stapinski's story, they are the heroes. How does *Murder in Matera* change the typical stereotypes and standards?

About the Author

HELENE STAPINSKI is the author of *Five-Finger Discount: A Crooked Family History*, which recounts her family's criminal history, and *Baby Plays Around: A Love Affair with Music*, which chronicles her years playing drums in a rock band in Manhattan. She has written extensively for the *New York Times* as well as for *New York* magazine, Salon, *Travel & Leisure* and dozens of other publications and essay collections. On the documentary based on *Five-Finger Discount*, she has worked as a producer and writer. Stapinski has been a radio newscaster in Alaska, has appeared on National Public Radio, was a featured performer with The Moth, has lectured at her alma mater, Columbia University, and has taught at Fordham University. She lives in Brooklyn with her husband and two children.